Visualizing
American Empire

Visualizing American Empire

Orientalism and Imperialism in the Philippines

DAVID BRODY

The University of Chicago Press   Chicago and London

DAVID BRODY is assistant professor of design studies at Parsons, The New School for Design.

The University of Chicago Press, Chicago 60637
The University of Chicago Press, Ltd., London
© 2010 by The University of Chicago
All rights reserved. Published 2010
Printed in the United States of America

20 19 18 17 16 15 14 13 12 11 10   1 2 3 4 5

ISBN-13: 978-0-226-07533-4 (cloth)
ISBN-13: 978-0-226-07534-1 (paper)
ISBN-10: 0-226-07533-8 (cloth)
ISBN-10: 0-226-07534-6 (paper)

Library of Congress Cataloging-in-Publication Data

Brody, David, 1958–
 Visualizing American empire : orientalism and imperialism in the
Philippines / David Brody.
       p. cm.
 Includes index.
 ISBN-13: 978-0-226-07533-4 (cloth : alk. paper)
 ISBN-13: 978-0-226-07534-1 (pbk. : alk. paper)
 ISBN-10: 0-226-07533-8 (cloth : alk. paper)
 ISBN-10: 0-226-07534-6 (pbk. : alk. paper)   1. United States—
Relations—Philippines. 2. Philippines—Relations—United States.
3. Imperialism in art. 4. Longfellow, Charles Appleton. 5. Morse,
Edward Sylvester, 1838–1925. 6. Philippines—History—Philippine
American War, 1899–1902. 7. Dewey, George, 1837–1917.   I. Title.
 E183.8.P5B76 2010
 327.730599—dc22

                                                    2009049567

♾ The paper used in this publication meets the minimum require-
ments of the American National Standard for Information Sciences—
Permanence of Paper for Printed Library Materials, ANSI Z39.48–1992.

To my family: James, Barbara, Dad Bro, JB, Mom Bro, and Nanny Helene.
In memory of Nanny Fay (1917–2006), Poppy Frank (1912–1984), and Poppy
Stan (1910–1990).

Contents

Illustrations

Introduction

President William McKinley prayed for answers to the question of what to do with the newly acquired Philippines. "I am not ashamed," he admitted to a group of clergymen, "that I went down on my knees and prayed Almighty God for light and guidance more than one night."[1] After the taking of the island nation, as a result of the brief Spanish-American War, a debate erupted about what America should do in the Pacific, and the president found himself in the middle of this maelstrom of political opinion. Many claimed the United States should walk away from the messy business of overseas empire, while others argued that the creation of such an empire was the answer to years of longing for further expansion, a desire for lands that had been a way of life in a world controlled from European capitals.

According to a report in the *Christian Advocate,* divine inspiration struck the president in a flash and "one night late it came to me this way,—I don't know how it was, but it came: (1) That we could not give them [the Philippines] back to Spain—that would be cowardly and dishonorable; (2) that we could not turn them over to France or Germany . . . that would be bad business and discreditable." Not satisfied with either of these two options, McKinley continued by listing the two concerns that would become most critical to American empire during the late nineteenth and early twentieth centuries: "(3) that we could not leave them to themselves—they were unfit for self-government—and . . . (4) that there was nothing left for us to do but to take them all, and to educate the Filipinos, and uplift and civilize and Christianize them, and by God's grace do the very best we could by

1

them, as our fellow-men for whom Christ also died."[2] In response to this impassioned realization, McKinley woke up the next morning and " 'sent for the chief engineer of the War Department (our map-maker), and told him to put the Philippines on the map of the United States' (pointing to a large map on the wall of his office); 'and there they are, and there they will stay while I am President!' "[3]

There was no easy path to fulfilling McKinley's ardent hopes. Indeed, after the Spanish-American conflict, which was, by most accounts, a rather quick series of events that led to the United States gaining a physical presence in a number of locations (including Cuba, Puerto Rico, Guam, and the Philippines), America then engaged in the very messy business of the Philippine-American War. The official dates of that conflict for colonial dominion are 1899–1902, but the actual years of the war against Filipino insurgents went well beyond the July 1902 cutoff date that president Theodore Roosevelt declared. Both the American government and other institutions, such as the dominant media, tried to stay on message about the Philippines, endlessly repeating McKinley's initial mandate for America's civilizing mission in the archipelago. This missionary attitude helped formulate the US ideology of "benevolent assimilation," an edict premised on bringing moral and intellectual uplift to a part of the world repeatedly perceived as inferior. Benevolent assimilation was also, it is critical to note, a directive predicated on a Christlike metaphor of selflessness in the face of a world order dominated by what many Americans conceptualized as the politics of European imperial greed.

What is most striking about McKinley's divine dictate is that he did not describe how the military facilitated his goal of empire, but instead he focused on the visually mediated task of mapping. By placing the Philippines on the map of the United States—by the very act of geographic inscription—McKinley incited the experience of empire. In the chapters that follow, this book explores how deploying the visual to signify empire helped further American imperialism in Asia. Through a close reading of a number of visual scapes—including the body, the decorative arts, the mass media, maps, the public spectacle of a parade, and architecture—*Visualizing American Empire* argues that different visual mediums furthered empire while concomitantly fostering a space where debates about empire could take place. Arjun Appadurai claims that our current global circumstance plays out in a world of scapes (from mediascapes to financescapes). These interrelated milieus foster our current world condition where fixity and stability are no longer feasible. These scapes are fluid and are constantly reinvented by the multifarious framework of our media-dominant world. Furthermore, these scapes are dependent on numerous points of view, and thus are not rigid, as their meaning morphs depending on context. Although Appadurai is describing our contemporary situation, his notion of scapes, and their amorphous quality, elucidates late nineteenth- and early twentieth-century American imperialism. The concept of scapes permits a sustained reflection on different modes of empire, which through a panoply of primary sources, especially those connected to the media, explains the anxieties and tensions that attended American empire.[4]

Visualizing American Empire starts with the historically conceptualized notion that the Philippines is part of the Orient and explains the early American colonial project in Asia (1898–1913) as a visually mediated experience. I contend that how we look (or visualize) is integral to the machinery that helps run the colonial engine. By attending to the visual, we gain a new perspective on the problematic circumstances that lead to and evolve out of the colonial process. This is not to downplay the power of words, and, in fact, the six chapters that follow often analyze written and spoken language in combination with images. Nevertheless, this book shows that images most influenced Americans' early perceptions of the Orient, and that images often created a space for a dialogue about empire that words alone could not nurture.

The debate about whether Filipinos were fit or unfit colonial subjects often took place under the auspices of how visual culture defined race. There have been countless academic studies that approach the peculiar relationship between empire and race through the lens of Orientalism. These theoretical assessments about Orientalism posit what we traditionally think of as the "Far East," the "Middle East," and the "Near East" as invented spaces in terms of their cartographic conceptualization by the West and as sites that host Western fantasies that transpire in the cultural sphere. Edward Said's influential work, which named this phenomenon, explains Orientalism as "the corporate institution for dealing with the Orient—dealing with it by making statements about it, authorizing views of it, describing it, by teaching it, settling it, ruling over it: in short, Orientalism as a Western style for dominating, restructuring, and having authority over the Orient."[5] Said considers American instances of Orientalism, but he focuses on the European version of Orientalism that uses what we think of as the Near East and Middle East as its knowledge-enhancing laboratory. Even so, Said's framework can help us elucidate American Orientalism and its motives behind representing Asia at the turn of the century.

I use Said's theory to investigate late nineteenth- and early twentieth-century American Orientalism. The United States took an active role in defining specific geographic locations through parameters that correspond with Said's thesis, yet there are places where my book raises concerns that others, who have used Said as a springboard, have mapped as integral to the colonial landscape. Homi Bhabha, for instance, has written about the ambivalence and hybridity found in colonial discourse; Aijaz Ahmad has insisted that scholars think about the importance of capitalist forces in relation to imperial conquest; Reina Lewis and Meyda Yeğenoğlu have asked that scholars study the relationship between gender and Orientalism; and Anne McClintock has claimed that technology, notions of time, and gender are critical components of colonialism.[6] Each of these critics' positions, often labeled under the umbrella of postcolonial studies and/or postcolonial theory, complicates my investigation of American imperialism in the Philippines.

Instead of reading the visual as a straightforward indicator of the American acceptance of colonialism, several sources will be deciphered as examples of the multifaceted discourse that emerged as a result of imperialism. For example, let us briefly consider a visual image that surfaces in chapter 3 and then returns in the final chapter. This is an 1899 drawing from the very popular newspaper the *World* that shows an American soldier, named Private Lapeer, being infected with leprosy by a group of Filipino insurgents. Filipinos stand over and around the soldier as he grips his arm in horror about what has just been presumably introduced to his bloodstream by injection (fig. 29).[7] The site of infection is a primitive hut, which would have made the incident even more uncivilized, raw, and sensational to the turn-of-the-century reader. A fear of Philippine savagery floods the visual field. Not only is this an overtly racist representation of Filipino culture, but it also speaks to contemporaneous American obsessions with bloodline, miscegenation, and an influx of foreign immigrants into American cities. The popular press repeatedly used the Philippines to play into American anxieties about racial impurity, cultural contamination, and Oriental contagion.

This cultural anxiety about race and the treacherous nature of Philippine disease splintered American opinion about imperialism. While many viewed empire through the lens of manifest destiny, or the notion of Americans' divine-given right to take lands, others contended that American imperialism was a waste of fiscal resources predicated on humiliating colonial subjects. Some Americans even looked to the Philippines with a sense of horror and could not imagine trying to tame a wild race of people who inhabited a set of Pacific islands thousands of miles from North America. Although we have no contemporary discussions about the leprosy image, outside of the text that appears in the newspaper, the rendering reveals conflicting political ideologies. The imperialist who wanted to bring benevolent assimilation—the policy that stressed how imperialism could reinvent the colony through the kind praxis of empire building—to the Philippines would have emphasized the leprosy narrative as an example of why Filipinos needed America. On the other hand, anti-imperialists would have understood the infection of the American soldier as a clear sign that the potential colony was too barbaric; regardless of the might of the American military, nothing good was going to happen in this uncivilized part of the world. Paul Kramer reveals that many anti-imperialists "saw Americans as empire's only victims and imagined this victimization as the United States' racial 'corruption' by potential colonial subjects."[8] Furthermore, a few of the more strident anti-imperialists would have discussed this image as an example of American troops receiving their comeuppance, as Filipinos returned the violence that Americans instigated. The possibility of these varied readings gives us a sense of how the mass media created a buzz about empire that culturally reverberated throughout turn-of-the-century America. Multiple constituencies would have been satisfied with Private Lapeer's story, making his narrative, told through both written and visual mediums, more compelling.[9]

A number of scholars have used the lens of visuality to assess imperial culture. Anthropologist James Clifford has problematized the link between cultural imperialism, vision, and anthropology, for example, while historians of the visual have examined cultural production and its link to national political agendas. Linda Nochlin and, more recently, Todd Porterfield and Darcy Grimaldo Grigsby have questioned the imperialist impulse found in nineteenth-century French painting. Beth Fowkes Tobin has revealed the imperialist desires in eighteenth-century British painting. Zeynep Çelik and Robert Rydell have assessed representations of colonial sites at the world's fairs of the nineteenth century. Benito Vergara has chronicled the use of photography in American colonialism. And, in the multidisciplinary model of American studies scholarship, Amy Kaplan has investigated the role of film in the promotion of American empire; Laura Wexler has studied photography in relation to the violence of imperial conquest; and Vicente Rafael has considered the efficacy of photography in disciplining colonial subjects (both alive and dead).[10] My project fills gaps in the field of colonial and postcolonial studies by looking at the American experience of empire through a multidisciplinary lens, thus following the lead of scholars like Kaplan, Wexler, and Rafael. Additionally, *Visualizing American Empire* is part of a growing body of studies that examines American empire in Asia and the history of

American Orientalism in the cultural sphere. This wave of recent books has been instrumental to my thinking about the US-Philippine nexus.[11]

Visualizing American Empire deploys the visual to link American interests in Asia prior to the Spanish-American conflict to colonial efforts in Asia after the war. This is not to say that there is a direct causal relationship between pre-1898 examples of American Orientalism and post-1898 imperialism. This prior interest in the "Orient" was not, in other words, a guise for empire lust. On the other hand, this curiosity in things related to the ambiguously defined Orient led to an American engagement with an early form of globalization that inevitably fostered a fascination with thinking about, defining, and claiming a better understanding of the larger world. Eventually this global perspective, or what Kristin Hoganson has helpfully identified as "cosmopolitan domesticity," cultivated a climate where Americans embraced ideas about empire with greater ease.[12]

Over the course of the late nineteenth century, visual representations of the Orient exploded into a tangled knot of discursive possibilities, and the first chapter of *Visualizing American Empire* examines the American interest in Oriental motifs in the 1870s before images representing the Philippines surfaced in the mass media. Specifically, chapter 1 considers the personal collection of Charles Longfellow, the extraordinary son of Henry Wadsworth Longfellow who spent several years traveling in Asia during the 1870s. Longfellow collected photographs, tattoos, and other material objects during lengthy trips to Asia. The poet's son is particularly intriguing because he went beyond the role of mere tourist; he actually lived in Asia for a number of years and also collected images of himself and others in the Philippines.

Chapter 2 turns to a popular American arts magazine from the turn of the century, the *Art Amateur*. The magazine, which had a circulation of over ten thousand, is representative of how the conception of the ideal, domestic space was often designed using fantasies of the representational Other, or Oriental. *Art Amateur* used racially motivated images to sell a commodified aesthetic to a middle-class audience. Before looking in detail at the pages of *Art Amateur*, this chapter explores the life of Edward Morse, a scientist turned art scholar who published widely on Asian art and design. His impulse to investigate the Orient, through the visual, is similar to the case of Longfellow, but the magazine and Morse made the Orient accessible to thousands of readers who could not experience Asia firsthand. Additionally, *Art Amateur*'s pages began to show an interest in America's movement toward empire in the late 1890s, and I assess the Colonial Revival and its place in relation to imperial fantasies.

These early forms of nineteenth-century Orientalism were fantastic and based not on a purely imperialist impulse, but rather on a desire to collect, curate, and domesticate objects from places Americans defined as exotic.[13] However, as Amy Kaplan has shown, there are "multiple historical trajectories" that furthered American empire, and this domestication of the racial Other prepared Americans for their eventual foray into overseas expansion.[14] My chapters on Longfellow, Morse, and *Art Amateur* help establish the interest in Orientalism that proliferated in late nineteenth-century middle-class culture. This global curiosity made Americans feel more cosmopolitan and nurtured fantasies about what the Orient held beyond its mysterious and nebulously defined borders.

The second part of the book details how the relationship between the United States and the Orient changed after the Spanish-American War of 1898. After growing tensions during the 1890s, the conflict began in earnest after the Spanish allegedly sank the USS *Maine*, an American battleship in Havana Harbor. America then attacked the Spanish fleet in both the Atlantic and Pacific Oceans, establishing military outposts in Cuba, Puerto Rico, Guam, and the Philippines.[15] When future admiral (then commodore) George Dewey maneuvered his fleet into Manila Bay and defeated the Spanish in a brief battle, it created a swelling of nationalistic pride. There were Americans who wanted Dewey to leave the Philippines after annihilating the Spanish navy, but Dewey and many in the American government saw future military opportunities in Asia and decided that the city of Manila should surrender to the American flag. President McKinley sent more troops to further Dewey's efforts, thereby instigating the Philippine-American War, which eventually led to the United States creating a colony in the Pacific.[16] The Orient now hosted the continuation of an American vision of manifest destiny.

Chapter 3 elaborates the connection between the Philippines and American empire by exploring how the American press depicted the Philippines as an Oriental nation devoid of civilization, a site waiting for American prayers as manifest in the pretense of colonization. Through a close reading of popular media sources, this chapter asks how Americans, in the context of their own homes (the same homes they often decorated in an Oriental manner), visually consumed the spectacle of America's new colony. Two New York–based newspapers, William Randolph Hearst's *New York Evening Journal* and Joseph Pulitzer's the *World*, and two national magazines, *Harper's Weekly* and *McClure's*, each represented the Philippines as an exoticized location with an Oriental nature.[17] The American media, controlled by individuals such as Hearst and Pulitzer, helped sell the war along with countless magazines and newspapers.[18]

Chapter 4 continues this assessment of the mass media by claiming that maps helped define Americans' experience of the Spanish-American and Philippine-American Wars. I then extend this notion of mapping by investigating how the American military and the nascent field of anthropology utilized ideas about mapping places and bodies to gather information about the new colony. The chapter contends that various forms of cartography helped Americans discern and generate imperial knowledge about the archipelago.

Chapter 5 continues exploring the mass media and assesses New York's 1899 welcome-home party for the victorious Admiral Dewey. This chapter argues that the visual spectacle of a military homecoming enhanced the American desire to colonize the Orient. Millions of New Yorkers attended this two-day event, which included firework displays, naval and land parades, the construction of a triumphal arch, and other cultural hyperbole, such as the publication of several hagiographies on Dewey.[19]

Chapter 6 begins on the domestic front and investigates the representation of the Orient at turn-of-the-century world's fairs. This chapter initially asks why Americans became so interested in representing the Orient through architecture at these expositions. Specifically, this final chapter focuses on the 1904 Louisiana Purchase Exposition in St. Louis. Here imported Filipino workers (directed by the fair's organizers) constructed a form of "native" architecture meant to frighten visitors, convincing them of the need for an American presence in the Philippines.[20] This chapter then moves from American fantasies about Filipino architecture on American soil into the Philippines by examining architect Daniel Hudson Burnham's presence in the Pacific from late 1904 to early 1905, detailing how the colonial administration implemented an architectural program of building imperialism. Once American colonial officials, with the help of Burnham's successor, architect William Parsons, executed parts of these plans, these alterations to the Philippine landscape established that the Orient did not have to be relegated to the realm of fantasy. This distant place had become a tangible location, appropriated for imperialist interests by building government structures and business venues. The creation of US government–sponsored architecture in the Philippines epitomizes how Americans wanted to replicate their vision of American ingenuity in the colonial zone.[21]

The conclusion returns us to the United States and the scape of the decorative arts in the context of America's most famous domicile, the White House. Specifically, I assess president William Howard Taft's redecoration of parts of the White House using Filipino furniture. Taft left an enormous record of his time in the Philippines, and the conclusion begins by looking at several of the colonial themes that his writing touches upon. After this discussion of Taft's overt interest in empire, the conclusion ventures into the space of the White House and reads the presence of this Filipino furniture as both a symbolic manifestation of Taft's own nostalgia and his never-ending quest for order in the American colony.

Each of these chapters uses examples of American culture and does not, except for one brief example in chapter 6, consider Philippine reactions to American empire. For the most part, my project focuses on a critique of sources produced by, or consumed by, white Americans. This is not to deny the importance of visual responses by the colonized, which have, as Jill Beaulieu and Mary Roberts explore in their edited volume *Orientalism's Interlocutors*, been an often under-told aspect of the colonial archive.[22] In fact, Filipino examples of these responses have been chronicled and assessed by authors such as Clodualdo del Mundo Jr. and Vicente Rafael.[23] Accordingly, more work needs to be done to evaluate the visual culture that Filipinos and other nonwhites produced in the face of empire. My hope is that my project will contribute to the continuing reevaluation of the vast visual record (American and Filipino) that attended the early colonial period.

Like the Philippines, other areas of the globe were—and still are—dealing with America's imperial presence. Because of what Frederick Jackson Turner termed the closing of the frontier, the United States looked beyond its own borders to places such as Cuba, Hawaii, Panama, Puerto Rico, Guam, and, of course, the Philippines, to fulfill the desire for territorial expansion. At the beginning of his famous 1893 paper titled "The Significance of the Frontier in American History," Turner claimed that "American history has been in a large degree the history of the colonization of the Great West."[24] Implicit in his thesis was the idea that the "Great West" was an ideologically closed zone (both the native population and ecological life had been destroyed for imperialist purposes); thus, it was time to move beyond the North American frontier and colonize other places that could enhance the American individualistic character.[25] The fantasies and military realities of empire would become more viable with the advent of cultural mediators who represented the arena of conquest through the multifaceted lens of visuality.

ONE

Strange Travelogues

Charles Longfellow in the Orient

Charles Longfellow (1844–1893) never intended to create an archive that would present an objective view of Asia. Nor did he have the patience for such an endeavor. "Charley," the eldest son of Henry Wadsworth Longfellow (arguably the most famous poet in nineteenth-century America) left Cambridge, Massachusetts, to travel in Asia from 1871 to 1873.[1] There are plenty of reminders, or souvenirs, of his adventure, including letters, photographs, objects, and journal entries, but nineteenth-century publishers never codified the record of his trip in books or articles. Charley kept a personal record. The tone of his visual and written account is not consistent with those of many artists, scientists, and thrill seekers who went east with the hope of plotting knowledge about Asia onto a grid of perception, providing their curious Western audience with information about the Orient through collections. Longfellow's chronicle is sexy, disorganized, and, most problematic to a researcher, fragmented; his representations of strange experiences would have befuddled most Americans seeking a sense of order about the world.

During the postbellum period Longfellow traveled to Japan, Cambodia, Thailand, China, Vietnam, India, and the Philippines. While his literary father repeatedly asked him to return home and stop spending the principal of his inheritance, Charley remained in Asia and never shied away from extravagance. Approximately 350 photographs, hundreds of objects, numerous letters, and pages of journals indicate his lack of interest in fiscal concerns. Longfellow materially exemplified his contemporary Ralph Waldo Emerson's notion of the "transparent eyeball," voraciously taking in everything that lay in his path and recording these impressions through the lens of his own writing, other people's cameras, and a capacious desire to collect. While the Longfellow archive is somewhat of an anomaly in terms of its unusual content, Charley's longing to domesticate, catalog, and stereotype Asia was a product of American Orientalism during the 1870s.

Although most nineteenth-century Americans traveling in Asia stayed in major cities and ports, Longfellow often left this well-mapped terrain to explore areas that enticed his curiosity. The writing he undertook and the photographs he collected in these remote regions, coupled with his impressions of metropolitan areas, form an early example of an American Orientalist archive. Longfellow's desire to gain a cultural understanding of these distant places is obvious, but what also emerges as we look at the copious material he left behind is one man's hope of attaining access to a part of the world that he understood as exotic, sensual, and completely separate from the Boston Brahmin upbringing he was trying to escape.

Longfellow struggled against the confines of his family's class consciousness; he seemed to loathe his refined childhood. While the Longfellows expected Charley to attend college, get a proper job, and heed the parameters of New England society, he refused to entertain his parents' wishes. At the age of eighteen, shortly after his mother's death, he left home and joined the Union cause in 1863. His father was dead set against him serving during the Civil War, but Charley saw the war as an opportunity that would help him quench his thirst for adventure. For ten months he was a second lieutenant, but during the Battle of New Hope Church he was injured. Photos of his shoulder and back display the scars of battle that forced Longfellow to return home and begin his unusual journey as an eccentric obsessed with travel.[2]

Longfellow's experiences in Asia are an early example of an American interest in gaining knowledge about the ambiguously defined Orient. The Longfellow archive is a visually mediated scape that showcases bodies, both his own and those of his "Oriental" subjects, as a manifestation of Orientalist desire. It was through the photographic representations of others and the decoration of his own body that Longfellow deployed the visual to incite fantasies about the cultural Other. His portrayal of the body signified stereotypes of non-Western cultures and portended the Philippines as a future site of American representational interests and global pursuits. Longfellow's travels were particularly important because he was one of the first Americans I have found who spent time in the

Philippines, the site in the Orient that became critical for the project of American empire at the turn of the century.

Life with the Ainus

Writing from San Francisco in early June 1871, Charles declared to his father that he "suddenly decided to sail for Japan today."[3] He arrived in Japan later that month and spent most of the summer traveling through various parts of the country and becoming acquainted with Yedo, the city that would become his home base. After this initial summer in Japan, Longfellow spent time with a native Japanese tribe called the Ainus, located in the northern part of the country. In September and October 1871, he wrote extensively about the Ainus, and he purchased photographs to document these "quiet, amiable people."[4]

One of the photo albums with Ainu images in Longfellow's collection has the name Nagootchi on a blue cover and displays an arrangement of twenty-one photos along with captions written in what was probably Nagootchi's (the possible photographer's) hand.[5] The Ainus would have interested Charley because they fit his notion of a travel oddity; they were so different from life in Cambridge that he quickly focused his attention on capturing their unique cultural features through writing and photography. The Ainus lived on the northernmost island of Japan, Hokkaido, which was far from the metropolitan areas of the nation that were struggling with an effort to modernize and remake their image as more Western during this period. When the emperor Meiji came to power in 1868, the Japanese government did not know what to do with the Ainus, whose customs were antithetical to the Meiji wishes for an industrialized and modern Japan. According to historian Richard Siddle, the Meiji enforced the transformation of the Ainus' landscape "into an internal colony of the new Japanese state, a strategic 'empty land' to be settled by Japanese immigration and developed along capitalist lines" and "these policies required the dispossession of the Ainu as a prerequisite."[6] Like the Native Americans, the Ainus hindered capitalist expansion. Thus, the Japanese government thwarted their preindustrial culture through an imperial project that posited the Ainus as subjects who needed to be assimilated.[7]

The blue photo album documents what Longfellow understood as an untainted people who had not yet faced radical changes brought about by modern life. For instance, the fifth image in Nagootchi's packaged ethnography of the Ainus represents huts and storage facilities (fig. 1).[8] The text explains that the "photograph represents the Ainos [sic] huts, and

This photograph represents the Ainos huts, and store house at Otarnari in a western coast of Yezo. These huts & store houses are thatched with bamboo leafs, the Ainos girl & boy carring a baby, the other two shoe their dress.

Figure 1 Nagotchi, photograph of Ainu huts and storage facilities, ca. 1871. Courtesy of National Park Service, Longfellow National Historic Site.

store house at Otarnari in a western coast of Yezo. These huts and store houses are thatched with bamboo leafs, the Ainos girl and boy carrying a baby, the other two shoe [*sic*] their dress." If we assume that Longfellow purchased this album as a souvenir of his trip—one of several souvenirs he took home from Asia—than this particular item, inscribed with exacting language where every caption begins with the phrase "This photograph represents," would have been very desirable. Whether the hand is that of Nagootchi or another individual who worked with Nagootchi, the author's attempt at providing definitive meaning and clear objectivity appealed to the American tourist.

The photographs, like the captions, create a sense of ethnographic certainty through declarative descriptions of the images. In the fifth image, several huts circle the ground at the center of the photograph. Each hut is, as the caption states, "thatched with bamboo leafs." In the middle ground of the photograph are five Ainus who are, without the help of the authoritative caption, not clearly discernible. Huts appear in several of the other images in Nagootchi's album. Even though many viewed the hut as the architectural prototype for future building, Western culture in general understood the hut's impermanence as uncivilized and culturally unstable, connoting the world of the primitive through its inhabitants' adherence to a type of ephemeral building.[9]

Longfellow wrote about Ainu dwellings in his journal. "They all seem poor, but to want for nothing, as all the houses we entered were comfortable in a smoky sort of way. But I must describe them! They are as a rule quite large, thatched walls and roofs, no chimney, but a large hearth in the center of the floor is what the fire is made on, the smoke finding its way out at the windows and sometimes by a small hole in the roof." He provided specifics about some of the objects in these spaces and ended his descriptive paragraph by noting that "scarcely ever in the day time does one find any young men about these houses, they all being off fishing or hunting."[10] Like the photographs of the Ainu homes, the journal lent an air of domestic regularity to these spaces; there were hearths, and men and women had separate functions within this sphere. Indeed, Charley's own sense of the domestic probably influenced his perception of Ainu housing.

Impermanent building was just one of the ways in which Longfellow signified the Ainus as ethnographically different. In 1871, on the last page of his journal, Charley wrote:

The name Ainu means hairy men in their language, which is quite different from that of Japan—the two peoples not understanding each other's language.

They were found in Japan by the Japanese occupying Nipon and Yesso, but many years ago, they had a severe war with the Japanese and were driven from the island of Nipon and the southern part of Yesso.

They are said to have been a very warlike people, but they seem very mild, devoting themselves to hunting and fishing exclusively, not tilling the soil.

They wear their hair and beards long and have a great deal of hair on their bodies even down the back bone. Their features are regular and some even fine looking. Their average height is about five feet seven or eight inches. They are as a rule very muscular.

Their women have a large mustache with pointed ends covering both the upper and under lip tattooed into their skins, or rather cut in with knives, at the age of fifteen or thereabouts.[11]

Although the Ainus were found on Japanese soil, they looked, acted, and spoke in a fashion that distinguished them from other Japanese people Longfellow encountered. His writing, like the photographs he collected, is akin to other examples of nineteenth-century ethnography in which categorizing difference, making distinctions, and pointing out racial characteristics are imperative.

The images of huts, and other photographs, such as a three-quarter-length portrait of an Ainu woman replete with a tattooed mustache, visually augment Charles's writing. Image and word worked together, allowing Charley to bring home souvenirs from his travels that would have reminded him of his trip and provided a venue where he could share his experiences with others. Susan Stewart claims that we "do not need or desire souvenirs of events that are repeatable. Rather we need and desire souvenirs of events that are reportable, events whose materiality has escaped us, events that thereby exist only through the invention of narrative."[12] Charles devised a travelogue about his own experiences in Asia through the interrelated acts of writing and collecting images. His photographic and journalistic souvenirs made his trip meaningful.[13] Indeed, the images of the Ainus constitute an artificial visual scape that Longfellow was able to carry as a souvenir when he returned to the United States. Longfellow may have orchestrated what photographs Nagootchi took and how his camera should frame these exotic natives. From there, the images were developed, ordered within the pages of the album, and made available for display to a Western audience. Again, these were not popular images—the photos probably did not circulate beyond family members and close friends—yet they manifest fantasies about other parts of the world that were becoming more widespread during this period. As later chapters reveal, these photos were typical for projects that visualized other geographic locations later in the nineteenth century.

Inking, Dressing, and Going Native

Perhaps the most peculiar piece of evidence that suggests Longfellow's commitment to the personal are the tattoos he brought from Asia, making his body into a visually mediated scape on which his travels were recorded in ink. "Injecting pigments" into the skin with needles creates tattoos, which have a long and complicated history in both Japanese and American culture.[14] Longfellow acquired most of his tattoos, which covered his arms, his back, and his chest, during the 1870s and 1880s. One of his tattoos, representing crossed flags on his arm, was completed during the Civil War while he served in the Union army. Included also in the hundreds of photographs he collected are images that show Japanese subjects with tattoos, such as the Ainu women with their tattooed mustaches.[15]

The riot of colors and shapes that covered Longfellow's body included a Japanese woman dressed in a kimono on his arm (a symbol of potential eroticism that reappears in numerous photographs that Longfellow collected), a large carp fish on his back (a symbol of virility), and an image of the Japanese goddess Kannon in the mouth of a dragon on his chest (a symbol of protection for sailors).[16] All these corporeal signifiers in ink were, like the photographs he collected and the writing he did while in Asia, souvenirs that marked, and in this case inscribed on his skin, the narrative of his travels. Longfellow's trip adorned his body. The tattoos were a form of writing, a type of language injected into the body that disclosed representational import.

Longfellow had photographs taken that reveal his desire to document how he inked and dressed his body with references to Japan in a fetishistic manner. Two photographs, one of his back (fig. 2) and one of his chest (fig. 3), depict his tattoos, but in both images his face is obscured. In the photograph of his back, dominated by the carp, his back is to the camera, and in the image of his chest, his face is hidden by the brim of a hat and a mask that covers his eyes. Longfellow tattooed his body as a way to subvert the cultural norms of genteel Brahmin culture. By dressing Japanese (fig. 4) and tattooing his body with Japanese imagery, Charley was reassuring himself and others that he had been in Asia.[17] Additionally, these portraits made Longfellow into a fetishistic site for the display of the cultural Other. By dressing up, or wearing the garb of the Other, Longfellow created a type of cross-racial identification.[18] Clothing, which he repeatedly deployed as a way to play Japanese, could be removed, while the tattoos were permanent, a type of indelible fetishistic mark. By capturing this transformation with a camera—the nineteenth-century's great documenting device—Longfellow recorded his fetish. He also created a fetishistic object, the photograph, by using his body as a subject. In short, Longfellow utilized his body and photographs of his body as visual scapes that represented his Orientalist fixation.

Longfellow's physical transformation exposed the ambiguities of his desire to become the Other, or the object of his own ethnographic gaze. He went to Asia to witness, observe, and become titillated. Charley collected photographs, wrote, and purchased souvenirs. The photographic and written collection he kept became a distancing mechanism that allowed him to separate himself from the subject of his gaze through the lens of the camera and the ink of his pen. However, wearing the clothes of the Other and being tattooed with Japanese imagery reveals a type of collecting that Charles did on his actual body. This brought the experience of Asia closer to his own physical sense of self; gone was the critical detachment of ethnographic observation. Take, for instance, the image that represents Longfellow in samurai garb (fig. 4). In this full-length portrait, he stands confidently in a photographer's studio, his body clad in the traditional layered robes of a samurai and his feet in sandals. In his

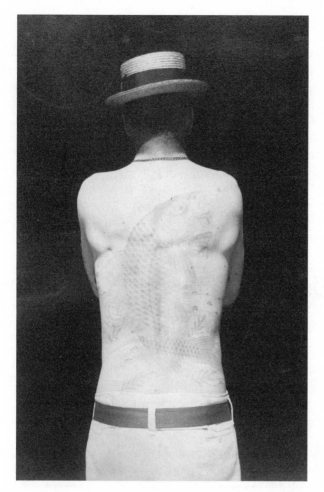

Figure 2 Photograph of Charles Longfellow, 1872. Courtesy of National Park Service, Longfellow National Historic Site.

right hand he holds a fan, and in his left hand he grips a samurai's sword called a katana. By taking on the sartorial signs of a Japanese samurai, Longfellow became a hybrid of both Western and Eastern cultures.[19] The trope of the samurai warrior heightened his own masculinity, as he created a self-made admixture of cultural typologies.[20]

Charley's turning away from the camera, his disavowal of self, is also significant in the tattoo photos (figs. 2 and 3). By refusing to face the lens in these two images (by either covering his face or turning his back) he shed his former self for a new persona. That Orientalized self, Charley's

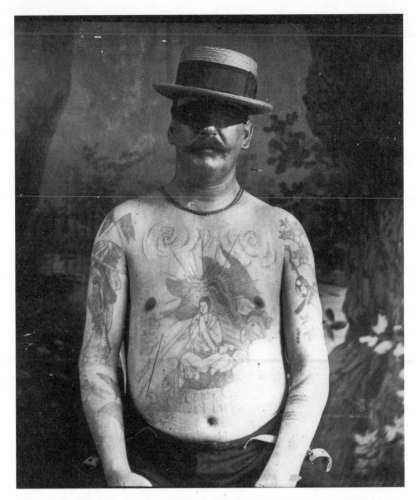

Figure 3 Photograph of Charles Longfellow, 1885. Courtesy of National Park Service, Longfellow National Historic Site.

new identity, obscured his Caucasian face, which appeared, in his estimation, too white, too refined, and too normative. He reinvented who he was while in Japan, and when he had completely transformed his character to the best of his abilities, he masked his former identity through concealing gestures, utilizing his body as a visual scape to cultivate a new identity that elided his former self. Longfellow knew that his white body lay behind the shroud of Asian symbolism, but the formation of a hybridic display (the combination of a white body with Japanese accoutrement) allowed him to represent his newly invented nature.

There are several moments in Longfellow's journals, letters, and collected photographs when his heightened interest in Japan relates to his desire for the company of Japanese women found in local teahouses. In August 1871, he wrote to his sister about a visit to a teahouse in Yedo. After being made comfortable in a room upstairs, Charles "heard a great tittering and laughing, and in trotted twenty-five singing girls, their bright eyes sparkling and white teeth shining as they came forward, knelt down, and bent down until their foreheads touched the ground. They knelt in front of us while we ate, helping us in the most graceful way, and going into fits at my bungling way of handling the chopsticks."[21] At the end of the meal, one of the "girls" offered each man a cup filled with sake. "After which if you like the girl and want to be gallant, you dip your cup in a bowl of cold water to clean it and hand it back to her. When she touches it to her forehead with a low bow, you fill it for her, and she drinks."[22] Once this drinking ceremony came to a close, "eight or ten of the girls ranged themselves in a row at the other side of the room, tuned

Figure 4 Photograph of Charles Longfellow in samurai garb, 1872. Courtesy of National Park Service, Longfellow National Historic Site.

19

their samisens and soon began to play and sing."[23] Longfellow never mentioned sex with any of these women, and the ceremonial proceedings he described were typical of what Westerners found in nineteenth-century Japanese teahouses. A number of photographs in his collection reveal an interest in the women he would have met in these teahouses. In one set of images, taken by the famous Venetian photographer Felice Beato, who moved to Asia in the 1860s and is well known for his photographs of everyday life in Japan, a group of four women is on the porch of Longfellow's house in Yedo. One of these images (fig. 5) portrays (from the viewer's left to right) an American friend of Charley's, three Japanese women sitting in the lotus position, Charley sitting in a chair with his chin in his right hand, and another Japanese woman who is standing.[24] Longfellow looks bored and contemplative, while the women appear more aware of the camera's presence.

Longfellow probably had sex with Japanese women while he lived in Japan.[25] Furthermore, there is a connection between Longfellow's collecting images of these women and the sexualized nature of these relationships. These photographs became a type of currency for Longfellow.[26] He could bring these photos home and display them in his family's house, thus deploying photography as a way to unravel the tangled narrative of his trip to Asia. Like the curios he collected and shipped to New England in crates, the photographs of his mistresses became souvenirs that reminded Longfellow of the pleasures made available to him in Japan.

Longfellow's sexual, intellectual, and spiritual involvement with Japan can be understood as protoanthropological in nature, and in the history of Western ethnography there is a long-standing tradition of confusing the boundaries of objective observation and subjective sexual curiosity. Marianna Torgovnick assesses the ethnographer's double bind of sexual attraction and objective understanding through a close reading of anthropologist Bronislaw Malinowski's work on, as he titled his most famous book, *The Sexual Lives of Savages*. This study, originally published in 1929, describes the intimate acts of natives from the Trobriand Islands. While anthropological jargon does not permit much unabashed sexuality to pervade the ethnographic descriptions in the text, Malinowski kept a journal of his time in the Trobriand Islands. His private record contains numerous passages about his sexual intrigue with what he saw while in the field. Ironically, Malinowski's wife found the diary after his death in 1942 and released its pages for public consumption.[27]

Malinowski's diary contains graphic descriptions of women's bodies he encountered in New Guinea. Torgovnick quotes one passage that is particularly charged: "At 5 went to Kaulaka. A pretty, finely built girl

Figure 5 Longfellow House in Yedo, ca. 1872. Photograph by Felice Beato. Courtesy of National Park Service, Longfellow National Historic Site.

walked ahead of me. I watched the muscles of her back, her figure, her legs, and the beauty of the body so hidden to us, whites, fascinated me. Probably even with my own wife I'll never have the opportunity to observe the play of back muscles for as long as with this little animal."[28] The racist vision that equates the "primitive" woman's body with an animal, who should be watched, observed, and cruised by a white man's gaze, is blatant. Even more telling is the irony that Malinowski spent so much of his time carefully examining the sexual lives of the people in New Guinea and insisting on a type of objective distance, while his private thoughts were nothing less than lustful. Torgovnick claims that for Malinowski "looking at 'natives' was a double act . . . the scientific act he claims in *The Sexual Life of Savages*, which cannot, he insists, 'be pornographic'; and the personal act—replete with longing—that left him night after night in moral agony beneath the mosquito net."[29]

This "double act" weighed on Longfellow's decision about what to report and to whom in relation to the visual scapes he created as souvenirs of his travel experiences. For Longfellow, the division between academic objectivity and sexual subjectivity was not that dichotomized. Indeed, the notion of Charley as an academic is rather absurd. He edited aspects of his travel narrative, however, depending on his audience. In letters home he never overtly discussed his sexual relationships. Neither, for that matter, did he express sexual longing in these missives or in his personal journal. The same can be said for the photographs on his porch in Yedo. Charley is there, the women are there, but they are on the perimeter of his home. They are in the architectural netherworld that the porch provides; they are neither inside nor outside. This liminal position leaves us with questions about what types of activities went on before and after Beato took these photos, but the imagery obscures any possibility of uncovering what exactly happened between Longfellow and these women. Longfellow did not present his "double act" as transparently as Malinowski; there is no secret diary that has been uncovered. As unconventional as his peers and family must have viewed his journeys to the East, Longfellow tempered the recorded history of his travels with careful prose and cautious camera direction.

Sunday Morning in Manila

In 1873, after two years in Japan and other Asian countries, Charley traveled to Manila, the capital of the Philippines. As he did in other locations, he collected photographs and wrote about his experiences. One particularly striking image from his time in Manila is labeled, in his own hand, "Sunday morning, Manila. 1873." The photo is set just inside the perimeter of a fence (fig. 6). Charley, wearing a hat and a dark jacket, sits to the back and right of a man in striped pajamas. Eight Caucasian men and one Spaniard surround him, and, in the background, encircling this group of Euro-Americans, are eight Filipinos. The Filipino on the far right, who stands at the ready with a fan to cool the tourists, signifies the status of these Filipino servants. The imperial setting is unmistakable as the natives attend to the needs of these non-Filipinos who appear relaxed and at ease in this Sunday-morning vignette.

Longfellow's presence in the Philippines is one of the earliest examples that I have found of an American in this part of Asia. Charley's trips to Japan and other countries were also early, but other Americans had visited and lived in this part of the world by the 1870s. Even more peculiar is the fact that Charley posed himself, and quite possibly the others in this group, in a type of archetypal colonial setting. Dark-skinned natives work as white men lounge waiting to be served cool breezes that would have been the product of these servants' labor. This photo was a harbinger of things to come. After the Spanish-American War of 1898 many Americans found themselves in the colonial setting of the Philippines,

Figure 6 "Sunday Morning, Manila, 1873." Courtesy of National Park Service, Longfellow National Historic Site.

a location that fell into US hands as a result of this conflict with Spain. "Sunday Morning, Manila" is the type of representation that proliferated during the Spanish occupation of the Philippines prior to the late 1890s, but was an anomaly when it came to the American understanding, or lack thereof, of the Philippines. Most Americans, prior to 1898, would not have been able to point to the Philippines on a world map.

Besides the image of himself, set in a protocolonial setting, Longfellow also collected photographs of Filipinos while in Manila. While he may have collected more, only ten images still exist in his archive that depict Filipinos (besides the Sunday morning photo). Most of these photos appear to be set in a studio, as the artificial backdrops and overly posed bodies of figures belie any attempt at candor. Although later images from the American colonial period would focus on cultural specificity and details, Longfellow probably bought these souvenirs from a local photo dealer without worrying about scientific accuracy or a specific colonial perspective. The popular press's stereotyping of Filipinos in the midst of the colonial conflict did not cross Longfellow's mind; nor did he hope to capture exact measurements of Filipinos. These images manifest Charley's fantasies of securing visual evidence that would showcase the exotic bodies he encountered during his travels.

The photographs that Charley purchased in Manila are, for the most part, simple interior scenes.[30] Out of these images, only two have specific marks on their verso sides. Both of these cartes-de-visite are from a studio called Honiss in Manila. In Charley's hand we read that one photo is of "Vicenta" (fig. 7) and the other is of "Vicenta's Sister" (fig. 8). The photographer, possibly under Longfellow's direction, has posed the women in a similar fashion. They turn slightly to their right without directly facing the viewer. They wear long dresses and white blouses that cover their upper bodies. Aprons have been fitted around their waists, and decorative collars, with crosses, adorn their necks. Within the Honiss studio are props and a wall drawing. Vicenta stands in front of one wall drawing that replicates decorative molding, replete with dentil work and ornate

Figure 7 Honiss Studio, Manila, "Vicenta," ca. 1873. Courtesy of National Park Service, Longfellow National Historic Site.

Figure 8 Honiss Studio, Manila, "Vicenta's Sister," ca. 1873. Courtesy of National Park Service, Longfellow National Historic Site.

swags. To her right is a table with turned legs, and she holds a fan in her right hand. Vicenta's sister stands in front of another backdrop that gives the impression of an expensive interior with paneling. To her right is a large chair with a caned back and to her left is a potted plant in a decorative urn that sits on a heavily carved pedestal.

Once again, Charley took the time to collect photographs of women in their native garb. Even though the sexual play that he wrote about in relation to the Japanese women he had photographed does not appear in these images (these women are not, for instance, on the porch of his house), it is curious that Longfellow possibly took the time and energy to stage these photographs and buy them from the Honiss studio. The photographs of Vicenta and her sister are, like the other images Longfellow brought back from his trips, souvenirs that document what he saw in the Philippines. The sisters' bodies have become visual scapes that Longfellow purchased as images to prompt his future recollections about the island nation.

Two other photographs from this set of Philippine images are even more racially charged. In one image two men hold roosters while standing in front of a backdrop that represents a landscape. One man is shirtless and the other man wears a long-sleeved shirt. Even though both men wear pants, neither wears shoes (fig. 9). In another photograph six figures (three men and three women) sit around a large table, playing a game. A dog appears in the foreground (fig. 10). The lack of shoes, the bare shoulders, and the half-naked man in the first photograph are typical of depictions of "native" peoples that would have circulated in the West at the turn of the century. However, there was also an attempt here on the part of the photographer to capture these Filipinos in an everyday scene. By posing this group in the fake setting of a studio, replete with props and overly staged scenarios, the influence of genre painting appears to have affected the photographer's decisions.[31] Perhaps the studio thought they could sell more of these photos if the Filipinos mimicked Western imagery.

The fact that these were images that Charley brought back to retell his travel narrative is significant, because here the photos enact a dual

Figure 9 Two men with roosters. Photograph from the Charles Appleton Longfellow Papers, ca. 1873. Courtesy of National Park Service, Longfellow National Historic Site.

Figure 10 Group playing cards. Photograph from the Charles Appleton Longfellow Papers, ca. 1873. Courtesy of National Park Service, Longfellow National Historic Site.

meaning. The Filipino figures appear different, as their dress, skin color, and overall appearance marks them as racially Other. They also perform in a visually staged way that would have made the American viewer more comfortable, since these representations of racial difference occur in a familiar setting. Of course, placing the figures in a photography studio would have made it easier to capture the image, given the long exposure time needed when using earlier cameras. Yet these interior vignettes also ensure a controlled narrative in which natives can look like natives but appear like their Western audience, through an enactment of bodily comportment that mimics their eventual observer.

The intertwined narratives about bodies and race depicted in these Filipino photographs are salient because they visually echo the material related to Longfellow's time in Japan. Charley appears to have used his experience in Japan as a model for how he would continue his collecting in the Philippines. The important difference is that in Japan the visual memories he stored in photographs and tattoos were private, as the images related directly to his own body. Recall the women photographed on the porch of his house, the portraits portraying Longfellow in Japanese garb, and, of course, the imagery he had inked into his skin. In the Philippines, his relationship with the subject matter is ambiguous. The only image we have that represents Charley in the Philippines offers no other explicit evidence outside of its city location (Manila), day (Sunday), time (morning), and year (1873). Longfellow wanted to capture his visual conception of the Philippines, a desire akin to what he did in Japan, but there is a critical distance in the Honiss Studio photos and in the Sunday morning image, since the highly personal nature of the Japanese material is absent. These photographs of the Philippines convey a distancing of subjectivity, as the manner in which Longfellow's own body participated in his travels through the archipelago remains a conundrum.

Almost thirty years later, images of Filipinos as visual scapes of corporeality would become integral to the American imperial project. Longfellow, and the natives represented, had no knowledge of this inevitable change in global politics, but Longfellow's intent on collecting photographs that cataloged Filipinos prefigures many of the same strategies of representation that propelled and sustained American empire at the turn of the century. In this instance, the photographs did not have a vast audience beyond Longfellow's immediate circle; nevertheless, as will soon become evident, various permutations of this type of imagery became very popular in the mass media several decades later when the Philippines became an American colony. Longfellow's presence in Asia might have been early, yet his strategy of stereotyping through written and visual texts is the underlying theme that the remainder of this book explores in an attempt to untangle the connections between Orientalist fantasies and imperialist practices.

TWO

Domesticating the Orient

Edward Morse, Art Amateur, *and the American Interior*

The beginning of William Dean Howells's novel *A Hazard of New Fortunes* narrates the experiences of a Boston couple, the Marches, as they search for a rental apartment in New York City. At one place for rent, the home of Mrs. Grosvenor Green, Mr. and Mrs. March encounter an impossible living space where "everything had been done by the architect to save space, and everything to waste it by Mrs. Grosvenor Green. . . . The radiator was concealed by a Jap screen, and over the top of this some Arab scarfs were flung. . . . Some red Japanese bird-kites were stuck about in the necks of spelter vases, a crimson Jap umbrella hung opened beneath the chandelier."[1] Howells's assessment of this apartment is a humorous ploy to encourage the reader to sympathize with the Marches' real-estate woes; the couple has, after all, the hardest time finding a place to live. Nevertheless, *Hazard*'s publication date of 1890 speaks to another narrative: those charged with creating stylish American interiors began to debate the Aesthetic period's clutter and exotic motifs. As a result, a new compulsion toward austere interiors started to dominate domestic design.

This debate about home décor reveals how Americans defined themselves in relation to a rapidly changing international political arena during the late nineteenth century. Indeed, the American "home front" was critical to the ideology of empire. As Amy Kaplan contends, the home front powerfully articulated the strange and fractured logic of empire in ways that historians often overlook.[2] Additionally, Kristin Hoganson notes that Americans brought an international panoply of decorative arts into their homes at the turn of the century under the auspices of "cosmopolitan domesticity." Hoganson explains how "foreignness seemed desirable to fashionable Americans in the late nineteenth century—so desirable that design writers stressed the virtues of authentically foreign appearances."[3] To unpack the tangled relationship between the home and empire, this chapter considers the material and visual culture that surrounded Americans during this period. While many historical studies of this epoch rely on written documents, I contend that Americans' interest in particular forms of material culture reveal their fantastical notions of their place in the world. In other words, peering into people's homes, and assessing how they decorated and put together their interiors, gives us a sense of why Americans made specific consumer choices and how these choices informed their perceptions of themselves and Others.

To glean why Americans, such as the fictive Marches, made specific consumer decisions, it helps to examine the network of influences that led to these design choices through the auspices of two interrelated archives. In particular I will focus first on the connections between the decorative arts and scientific intrigue explored by the scientist and art critic Edward Morse. I will then turn to representations of the Orient in arts periodicals and assess how the magazine the *Art Amateur* (1879–1903) represented the interior of the American home as a site where the decorative arts signified the Orient. *Art Amateur* repeatedly employed the trope of Orientalism as a marketing tool. Most of the issues between 1879 and 1890 mention Asia, while also dealing with a variety of topics, including artists' biographies, embroidery, new books, design plates, and flower arranging. The magazine's pages fostered stereotypes about the Orient that supplemented detailed descriptions of what the editors promoted as ideal art and design.

After investigating Orientalism, I will trace how racially charged fantasies about the Orient began to be accompanied by the Colonial Revival in late nineteenth-century America. This growing fascination with a nativist design motif did not mean that the trope of Orientalism disappeared. In fact, the pages of *Art Amateur* reveal a back-and-forth, and a sense of ambivalence, between these two aesthetics that emerged in the second half of the nineteenth century. Nevertheless, the rising importance of the Colonial Revival speaks to American interests in the actual practice of empire and the escalating militarism and masculinity that spread with viral-like potency in the late 1800s. Thus, the Colonial Revival was a concomitant to the overseas imperialism that attended the Spanish-American War. Indeed, the turn-of-the-century domestic sphere was frequently defined through the parameters of race, which included fantasies of the Other and ideals about what constituted a purified vision of American racial identity.

Orientalism and Edward Morse's Classificatory Mind

Edward Morse was born in 1839 and began collecting shells at the age of fifteen. He was the type of daydreaming boy who always thought about ideas and places not within his immediate reach. Morse, at a young age, traveled from his home in Portland, Maine, to Boston, where he studied zoology. He quickly developed into an active scholar, and the Boston Society of Natural History elected him as a member in 1859. Shortly thereafter he started working for Louis Agassiz at Harvard, helping the famous Swiss naturalist assemble what would become the world's largest museum of comparative zoology. Although he was only making a small amount of money, Morse's interest grew stronger, as did his enthusiasm for a new life far removed from the drudgery that he associated with Maine. By the 1870s, Morse became well known as a scientist and toured the country lecturing about the natural world to enthusiastic audiences. He traveled to the Western United States in 1874, and it was in San Francisco that he learned for the first time about the complexities of Asian zoology. His enthusiasm for Asia led him to move to Japan, where he began teaching and conducting research at Tokyo University in 1877. This relocation would soon make Morse into an acclaimed expert on Japanese art and culture.[4]

Before traveling in Asia, Morse asked the readers of his popular *First Book of Zoology* to collect and classify insects. "It is a part of the lesson to know how and where to collect, and above all to know how to preserve the specimens collected."[5] Morse explains that the insects' display should be established through the construction of "insect-boxes . . . having a depth of not over two and a half or three inches, and furnished with a lid. A shallow cigar-box will answer the purpose."[6] He provides details about how these boxes should appear: "The bottom of the box may be lined with strips of corn-pith, or slices of cork, into which the pins can be easily stuck. . . . The insects, when collected, are to be pinned to the cork in the way figured, leaving the head of the pin sufficiently above the insect to grasp with the fingers."[7] He included his own drawings of both *Sliced Cork for Insect-Box* and an actual *Insect-Box* (fig. 11). The insect box is, just

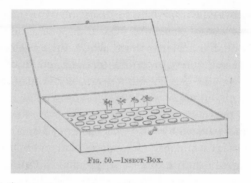

FIG. 50.—INSECT-BOX.

Figure 11 Edward Morse, *Insect-Box,* from his *First Book of Zoology* (New York: D. Appleton, 1875), 50. General Research Division, The New York Public Library, Astor, Lenox and Tilden Foundations.

as he suggests, a cigar box transformed into an entomological display kit. The open lid reveals four rows of circular pieces of cork. In the last row of the box, or the row farthest from the viewer via perspective, Morse drew four insects stuck into pins that rise out of the circles of cork. "Care," he explains, "must be taken not to have the insect too far down on the pin, as its legs in that case would touch the bottom of the box, and break off. Insects may be killed by immersing them in alcohol for a few minutes."[8] The drawing ensures that the reader understands that proper display can lead to viewing the insect in the round. The necessity of seeing the insect in its entirety, legs and all, was essential to Morse's project. It is from this visually mediated experience that readers may compare their collections to Morse's drawing and make classificatory sense of what they have procured from nature.

Morse's approach to collecting has nineteenth-century precedent. One of the more entertaining characters in the world of nineteenth-century zoology was the famous Philadelphia artist, political activist, and naturalist Charles Willson Peale, who set out to create a miniaturized version of the natural world within his Philadelphia museum in the early part of the century. In his famous self-portrait, *The Artist in His Museum* (1822, fig. 12), Peale gestures to his audience to enter into the world of collecting he has assembled for public edification. He has arranged nature in an obsessive fashion and placed preserved specimens in a specific order revealing nature's classificatory narrative according to scientists, such as Carolus Linnaeus, whose theories Peale understood as scientific fact. One of the most telling iconographic tricks found in this 1822 self-portrait is that Peale, like the animal life in the background, is a specimen placed in a box format; he has been put on display as the highest form of animal life within the visual field.[9] Peale, in other words, is akin to the birds seen to the viewer's left, but Peale is larger, centered, and the compositional highlight of the foreground. Peale, like Morse, discursively inscribed the parameters of collecting and placed that narrative in an enclosed setting. While Peale's display box was the actual space of a museum in Philadelphia, and Morse's box was a simple container for cigars, both scientists attempted to redact the natural world into a miniaturized, encyclopedic whole.

Susan Stewart views the collection as a "form of self-enclosure which is possible because of its ahistoricism. The collection replaces history

Figure 12 Charles Willson Peale, *The Artist in His Museum*, 1822. Courtesy of the Pennsylvania Academy of Fine Arts, Philadelphia. Gift of Mrs. Sarah Harrison (The Joseph Harrison Collection).

with *classification*, with order beyond the realm of temporality. In the collection, time is not something to be restored to an origin; rather, all time is made simultaneous or synchronous within the collection's world."[10] The collection is an artificial construct where bits and pieces of an imagined whole are brought together under one roof—or lid, in the case of Morse's cigar-box display. Stewart reveals, "The archetypal collection is Noah's Ark, a world which is representative yet which erases its context of origin."[11] Noah's collection can be compared with Morse's and Peale's separate intentions of constructing a space where man delineates animal life through naming. During the nineteenth century, naturalists ventured out into nature to gather specimens, and then placed their samples in containers of knowledge and understanding. The visual always mediated these projects.

What is unusual about Morse is that the focus of his compulsive collecting changed in the 1870s. As a result of traveling to Asia to work as a zoologist, Morse's passion turned from nature toward art and interior design. While in Asia, he wrote articles and books about Japanese and Chinese décor and began an important collection of Asian art that he eventually left to the Peabody Museum in Salem, Massachusetts (now the Peabody Essex Museum) and the Museum of Fine Arts in Boston. Morse was part of a larger late nineteenth-century group of Americans that set out to understand the art and people of Asia.

Morse's study of Japanese material culture reveals two interrelated issues. First, for all his claims of ethnographic sensitivity, an attribute that he believed he possessed, Morse fell into the same stereotyping practices found in other late nineteenth-century American analyses of Asia (think back for a moment to Charles Longfellow's stereotyping). Japan became a critical location for the development of an American version of Orientalist discourse. Second, Morse's earlier work on classifying nature informed his study of Japanese arts. In fact, there was a similar cultural impulse to name, label, classify, and, ultimately, collect and domesticate Asia in a way that emulated his desire to develop a taxonomic grid of the natural world. As in his work in zoology, Morse used numerous examples to describe, as he titled one book, *Japanese Homes and Their Surroundings*. His writing worked in tandem with his drawings to represent furnishings and aesthetic principles that created a fantasy about Japanese domesticity.

Morse, for example, describes a tranquil library space in a Tokyo house as separate from the rest of the home by cloth hung from a bamboo frame, "and when the owner went in search of some object on the other side of it, I could trace him by his candle-light as he wandered about behind the curtain. The furniture used in the room, and shown in the sketch,—

consisting of bookshelves, table hibachi, and other objects,—was in nearly every case precious antiques."[12] Unlike the precise renderings that enhance his images of insects and arachnids, where every surface of the specimen becomes magnified and clearly demarcated, the Japanese home has corners and crevices not available to the curious Western eye (fig. 13). The image of the veiled individual moving through this Japanese interior would add a sense of mystery, while the corresponding drawing reins in the written flourishes by simply depicting the corner of this library. Neatly stacked books are on shelving in the back of the room, and carefully arranged low tables, chairs, and mats are on the remainder of the floor.

Like the insect-display cases in his zoology book, the library in Tokyo is a staged scape of objects that Morse understood as worthy of collecting. This room, like the cigar box, is an exemplary collection that Morse rendered to inspire the reader to learn further. He wanted his American audience to take the visual clues, illustrated through his writing and drawing, and use Japanese art as a source for inspiration. At another point in *Japanese Homes*, Morse clarifies how Americans can learn from the Japanese sense of design: "After studying the Japanese home for a while . . . one comes to realize that [American] display as such is out of the question with them, and to recognize that a severe Quaker-like simplicity is

Fig. 137. — Room in Kura fitted up as a Library, Tokio.

Figure 13 Edward Morse, *Room in Kura Fitted Up as a Library, Tokio*, from his *Japanese Homes and Their Surroundings* (Boston: Ticknor and Company, 1886). Art & Architecture Collection, Miriam and Ira D. Wallach Division of Art, Prints and Photographs, The New York Public Library, Astor, Lenox, Tilden Foundations.

really one of the great charms of a Japanese room." He continues, "Absolute cleanliness and refinement, with very few objects in sight upon which the eye may rest contentedly, are the main features in household adornment which the Japanese strive after, and which they attain with a simplicity and effectiveness that we can never hope to reach." To the Japanese, "our rooms seem . . . like a curiosity shop, and 'stuffy' to the last degree."[13]

Morse contended that the Japanese had perfected the art of household decoration and that Americans should aspire to the lack of visual clutter found in Japanese homes. His work questioned the typical Aesthetic movement interior in the 1870s and 1880s when Americans filled their homes with material clutter that signified a global sensibility. Rooms, as depicted in magazines, paintings, and period photographs, were bursting at the seams with what social critics referred to as bric-a-brac, or those objects that sat on every surface, filled every corner, and saturated every nook and cranny. This was precisely what incited Howells to describe the peril of clutter in *A Hazard of New Fortunes*. Morse believed that the Japanese understood the value of living simply and condemned those in his American audience who continued to waste space with an abundance of décor.

Morse collated his imaginings about Japanese aesthetics in the pages of his book, which became a type of ethnographic collection for his American readers. His stereotyping about this distant location exemplified his need to understand another part of the world that Americans viewed as exotic, sensuous, and filled with mysteries that lurked behind veiled spaces. James Clifford examines the link between the impulse to collect and the desire to gather objects that signify the cultural Other. Clifford, like Stewart, notes that a collection is "an exercise in how to make the world one's own, to gather things around oneself tastefully, appropriately. The inclusions in all collections reflect wider cultural rules—or rational taxonomy, of gender, of aesthetics. An excessive, sometimes even rapacious need to *have* is transformed into rule-governed, meaningful desire. Thus the self that must possess but cannot have it all, learns to select, order, classify in hierarchies—to make 'good' collections."[14] Clifford details how the West began the process of accumulating non-Western material culture. He identifies a particular power dynamic that unfolds when the West exhibits the Other. In these instances, there arises the imperative "for different peoples to form complex images of one another." In turn, these images "are constituted—the critique of colonial modes of representation has shown at least this much—in specific historical relations of dominance and dialogue."[15] Through the act of classifying, non-Western cultures are appropriated within the collection and this, in turn, supports the belief that there is an understanding of what lies behind the enigmatic mask that shrouds these distant lands. Through this process, cultural arbiters like Morse get a sense of what is happening behind the library curtain. That sense is, however, a phantasm predicated on racially motivated guesswork. To collect is to appropriate, and these spaces and objects activate the problematic language of stereotype that incites a fantastical form of armchair travel.[16]

Morse was not alone in stereotyping Asian art and design at the turn of the century. Countless artists, interior designers, furniture makers, and architects looked to the East as a site for artistic inspiration. In June 1879, for instance, the first issue of the *Art Amateur* included an article titled "The Harmony of Colors." "With some of the Oriental nations," the author notes, "especially the Japanese, who have taught us so much in Decorative Art, the knowledge of harmony in color seems to be intuitive. The commonest designs of the Japanese artist or even artisan show how rarely the judgment of the workman is at fault in this regard." Using the same pedagogic device of cultural comparison encountered in Morse's work, the author explains that with "Americans, however, it is different. Those who understand the combination of colors with reference to artistic effect are decidedly in the minority."[17] In another *Art Amateur* article from September 1880 titled the "The Superb Japanese Lacquer Screen," the author proclaims that "Oriental artisans" appear to be "supernaturally endowed with patience, and . . . possess a peculiar delicacy of touch which enables them to effect without difficulty what to the heavy-handed Caucasian artisan would be impossible."[18] Japan, and the larger ambiguous geographic realm named the Orient, would repeatedly be stereotyped through what Thomas Kim has described as "aesthetic ethnography," a discursive strategy that enabled Americans to use art objects to construct an ambiguous understanding of the Orient as both inside and outside the cultural establishment.[19] The Orient was a site that was decidedly different, but Americans wanted to possess and emulate this unusual place, because Asians, according to the language of aesthetic ethnography, had natural talents in art and design.

Orientalism and the *Art Amateur*

Orientalism has an extensive history in American art and design. Throughout the eighteenth and nineteenth centuries the influence of the China trade could be seen in the homes of those Americans who had the money to purchase handcrafted decorative arts. Because of an inability to mass-produce these goods, the material culture related to the China trade entered homes only on the upper end of the socioeconomic ladder. Thus, this initial engagement with an Asian artistic style was quite different from the American interest in Orientalism found during the Aesthetic period of the late nineteenth century, when factory production permitted an enormous output of goods related to the Orient. The China trade is also dissimilar from later experiences with Orientalism because it flourished, for the most part, as a result of buying goods from China. During the nineteenth century, Americans would continue purchasing things from Asia, but they also began producing their own versions of Orientalist art objects.[20]

The explosion of interest in Asian art can be traced to the years 1853 and 1854, when the American trade relationship with Asia changed as a result of commodore Matthew Perry's landing in Japan. Perry and his Japanese counterparts began to exchange gifts, and this initial act of trading incited the explosion of what has been termed *Japonisme*, or a fascination with the art of Japan. This encounter with Japanese arts would lead to more popular venues for Asian objects at places such as the Philadelphia Centennial Exposition of 1876, which historians view as the initial mass display of the "Japan Craze" in the United States. Centennial visitors found an abundance of mass-produced souvenirs at the bazaar that sold Japanese products.[21] Decorative arts historians have noted that during the latter part of the nineteenth century, the term "Japanese" referred to a number of Asian cultures. Chinese, Japanese, Turkish, Indian, and other Eastern countries were often placed under one rubric of Oriental desire.[22] Edward Morse's keen interest in deciphering differences between Asian nations was unusual, as most Americans understood the Orient as a whole, as an entire entity with cultural parts and pieces that could be assembled, disassembled, and reassembled to form a Western fantasy.

Art and design from and relating to the Orient proliferated in late nineteenth-century America, creating visual scapes of exoticized decorative arts. It was possible for more Americans—outside of those wealthy enough to travel across the Pacific like Longfellow and Morse—to bring Asia into their own homes. Indeed, the Centennial of 1876 was a type of sales agent for Oriental goods that could be bought and appropriated for the domestic sphere.[23] After the Centennial, a number of arts magazines began to illustrate and extol the virtues of bringing Asian motifs into the parlor.[24] Titles such as *Art Interchange*, *Art Age*, and the *Art Amateur* are similar in their engagement with the aesthetic presentation of the domestic sphere. However, *Art Amateur* is unusual because its circulation was about ten thousand, making it (along with *Art Interchange*) one of the most popular arts periodical at this time.[25] The magazine was an integral voice in the American art establishment's newfound interest in modernist aesthetics and interior design.[26]

In 1886, the editors of *Art Amateur* claimed to "give the term 'Oriental' a wide latitude of interpretation, letting it embrace Turkish, Egyptian, Persian and Indian. Japanese and Chinese belong to a somewhat different genre; but even in many articles—especially of the decorative kind—wares of those people would be cordially welcomed to help out the general scheme of Eastern luxury."[27] American Orientalism from the 1870s into the 1890s was diverse in its scope of inquiry.[28] Photographs, travel memoirs, paintings, architecture, sculpture, scientific studies, and the first stages of anthropology reveal attempts to secure a discursive grip on what Americans could learn about the "mysterious" East. However, art and design held a special place in the field of Orientalist studies because it was Asian, North African, and Middle Eastern material culture that Americans wanted in their homes. The success of Orientalism in venues such as *Art Amateur* was predicated on Americans bringing fantasies about the cultural Other into their daily lives.[29]

Montague Marks, *Art Amateur*'s first editor, began publishing the journal in 1879, at the same time that the Orientalist craze proliferated in the decorative arts market. In 1897, he sold his business to John Van Oost, who acted as publisher and editor from December 1897 through the final issue in September 1903. During its twenty-four years of publication, the magazine's central offices remained in New York City, but the editors occasionally mention other locations of publication (Boston and London), signifying the magazine's cachet as an international presence.[30] In short, the magazine was a critical voice in the growing discourse of popular literature that gave advice to Americans on how best to fill their homes with commodities that signified "cosmopolitan domesticity."

This international sensibility was dependent upon positing women as the ideal consumers who could fill the home with status-laden goods. In the magazine's first issue in June 1879, the lead article, "Rise of Art in the Household," places decorative responsibility in the hands of women. The author relates that "the influence exercised by ladies on the formation of modern art has never been fully realized by art historians. It was very great, and the medium through which it made itself felt was the household."[31] By employing the word "modern," this statement asks the reader to think of this feminine influence as a specific historical occurrence. The author clarifies this historical moment by noting that over "the last fifty years one of the principal elements of domestic life, the so-called home industry, has almost entirely disappeared." And, because of this dramatic event, "something must take the place of the occupation lost."[32] This was the transformative moment in nineteenth-century American domesticity when the economy of home-based production, where workers and masters lived and manufactured goods all in the same location, moved to an economy that enforced the separation between work and home.[33] *Art Amateur* clarified which gender was responsible for filling this new void in the American home:

Empty hands give empty hearts. The reason why Eve listened so willingly to the serpent was, no doubt, that she had nothing else to do. Now, having once risen from drudgery to home-industry, the household cannot go back to drudgery in order to get something to do; on the contrary it must rise one step higher and fill the vacant place with something still nobler: it must move onwards from home-industry to art occupations; and it is in this great movement, from which an elegant household can emancipate itself, which we beg leave to offer our assistance.[34]

American domesticity had changed, and the gendered household had to occupy itself with a different type of production—specifically, artistic production. There was no feeling of loss for the magazine's editors, only excitement about what Americans could focus on to formulate an artistic vision predicated on consumerist desire.

Who does *Art Amateur* hold responsible in its call for artistic action? Not only is Eve a biblical figure, but she is also religiously posited as the first woman. As the author reminds us, when Eve had nothing to do she got herself into trouble and bit the apple. This employment of Eve as the universal signifier of woman essentializes women and calls attention to the possibility of their transgressions when they are idle. *Art Amateur* demands that the household provide an environment conducive to a new format of work for middle-class women; this is a model of work that engages their abilities as homemakers through physical labor, amateur artistic talent, and consumerism. Now that middle-class Americans had time to use their homes (or, their new Edens) for purposes outside of the drudgery of production, they had to create a realm of domesticity that could complement this new way of living. Women had to keep busy and "buy into" these artistic concerns so that they could avoid the perils of leisure that faced the "first" woman.[35]

The cover of the December 1881 edition of the magazine includes a drawing of two Japanese-influenced vases on a table (fig. 14) that stresses the predominance of feminine themes in these interiors.[36] The face of each vase depicts a Japanese woman. On the left vase, a woman plays a

Figure 14 *Japanese Bronze Vases with Inlaid and Relief Decoration*, *Art Amateur* (December 1881).
Courtesy of the Boston Public Library, Fine Arts Department.

percussion instrument as she looks out over a body of water. The vase on
the right shows a woman looking over her shoulder on a moonlit porch
also set on the water. These are not simply innocent images of women
by the sea. The elongated bodies of these figures and the sultry lighting
of the moon are overtly erotic. The written text describing these vases is
particularly sexual and "cannot help calling attention to the charming
sentiment of the little pictures in metal of Japanese aesthetes. The air of
the love-sick maiden bathing in the moonlight is really delicious."[37] The
maiden is a fantasy displayed in the context of Orientalist desire; thus
inscribing her onto the surface of these objects would make the vases
more sought-after within *Art Amateur*'s pages. Her sexualized depiction
increases the vase's desirability.

The drawing of the vases by Camille Piton promotes the Western fantasy of Japanese exoticism. Through the use of perspective, Piton makes

it appear as though the women are caught, or trapped, in these aesthetic containers. Placed on a shelf and centered so that we, the *Art Amateur* reader, can get easy visual access, the "maidens" are made submissive; they are stuck, like genies in a bottle, in a container that holds and prepares them for our ocular attention. The interplay between the gendered theme of the vases' narrative and the way in which Piton's image creates a sense of perspective, which makes it look as though these women are on a proscenium, enacts an erotic performance. It becomes difficult to imagine the maidens outside the confines of their prison-like vessels.

In 1881, the same year that they saw Piton's drawings, *Art Amateur*'s subscribers received a gift: one of two sets of four menu cards designed by Tiffany and Company.[38] The Tiffany menu cards would have been used to display the courses of food at a middle-class dinner party.[39] In one set, the first two cards are a combination of American, European, and Japanese motifs. The third and fourth cards are where the inclusion of Asian imagery permits the conflation of the Oriental and sexuality. The third card represents an interior (fig. 15). Tiffany renders a large bamboo screen with a pink covering at the center of the image. A Japanese woman, who is on the left side of the screen, has a white napkin in her mouth. She looks to her left with an erotic smile, and directly in front of her is a three-legged table that holds fruit and a carafe of wine. The fourth card also depicts a room. Here a bamboo screen, with the phrase "After Dinner," stands between two Japanese women and a man. They appear to be playfully chasing each other around the prominent partition (fig. 16).[40]

Given the proliferation of Orientalist tropes in *Art Amateur*, the presence of these women dressed like geishas is not surprising. As Charles Longfellow made clear, the representation of Asian sexuality was an important part of American imaginings about Asia. The geisha became a projection for the Western erotic gaze, offering fantasies about sexuality that would not have been acceptable within the context of late nineteenth-century mores. Both menu cards focus, quite openly, on the relationship between sexuality and eating. Beyond their mere function as menu cards, the third card shows a woman eating and sucking on a napkin, and the fourth card announces the time of this chase as "after dinner." The images employ Orientalism to permit the expression of sexuality. These are not American men and women looking demure, sucking on napkins, and chasing each other, but American conceptions of an amative Japanese culture. Americans would never act this way at a Gilded Age dinner party that used Tiffany menu cards, but they could announce their meal with sexuality, if artists rendered that eroticism through an Orientalist context.[41]

All the figures on the menu cards wear kimonos that denote their

Figure 15 Tiffany and Co., menu card, *Art Amateur* (1881), insert. Courtesy of the Boston Public Library, Fine Arts Department.

nationality. Kimonos flourished during this period as a result of the fashion for women to get out of their corseted dresses into looser clothing. Americans saw the kimono as that which could free the body from the constraints of a previous style, while upholding its connotations of sexuality associated with Japan.[42] The sexuality found in these images becomes more overt if we look at the Japanese print sources for the Tiffany-designed card of the single geisha in front of the screen. A number

43

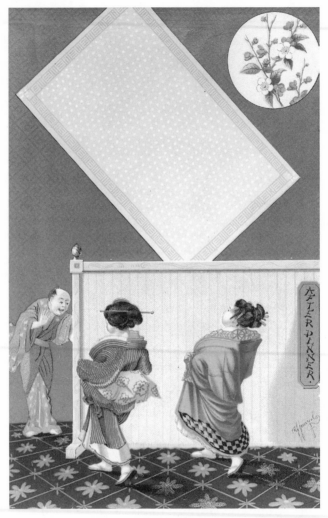

Figure 16 Tiffany and Co., menu card, *Art Amateur* (1881), insert. Courtesy of the Boston Public Library, Fine Arts Department.

of late eighteenth- and early nineteenth-century Japanese prints display geishas with tissue paper in their mouths, and their bodies have the same type of subservient pose that signifies a recoil away from a dominant figure, presumably the male, who, as in the Tiffany image, is absent. In Kikugawa Eizan's *Geisha with Umbrella* (ca. 1810s), for instance, the geisha's coy pose and the tissue hanging from her mouth are remarkably similar to the image on the menu card (fig. 17). Geisha imagery that includes an oral play with tissues suggests a number of sexual themes—longing, sensuality, and even an implied sense of cleanliness that the cloth would have allowed for postcoitus—referenced in Japanese prints through the iconography of napkins, tissues, and cloths.[43] These cards adhere to fantasies about the sexualized role of the geisha that were integral to imaginings about the Orient.

Like the sexuality that attends these menu cards, other descriptions in *Art Amateur* permit a retreat from everyday life within the fantasy space

Figure 17 Kikugawa Eizan (Japanese, 1787–1867), *Geisha with Umbrella*, color woodcut, 730 mm × 245 mm. Chazen Museum of Art, University of Wisconsin, Madison, Bequest of John H. Van Vleck, 1980.683.

of Oriental settings. In the April 1886 edition there is a description of the ideal "Oriental Lounging-Room": "We have long dreamed of a delightful little retreat . . . with everything suggestive of comfort combined with ideal idleness—a place where . . . the master of the house might retire and smoke his pipe with perfect rest. There . . . he would be in his glory, accessible to wife and babies and intimate friends, but none others could cross the threshold of the sanctum."[44] The best way to produce this mode of relaxation for the "master of the house" is within an Oriental environment. This "Oriental retreat" is a place where "we would have the room greatly subdued in the matter of illumination. . . . Books should be banished for the nonce, with the possible compromise that, for occasional sulky hours, a luxurious novel might appear as an agreeable companion."[45] Gender, and the construction of the Orient as a world of fantasy, defines this retreat. This space for relaxation is a place of escape for a man. His wife, children, and good friends can visit him in this inner "sanctum," but the entire room is built for his pleasure. This room, like the Tiffany menu cards, represents a sensual interior isolated from the commotion of Gilded Age, urban life. In late nineteenth-century America, a man could leave all his troubles behind if his sanctuary of repose signified the exotic Orient.[46]

The drawing that accompanies the article about the lounging room enhances the notion that this is a separate space constructed for a type of gendered isolation within the home (fig. 18). Like so many images of Oriental interiors, the drawing, completed by an artist identified only as L. F. W., depicts the corner of a room. The image includes a three-legged table, a hanging light fixture, a pierced wooden frieze, a print rack, and heavy fabrics. The article's reference to many of these objects as "Moorish" in design (for example, the pierced woodwork is described as Moorish) would have connoted a masculine space to the *Art Amateur* reader. Remember, the text details the importance of understanding this interior as a male domain, and the historical connection that readers would have made between these masculine objects and an understanding of the Moors as entangled with a history of conquest is significant.[47] Moorish history was part of American popular culture during the nineteenth century when books such as Washington Irving's *The Alhambra* enticed readers with narratives about the Moors' presence in Western Europe.[48]

The importance of collecting as the driving impetus behind the magazine's discussion of these Oriental interiors becomes apparent in the drawing "Oriental Lounging-Room." The artist renders the objects across the middle ground of the image to display these items as potential collectibles. The objects look as though they are in a display window ready for our visual consumption. These furnishings reveal the collection as an

Figure 18 L. F. W., "An Oriental Lounging-Room," *Art Amateur* (April 1886): 111. Courtesy of the Boston Public Library, Fine Art Department.

artificial construct where objects illustrate their owner's ability at assembling a miniature world within the domestic sphere.[49] In this instance, the collection signifies both the worldliness of the consumer and the gendered sensibility of this room within the Aesthetic-period home.

There are several places in *Art Amateur* where the fashion for Orientalism is given only the corner of a room. These so-called cozy corners were spaces within the parlor that allowed Americans to retreat from the unbending performance of middle-class mores.[50] Late nineteenth-century Americans understood the parlor as the best room in the house. Here they would meet their guests from the outside world and perform their gendered and class-bound roles in a highly staged manner, enacting what middle-class Americans defined, in the pages of the popular press and a wide range of prescriptive literature, as normative.[51] Decorators designed the cozy corner as a cluttered space that became a repository for objects that signified exoticism, racially marking an area within the parlor that permitted less formal behavior. Not only did these non-Western objects speak to the concept of retreat from polite society, but often the seating arrangement found in these spaces, replete with sofas ensconced with heavy pillows, allowed for a type of corporeal repose.[52] The eye could

Figure 19 W. P. Brigden, "Corner of a Reception-Room, with Japanese Furnishings," *Art Amateur* (December 1897): 17. Courtesy of the Boston Public Library, Fine Arts Department.

wander around these object-laden corners, while the body rested on comfortable fabrics that permitted relaxation not allowed in the other regions of the formal interior.

W. P. Brigden illustrates an ideal cozy corner in a drawing captioned "Corner of a Reception-Room, with Japanese Furnishings" from the December 1897 issue of *Art Amateur* (fig. 19). Brigden creates a triangle of space that leads us into one corner of this larger room. A bamboo screen separates the cozy corner from the rest of the parlor, and draped curtains, of "Chinese silk," segregate these Asian-influenced furnishings from the rest of the home. Brigden frames the entrance with two carved stands made from teakwood. The vase on the left stand contains a dwarf pine tree and the vase on the right stand has a sheaf of cattails that Brigden places next to a pair of Japanese fans attached to the screen. The bamboo screen is embellished with embroidered drapery that represents flowers and Japanese figures. Underneath this heavy fabric is a "cushioned lounge" that has several overstuffed pillows on its surface.[53] The separation of space between the inside and the outside of the cozy corner delineates how this parlor should be used. The world outside the cozy corner is for a type of regulated behavior that the parlor sanctions through its regimented space, while inside the cozy corner one can relax in an environment that signifies exotic difference. The screen functions as a barrier demarcating where and how one can act within this staged realm. To accentuate this division of space, Brigden depicts the bamboo screen's curtains as coming out from the mouth of a "Japanese mask"; the mask's eyes questioningly glance toward the room's entrance to the viewer's right. Even more peculiar are the implied hands that support two swags of the curtain on either side of the mask's face. The mouth of the mask seems to mimic the opening, or entrance, to the cozy corner, thus anthropomorphizing this interior and making this point of egress appear as a type of corporeal opening. Like the enigmatic world hidden within a body, the cozy corner offers the mysteries of a dark, unknown place.

Brigden's cozy corner displays an Asian-influenced collection. A religious symbol, which the written text describes, adds legitimacy to this "real" Oriental location: "Over part of this [embroidered drapery] hangs an old Buddhist Kakemono painted on brownish silk and mounted with old brocades—perhaps the most costly object in the room, as all good works of the sort are old, and therefore precious."[54] This hanging is, in other words, an antique with an Asian provenance. We do not know this object's exact origin, and, in fact, all that matters to this writer is that it is an authentic piece of Asia. Geographic precision is not important in a room that combines, in a hybridic mélange, so many objects from so many different countries. For instance, think about the national combination in this sentence, part of which I already quoted, "The drapery falling from a large Japanese mask over the opening in the screen of thin Chinese silk, of a delicate celadon green, embroidered in bright colors and gold."[55] Many of the objects found in these types of interiors were made in America, or in Asia, to satisfy Western customers, but the editors represent this Buddha as a piece of material culture that signifies the history of the Orient, the place that the entire room symbolically embodies.

Brigden's rendering domesticates the Orient through the machinations of design. Anne McClintock suggests that "the verb to domesticate is akin to dominate, which derives from *dominus*, lord of the *domum*, or home." From a historical perspective, "the verb to domesticate also carried as one of its meanings the action 'to civilize.'"[56] Bringing the material world of the Orient into the home, regardless of the fact that this conception of the Other was purely fantastic, reinforced the Western belief that these Oriental cultures, these unknown geographies that enticed through stereotype, could be tamed and shaped into a domesticated collection.

Americans inextricably linked domesticity to the cultural construction of race at the end of the nineteenth century. The strength of American fantasies about domesticity relied on the idea that outside the domestic realm were other locations, other races, and other peoples who reified American domesticity through what the West inscribed as cultural difference. The inclusion of Oriental objects within the American domicile points to an obfuscation of these racially charged political issues. Laura Wexler has described this phenomenon as the performance of "tender violence." The oxymoron explains the turn-of-the-century impulse toward domestic harmony predicated on a racially motivated discourse that covered up acts of violence.[57] The images of Orientalized interiors that I have been exploring do present a form of "tender violence." Although these descriptions of the perfect domestic sphere contain images and writing related to sentimentality, they repeatedly signify racial difference in ways that essentialize the East. In all the examples explored here, from the Tiffany menu cards to Morse's ethnological study of Japanese interiors, the Other is exoticized, but also bridled within the confines of books, furnishings, and collections. Represented as a curiosity to be emulated, the presence of Asian motifs in late nineteenth-century American design evidences the larger American project of trying to gain cultural control over the geography of the unknown. The stereotypes may have been positive and "tender" in tone, and the texts may have displayed numerous objects that were expensive and desirable, but the overall aesthetic mandated cultural appropriation and control conducted through the power of stereotype. Often pushed into the realm of the cozy corner, non-Western décor was surrounded, in a type of decorative-arts pincer movement, by the civilizing force of Western furnishings.

The civilizing trope of domestication is closely related to the empire building that I discuss in the remainder of this book. We cannot look at America's fight for overseas expansion during this period without questioning how events on the home front helped to bolster these military efforts. A symbiotic relationship existed between the American home and American empire that, while not part of a simple cause-and-effect scenario, does help explain the US interest in colonial endeavors from this period.[58] Rather than seal them off and keep them sheltered from other national interests, American fantasies about the domestic, whether lived or imagined, need to be historically contextualized as part of a fascination with other places that lay outside of the purview of everyday experience. Middle-class Americans saw their homes as experimental laboratories where the material culture they bought and displayed signified their growing fascination with an increasingly global economy and rapidly changing world political order.

Interior Scapes and Nationalist Fantasies

Another style of decoration, which celebrated the diminution of the exotic flourishes found during the Aesthetic period, emerged in the 1870s and became popular by the late 1880s. In July 1888, an article on domestic design in *Art Amateur* claimed that it "is not desirable to convert a family gathering place into a studio. . . . In the house of the average man . . . it is best to avoid artistic jumble."[59] The reign of Orientalist irregularity was giving way to images that showed the home as devoid of non-Western objects. The drawing underneath this article about the suitable home renders a sparse setting with little clutter (fig. 20). The room has wood paneling, exposed ceiling beams, and a Windsor chair, which were all details signifying the Colonial Revival.

Figure 20 "Cozy Fireplace Corner in the Hall," *Art Amateur* (July 1888): 38. Courtesy of the Boston Public Library, Fine Arts Department.

Figure 21 "Dining Room in 'Colonial' (Adam) Style, in the House of Mr. Frank Wallis, Architect," *Art Amateur* (March 1896): 95. Courtesy of the Boston Public Library, Fine Arts Department.

This move from Aesthetic period exoticism to the Colonial Revival be-came more pronounced during the 1890s. The turn toward an American fantasy about its colonial past was, in part, a reaction against the Aes-thetic movement. Interiors that signified the Colonial Revival contained fewer objects, utilized lighter colors, and accentuated verticality instead of the horizontality found in spaces laden with bric-a-brac.[60] An image from the March 1896 issue of the *Art Amateur* depicts this restrained deco-rating scheme in "Dining-Room in 'Colonial' (Adam) Style." The Oriental influence is absent in this drawing (fig. 21). The tiled fireplace, Chippen-dale chairs, Federal-style sideboard, basic mahogany table, and overall "chaste simplicity" (to use the caption's terminology) of the room reflect an adherence to this new decorative interest in America's culturally con-structed colonial past.[61]

Through advocacy of a material culture that emphasized spinning wheels, hearths, Chippendale and Queen Anne furniture, and other fan-tasies about an indigenous past, Americans looked inward for inspiration that would upend the exoticism of the previous decades. This new inter-est in the colonial created a jingoistic disposition that would ideologically support the growing sense of nationalism that became more pronounced during the 1890s. The Colonial Revival was part of the same period of history that witnessed a trend toward imperialist and militaristic practices. Representations of the Orient continued to fill the popular press and the pages of American art journals. For instance, the cozy corner dates from 1897, but there was an increasing movement away from the exotic toward a more austere sense of décor. Howells's characterization of the Marches, introduced at the beginning of this chapter, indicates this mind-set as they shun Mrs. Green's impossibly cluttered interior. Furthermore, Edward Morse foreshadowed this new style with his demand for fewer furnishings. The *Art Amateur*, while still committing itself in a limited way to exoticism, adhered to a colonial aesthetic that used design to celebrate pride in America's heritage.

This nationalistic aesthetic was made very apparent in a February 1899 article about two different children's bedrooms, one for a boy and one for a girl. The article and attendant imagery posit a connection between childhood culture and American success during the Spanish-American War of 1898, which brought the United States onto the international stage of militarism. The editors explain that the "young man's bedroom is evidently that of a person of military and sporting proclivities, as most young men are. The trophy over the bureau suggests that he may have smelled powder at Santiago; while if an army man, he must be credited with a generous enthusiasm for the deeds of our navy also, for what else can the model of the man-of-war on top of the bookcase signify?"[62] The mentioning of Santiago (a battle during the Spanish-American conflict) and other rudiments of military culture would have reminded the reader of the Spanish-American War and answered the author's rhetorical inquiry. The bedroom suggests what Lisa Bloom has identified as the turn-of-the-century "relation[ship] between *masculinism* and *nationalism*."[63] Every surface in this room contains tropes of masculinity that would, the editors hoped, facilitate the healthy development of an ideal American boy.

These children's interiors, with their lack of exoticism and inclusion of ladder-back chairs and decorative swags and wreaths, clearly invoke the Colonial Revival. In this instance, the rustic colonial past, represented in the boy's room through heavy woods and sharp angles, accentuates an overtly male-identified aesthetic. The girl's room, however, deploys tropes from the Federal period, which would have signaled a more feminine sensibility.[64] The emphasis on space defined through gender becomes even more apparent if we compare the drawings by W. P. Brigden of the "young man's bedroom" and the "young girl's bedroom" in greater detail (figs. 22 and 23).[65] The focus in the young man's room is on his possessions, which reveal his desire for competition and, to use Theodore

Figure 22 W. P. Brigden, "A Simple Arrangement for a Young Man's Bedroom," *Art Amateur* (February 1899): 68. Courtesy of the Boston Public Library, Fine Arts Department.

Roosevelt's phrase, "the strenuous life."[66] Besides the man-of-war, a gun and sword are on the left side of the drawing, and two tennis racquets are over the room's doorway. To stress competitiveness, the only readable framed picture in the room represents a battle. The artist constructs the girl's room in an entirely different fashion. The bed, which acts merely as negative, foreground space in the young man's room, is more prominent in her room. Furthermore, her interior lacks all signs of war and competition. Her writing table is open, a number of photographs are on the bookcase, and the only readable framed image is a tranquil landscape.[67] The design of the young man's room focuses on the world of belligerence outside the home, while the girl's room contains objects that refer to the domestic sphere. The bed is for sleeping, the desk is for writing, and the photographs on the bookcase are for looking. The material culture of this girl's room is for in-house use, and the boy's room becomes a space for fantasies about American military triumphs that would take place outside the home.[68] The boy's room, especially when compared with the girl's room, is a vivid example of the turn-of-the-century interest in the masculine nature of war.[69]

The Colonial Revival enabled Americans to utilize material culture to construct an imagined sense of nationalism.[70] Thus, *Art Amateur*'s readership constituted a coterie of those with art-world interests who promoted this new nation-based aesthetic. Seeing the magazine in the homes of other middle-class design aficionados would have fostered a type of camaraderie among readers of this evolving and popular arts press. In short, *Art Amateur*'s advocacy of the Colonial Revival through its widely disseminated pages helped devise American thinking about its exceptionalism. This, in turn, went hand in hand with the revival of a decorative arts style that contained narratives about the nation's shared, yet fantastical, sense of the past. In the case of the Colonial Revival, Americans constructed their own sense of a superior past through a decorative tribute to a mythic conception of American history. The ongoing promotion of this revival worked well with narratives about masculinity, militarism, and imperialism that were omnipresent at the end of the nineteenth century.[71]

Figure 23 W. P. Brigden, "A Simple Arrangement for a Young Girl's Bedroom," *Art Amateur* (February 1899): 69. Courtesy of the Boston Public Library, Fine Arts Department.

Although the Colonial Revival eliminated much of the exoticism of the previous decades, the break from Orientalism was far from clean. There was ambivalence about décor, or a back-and-forth between the austerity of the Colonial Revival and the exoticized abundance found in places like *Art Amateur*. These two opposing discourses needed each other to survive. Just as Americans domesticated the cozy corner within the parlor, these same Americans often tamed the exoticized interior with the countering discourse of the Colonial Revival. Periodicals committed to interior design reenacted this spatial conflict through alternating points of view. In one article, the Colonial Revival became the focal point; on the next page, or issue, the exoticism of the Orient found praise.

Art about War and the Philippines

Later editions of *Art Amateur* contain reactions to the Spanish-American War that move outside the American domestic sphere into the hotly contested colonial zone of the Philippines. In an article from the February 1902 edition of the magazine titled "Art in the Philippines," G. D. Rice writes about artistic changes in the Philippines since the advent of American colonialism. He comments on photography, woodcarving, and lettering. During his discussion about photography, Rice notes how "there is a very good business being done by the photographers throughout the islands. Some of the proprietors of the photographic galleries are Spanish and Filipinos, while one often sees that the proprietor is an American." American "soldiers have in some cases undertaken the business, and they are making money at it. I know of a number of ex-soldiers who are deriving good incomes from small outfits they put in recently. The natives have a great love for photography, and they will pay high prices for two or three inferior pictures of themselves in best attire."[72] Soldiers who had invaded the islands four years before, and who probably had engaged in the Philippine-American War, were now selling what Rice describes as inferior art for a profit. Later in the same essay, he mentions the recent proliferation of sign painting in the Philippines. He explores this art in detail and includes a drawing of sample letter styles and sign painting equipment. Over the course of "the past year a large number of new stores and manufacturing places were opened in Manila, Iloilo, and other places on the islands, and nearly all of the proprietors required signs of some sort. In many cases the owners need two sets of signs, one set in English and the other in the local language."[73] Rice promoted the American imperialist cause through his commentary about the need for English signs. This influx of English is exemplary of what American imperialism brought to the Orient; now even the lingua franca of the Philippines began losing its authority.[74]

Rice's essay reports on Americans bringing commerce to "native" Filipinos in a way that will increase the colony's fiscal success. This is not *Art Amateur*'s typical artistic appropriation of a fantastical Asian culture, but a type of political journalism that details American entrepreneurial accomplishments in the new colony. Rice idealized the American intervention and how the American presence in the Pacific was (when read through the experience of the arts) a story about the spread of English, and, most importantly, the influence of financial savvy in a part of the world that appeared inferior in the pages of the mass media.

In the articles about the two children's bedrooms, and in Rice's description of Philippine arts, the Spanish-American War remains subtextual; each author elided the actuality of war because of its political implications. In the October 1899 edition of *Art Amateur*, however, Charles Niehaus wrote specifically about the Spanish-American War and the Dewey Arch, which the National Sculpture Society built in New York City to commemorate Admiral Dewey's decisive victory in the Philippines over the Spanish in May 1898 (fig. 24). A member of the Sculpture Society who

Figure 24 The Dewey Triumphal Arch and Colonnade. Image from Moses King, *The Dewey Reception Committee of New York City* (New York: Chasmar-Winchell, 1899), 8. Courtesy of the Library of Congress.

worked on the arch, Niehaus detailed who built the arch and how it appeared.[75] On the page after Niehaus's report, in "The Note-Book" section of the magazine, a paragraph described how "the patriotism of the sculptors who volunteered to decorate the Dewey Arch has unfortunately resulted in the death of two of their number, and the prostration, through an attack of paralysis, of a third."[76] *Art Amateur* conflated artistic production with death, elevating the status of this sculptural monument beyond a mere celebration of military victory. The actual building of the arch recreated the war by representing the artisan as an individual who sacrificed his life in a type of artistic battle. In other words, the construction of the Dewey Arch replayed the heroic sacrifice of war.

The commentary on the Dewey Arch elucidates how interest in the Orient intersected with issues related to American colonialism in the late 1890s. Narratives of heroism, such as triumphal and tragic stories about building enormous works of sculpture, supported imperialist aspirations. The Orient had been a distant place that could be bought, displayed, and misappropriated in art journals, books, and personal archives, but now it was a potential colony. Thus, the collector's impulse to isolate the Orient as a site that could be studied, as if under the lid of a cigar box, was now a focal point of American visual and material culture that accompanied the mounting concern with overseas interests. There was an increasing fascination with Asia as a site that could become an American stronghold for colonial activity. This imperial incursion centered on military might, commercial success, and the constant refrain of benevolent assimilation conducted under the pretext of civilizing missions.

Art Amateur stopped publishing in 1903, and Edward Morse continued to publish books about Asia well into the twentieth century.[77] However, the dissemination of artistic Orientalism throughout the Gilded Age by Morse and the magazine's editors exemplifies their position as early agents of American interest in Asia. They asked their readers to purchase Oriental objects and place these goods in their artistic homes; they discussed these exoticized interiors in a manner that employed Oriental fantasies to represent a commodity aesthetic. In short, this process helped to introduce many middle-class readers to an ever-growing interest in Asia, as exemplified in *Art Amateur*'s eventual foray into the politics of war and empire. Indeed, through the circulation of this expanding Orientalist discourse, *Art Amateur* eventually commented on and approved of the American intervention in the Philippines, rendering this distant place as a location that could help satiate America's need for an imperialist future.

THREE

Disseminating Empire

Representing the Philippine Colony

At the beginning of the twentieth century, the Orient remained, in part, a phantasmatic site, a place where Western
imagination continued to envision exoticism and peculiarity. This imagination grew into ideas about how this
location could be controlled through the machinations of
empire building. As discussed in the previous chapter, the
editors of art and décor journals acknowledged this shift
in American Orientalism by commenting on the American
presence in the Philippines. In 1902, *Brush and Pencil* published an article "Native Art in the Moro Country," paying
tribute to a region of the Philippines the media often described as untouched by Western influence. Author George
Reece explains his journalistic mission: "As your correspondent has been sketching and photographing in the island
of Mindanao, where white man never trod before, perhaps
an account of the trip, especially of the methods of Moro
artists, may be of interest to the magazine's readers." Before looking at Moro art in detail, Reece reports that the
Moros' isolation from the rest of the world is a product of
a "sultan and dattos" who "do not encourage visits from
foreigners. They prefer to be let alone." Reece claims that
the only way to penetrate this "forbidden portion of the
island" is with the help of "the American column of United
States soldiers."[1]

The Philippine landscape was repeatedly posited as a forbidden locale, a place of treachery and fear, as Americans
began to explore the colony. Reece's description of Moro

art reinforced his account of the Moros' primitive state. "The native artist depends largely upon what he can collect about him. He does not use much pottery or metal wire. He can get a form of dish for mixing purposes by cutting out a section of wood from the nearest bamboo-tree."[2] Reece commented on other artistic equipment, including "a Moro mallet of wood for reducing pieces of mineral stuff," only to conclude that the "Moro artist is of course greatly handicapped in his work. He must not only make nearly everything he uses, but he must hustle for supplies."[3] Since the magazine contained countless articles describing the ease of acquiring store-bought art supplies, the notion of hunting for equipment in the wild would have been anomalous to *Brush and Pencil*'s readership. The native Filipino artist, according to Reece, has suffered as a result of a lack of industrialization. The brushes and pencils that the periodical's audience would have been able to procure would have been unthinkable to the Moro artist, whose ability to get supplies was made analogous to the prehistoric acts of hunting and gathering.

Reece's understanding of Moro art encapsulates several of the themes that this chapter explores in its assessment of how the media disseminated American empire through the visual scape of news coverage. In Reece's narrative, the Moro artist becomes a subject that can be fixed, represented, and disciplined through the efforts of benevolent assimilation, which was the official American colonial policy formulated to make the Filipino people more Occidental and less Oriental. Vicente Rafael has interrogated the American colonizers' notion of paternalistic and civilizing change by "suggest[ing] that the link between benevolence and discipline was made possible through representational practices that recast Filipino appearances. The re-formation of natives as colonial subjects required that they become visible and therefore accessible to those charged with their supervision."[4] Reece placed the Filipino artist on view and in clear sight for the visually mediated experience of American imperialism. The savage became a signifier of an earlier period and it is, Reece tacitly argued, the responsibility of colonialism to rescue the Moro artist from his modern-day anachronistic life.

There are hundreds of magazines and newspapers from this period that assess the Philippines as a location for American imperialism. Several of these sources take an anti-imperialist stance and maintain that the United States had no business abusing the political and economic resources of another country. In 1901, for instance, Mark Twain wrote his famous essay "To the Person Sitting in Darkness" for the *North American Review*. Twain describes American colonial interests in the Philippines as "a pity; it was a great pity, that error; that one grievous error, that irrevocable error."[5] To Twain, getting involved with the Philippines was a diplomatic nightmare and a moral blunder. While begun under the guise of freedom, colonialism was in reality the unyielding American practice of pilfering Philippine land through violence. The overriding sentiment of the American press, however, was enthusiasm for war and empire. Even when the popular press protested American colonialism, it was often done in outrageous ways through racially charged representations of the archipelago. This tactic would, ultimately, sell more newsprint. The excitement about war fed the American public's desire for media coverage about those parts of the world understood as exotic. Newspapers such as William Randolph Hearst's *Evening Journal* and Joseph Pulitzer's the *World* drove American interests in the international arena through exaggerated imagery.[6]

This chapter looks at this imagery and argues that the visual scape of news provided an ideal venue for debates about colonialism during the late nineteenth and early twentieth century. In particular, it is the images—the photographs and drawings—that promulgated the most racially loaded representations in the expanding popular press. The mass media depicted the Philippines as a visually curious site where civilization did not exist and all that could be found was the taint of exoticized bodies, odd customs, and contaminated blood. Ironically, the barbaric Philippines was also understood as a potential site for commercial activity, especially after American technology could be deployed to help ease the flow of capital. Thus, this chapter concludes with a discussion about how the media portrayed the commercial viability of America's colonial outpost.

Ethnographic Curiosity

Hearst's *New York Evening Journal* devoted a full page of coverage to the 1901 capture of Emilio Aguinaldo, the leader of the Philippine insurgency movement. After being celebrated by the Americans in the hope that he would facilitate the Spanish defeat, Aguinaldo fought against the American military forces led by brigadier general Frederick Funston. Headlines such as "Prison for Aguinaldo" and "Funston's Companions" are neatly boxed into articles on various parts of the page. Along with this serious copy are more facetious headlines, such as "Spank Him" and a poem entitled "No Foozle for Funston." Next to this written text are four separate images taken from photographs representing Funston's eyes, Funston's chin, Aguinaldo's eyes, and Aguinaldo's mouth (fig. 25).

Figure 25 "Funston's Nerve Took Wily Filipinos Off Their Guard," *New York Evening Journal*, March 28, 1901. Courtesy of Harry Ransom Humanities Research Center, The University of Texas at Austin.

Each image has a caption about these physiognomic depictions. Under the title "Funston's Typical American Eyes (from a photograph)" is a rectangular box with a visual cross-section of Funston's face. These unusual juxtapositions need to be read in conjunction with the passage beneath the images: "Funston has the eyes of a woman when he is not stirred up. . . . But they are deep set, and the softness changes to sternness when he has a difficult job on hand. He is a man absolutely without fear." Across the page are "Aguinaldo's Remarkable Eyes (from a photograph)" with the written text "The captured leader of the Filipinos is said to have the most remarkable eyes—almost of hypnotic power and at times savage. They are coal black and piercing. He has the power to control men with them."[7] The representation of Aguinaldo's eyes is similar to the facial cross-section in Funston's depiction, but the Filipino's eyes do not stare at the viewer with purpose. It is as if his savage eyes are too powerful to allow the reader a full-frontal view of their entrancing depth.

The images of Funston's chin and Aguinaldo's mouth are stacked vertically, and Funston's bearded lower face receives top billing. Under the depiction of "Funston's Strong Chin (from a photograph)" is a physiognomic explanation of his character: "Funston's mouth and chin denote determination. It is strong in every particular. His jaws come together like a bulldog's. A man who knows him well, describing his chin, said—'God almighty knew what he was about when he put that chin on Funston.'" Directly below this description is "Aguinaldo's Savage Mouth (from a photograph)" and writing that details how "Aguinaldo's mouth denotes the savage. His lips are red and thick. The lower lip hangs down heavily. The upper lip turns up coarsely. His brutality is plainly shown."[8] In an increasingly urbanized world, physiognomy, a pseudoscience that connected body parts to character analysis, flourished. Physically based tests, given in an instant, could reveal the "true nature" of a neighbor or stranger. John Kasson notes that much of this physiognomic "science of reading temperament and character from the appearance of the body and particularly the face . . . was a pursuit that thrived in the social conditions of the metropolis, which brought a vast array of human types into intimate proximity."[9] The media used this "science" in the colonial setting, where reading Philippine culture was problematic guesswork. By formulating a comparison between American and Filipino physical traits, the *Evening Journal* constructed Funston's physical appearance using "American" characteristics, such as determination, fearlessness, strength, and an ability to show a kind, "feminine" side. Aguinaldo's mouth and eyes, in contrast, "denote" the antithesis and signify the uncivilized state of the Philippines. An American consumer of newspapers could have utilized these media portrayals to construct the Philippines as a place that could benefit from American colonial control. On the other hand, anti-imperialists could have pointed to Aguinaldo's frightening body as the reason to avoid the savagery found on the other side of the Pacific. Ethnographic renderings of a putatively uncivilized Filipino culture translated into cultural inferiority, an inadequacy that many claimed should be avoided and others thought could be enhanced through benevolent assimilation.

Headlines note that a photographer rendered Aguinaldo's and Funston's body parts (note the phrase "from a photograph" included above each image). This was a meaningful caveat that validated these representations. Although these images are not actual photographs (they are engraved tracings of photos), the mere mention of the photographic method explained their portrayal as trustworthy. The editors' use of close-up and cropping techniques, which help make these images readily legible, permitted conclusions based on the biased text found above and below each depiction. The newspaper's readers would have recognized these details of Funston's and Aguinaldo's bodies, along with the physiognomic comments, as documentary truth.[10] The media magnified stereotypes of the Orient through the rendering of Oriental and Occidental bodies, and the juxtaposition ensured the colony's subaltern position.

A year after Aguinaldo's capture, the Americans released him from prison with amnesty. By May 1902, the colonization of the Philippines putatively appeared complete; although fighting continued, president Theodore Roosevelt declared in the summer of 1902 that the islands in the Pacific were under American control. Aguinaldo and his body, however, remained a physiognomic curiosity. In October of the same year, the *World* published a lengthy article and images from a recent American media junket to the insurgent leader "on his homestead near Manila since he received full amnesty." The article, written by William Dinwiddie, details the living situation of the Filipino leader during his captivity. Dinwiddie reveals that the "more one studies Aguinaldo's face the greater is the impression of general strength. His forehead is high and straight. . . . The chin and jaw are strong, far stronger than those of the average representative of his race, and the teeth are always closely set together, as is the habit of determined men." These physical descriptions attain more authorial validity through photography. "The photograph of Aguinaldo and Lieut. Johnson, his last keeper, taken together, gives opportunity for comparison of two races, for both have a general similarity of head" (fig. 26). The physical likeness between Aguinaldo and his American counterpart belie the striking differences the *Evening Journal* posited between Aguinaldo and Funston. It was no longer necessary to represent Aguinaldo as a barbarian, because he had been caught, and "the closing days of . . . [his] long military confinement were rather pathetic, for the little man had eaten his heart out in the silent misery of a lost cause."[11] Aguinaldo, removed from the role of insurgent leader and domesticated on a couch, had been defeated.

THE WORLD: SUNDAY. OCTOBER 5, 1902

as a *Prisoner* at *$4 a Day*

Vanquished Filipino Leader in Captivity

cted. How He Looked. What He Said
to Say—His Life as a Farmer on His
to Since He Received Full Amnesty

Figure 26 "Aguinaldo as a Prisoner at $4 a Day," *World*, October 5, 1902. General Research Division, The New York Public Library, Astor, Lenox and Tilden Foundations.

The popular press also used markers of physical difference to discern tribal affiliations in the Philippines. Before Aguinaldo's capture in 1901, the press assumed that a group of Filipinos, known as the Igorots, had killed him in May 1900.[12] The year before the release of this *Evening Journal* article about Aguinaldo's possible death, *Harper's Weekly* published "Philippine Ethnology" by Marion Wilcox, who described the Igorots' ferocity. Wilcox divided native Filipinos into seven distinct tribal groups and wrote extensively about the Igorots. Wilcox assessed their physical traits with frank precision: "The Igorrotes are tall, robust, and well proportioned, we are told. Their skin is brown, their hair is black, straight, and very thick, cut short over the forehead, and hanging loose over back and shoulders. They have high and vertical foreheads; large, black, expressive eyes (sometimes with a slight inward tendency). . . ."[13] The article about the rumored death of Aguinaldo in the *Evening Journal* includes a photograph of an Igorot that corresponds with Wilcox's writing (fig. 27). In this image, "an Igorrote Warrior" stands erect with his arms down at his sides. He holds his spear upright in his right hand and engages the viewer with a direct stare, revealing a readiness for battle. Showing an image of an Igorot allowed the American reader to participate in a new form of armchair travel; the primitive fighter could enter the American domestic realm at a safe distance, encapsulated and categorized within a photographic representation.[14]

Journalists described the savage qualities of the Igorot in detail. Wilcox, for example, warned that the "Igorrotes are the wildest and most savage of all the . . . island tribes in the archipelago."[15] Indeed, "In time of war they paint their bodies and faces. Our North-American Indians so

Figure 27 "An Igorrote Warrior," *New York Evening Journal*, May 3, 1900. Courtesy of the Harry Ransom Humanities Research Center, The University of Texas at Austin.

thoroughly interpret to us this type of humanity that we shall presently hear of a Pacific discovery of America, and maybe find that some of our present hostiles are blood-relations to the poor foes of the Pilgrims and Puritans."[16] The Native American had, by this point, established an inferior position in the minds of middle-class American readers. Thus, the Filipino could be constructed as a barbaric savage through a comparative ethnographic stereotype that purported racial inferiority predicated on the possibility of a similar bloodline.

Other media descriptions portrayed Filipinos as wild and belligerent by using familiar tropes related to representations of Native Americans. In February 1899, the *Evening Journal* published a drawing with the caption "Formidable Knives of Filipino Warriors." These six knives, lined up in a row, all appear threatening, especially the first knife on the right side, which has a lock of hair hanging from its handle (fig. 28).[17] The ominous nature of this weapon goes beyond its sharp and dangerous appearance; here a symbolic manifestation of a maimed body—a lock of disembodied hair—is present. During the initial days of the American invasion of Manila Bay, reporter John Dwyer explained, "They [the Filipino natives] have long knives which they use with the utmost proficiency, and which are keen enough to cut a man's head off at a blow." An American audience looking at the drawing of knives might have accepted the idea of American intervention in a location where "heads of . . . victims are spiked as landmarks."[18] This visual representation of decapitation, where the only indication of the missing head is the synecdoche of hair wrapped around the knife's handle, would have reminded American readers of narratives about Native American barbarism. Stories about the Native American practice of scalping were quite popular in the nineteenth century, thus the press provoked more fear and fascination about the Philippines by reporting on these supposed native Philippine practices.[19]

While fervor for imperialism may be part of the logic behind these images, an anti-imperialist mind-set can also be attributed to this media discourse. Anti-imperialist sentiment spread widely during this period and many questioned these representations of Philippine barbarism. Sixto Lopez, for instance, a Filipino member of the Boston Anti-Imperialist League, took umbrage with the popular notion of Philippine savagery. In his essay *The "Wild Tribes" and Other Filipinos*, published by the league, he contends that in "the official census of March 2, 1903, taken under the directorship of General I. P. Sanger, the population of the Philippines numbered 7,635,426. Of this number 647,740 (including the Moros) are classified as 'wild and uncivilized, though not without some knowledge of the domestic arts.'" Lopez notes that these "figures may or may not represent the actual facts. It depends, not on the accuracy of the count, but on whether the line between civilized and wild has been accurately drawn. The absence of European clothing, or of a particular form of religion, does not in itself furnish evidence of being uncivilized."[20] His understanding of cultural relativism was unusual for this period, especially at a moment when anthropology, along with its initial commitment to ethnocentric points of view, was beginning to take shape as an academic discipline. While Lopez would have been upset with depictions of Filipino knives

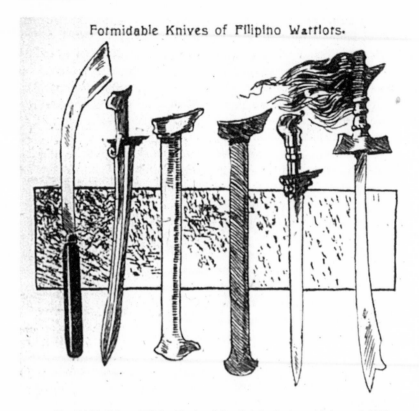

Figure 28 "Formidable Knives of Filipino Warriors," *New York Evening Journal*, February 6, 1899. Courtesy of the Harry Ransom Humanities Research Center, The University of Texas at Austin.

and discussions about decapitation, another mode of anti-imperialism can be attributed to these media representations of Philippine savagery. Indeed, many would have argued for turning away from a part of the world that supposedly engaged in scalping and other questionable practices. To anti-imperialists, these media representations were exemplary of why it was essential to remain out of the international political arena; headhunters, death, and an overall predilection for savagery were exactly what many Americans feared. By making these portents of barbarity come to life, the media played into the fears of those who advocated an isolationist attitude, while concomitantly providing evidence for those pro-imperialists who adhered to the government-sanctioned program of benevolent assimilation.

The dominant narrative repeated in many of these articles about Filipino natives is that savagery, obsession with revenge, and an overall uncivilized nature are characteristics flowing through Filipino blood. An article in *Harper's Weekly* titled "Filipino Characteristics" describes the "mixed blood" as "any cross of Malay-Spanish, Malay-Chinese, or Malay-English. . . . The Malay-Chinese unquestionably produced the best results—quick mentally, and honest commercially, in both respects fully up to European standard."[21] Another article from *Harper's* declares that "conceit, which like the spirit of revenge, is one of the dominant characteristics of every human being who has a taint of Malay blood in his veins, is somewhat modified in its influence by the councils of a few experienced and educated Filipinos who have traveled abroad."[22] *Harper's* furthered the quest for American superiority by adhering to the theory that blood infuses racially based characteristics.

Outside of the transmission of racial defects, the popular press also imagined blood as the carrier of diseases in the Philippines. In January 1899, the *World* published an article called "The Revenge of the Filipino" about two men who used a syringe filled with leprosy bacteria to infect an American soldier. The article opens with a brief passage from a Rudyard Kipling story entitled "The Phantom Rickshaw," which includes, within the context of its Orientalist narrative, details about leprosy.[23] The anonymous writer introduces the reader to private William Lapeer, "a returned soldier from the Philippines, tossing on a bed of pain in his father's house in Richmond," who "told The World why he fears that there is in his veins a poison subtler and more insidious than that of tropic fever."[24] The author situates the hyperbole of this article by opening with this dramatic point of view and explaining that Lapeer's experiences will be as spellbinding as Kipling's popular fiction.

Lapeer's narrative maintains the initial promise of its sensationalist tenor. The private explains that he and a few American soldiers got into a quarrel with a group of Filipinos that resulted in the Filipinos drugging his drink and bringing him back to "a dirty little room." Lapeer awoke from his drug-induced state to a group of Filipinos, one of whom was a leper. The soldier relates, "He was the worst-looking leper I'd seen on the islands. His fingers had fallen off, his face was covered with white, chalky knobs and scales, and his joints were so stiff he could hardly walk." Then the leader of the Filipino group "laughed and said I'd [Lapeer] be like that soon. He told me that he and his friend had squirted the leper's blood into me while I lay unconscious." Lapeer (did the turn-of-the-century reader get the pun?) describes his emotional state as so precarious since then that before "rotting" to death like the lepers he has seen in Manila, he will first "blow [his] brains out."[25] Turn-of-the-century Americans would have been very familiar with discussions about racial connections to blood as a result of slavery and its deep commitment to bloodlines as an indicator of racial typology. Anxieties about tainted blood translated into a growing fear of the developing American colony. The idea of being "contaminated" was enough to make many Americans terrified about the prospect of being surrounded by Filipinos.[26] As Warwick Anderson writes, "All the fauna in the archipelago, whether human or nonhuman, seemed increasingly duplicitous, ready at any moment to come into focus, to sting, to infect, to shoot."[27] This upset over what Anderson elucidates as "colonial pathologies" led to the creation of a colonial medical administration that attempted to sanitize the colony to quell the hysteria that accompanied supposed threats to white colonists. The perception of the Philippine body as diseased was a cornerstone of American colonial policy. In the colonial zone, American officials believed that race and disease were intricately linked; thus, specific ailments, such as leprosy, symbolically transmitted the anti-imperial fear that some Americans had of Filipinos and the need for benevolent assimilation that others advocated.

Images enhanced the horrific quality of the written text from this article (fig. 29). The central drawing represents Lapeer crouched next to the wall of a hut examining his arm, which has been injected with leprosy. Six Filipinos surround him. The American appears innocent and helpless, while the bodies and faces of the Filipinos contort with laughter; they are carelessly smoking cigarettes and are boisterous with enthusiasm because of their ability to humiliate the American soldier. Above this scene is a strip of drawings that represent four different "Types of Native Filipinos" and a hut captioned "In such a hut as this the incident happened." This conflation of architectural and facial stereotypes would have accentuated the foreign, and therefore frightening, aspects of this scene. It is difficult to read these shadowy faces, and the hut would have looked mysterious to a turn-of-the-century reader because it was an architectural manifestation of an unknown and uncivilized culture. On the right side of the central scene, functioning as the newspaper audience's ethnographic contrast, is a full-length portrait of "Private Lapeer From Photo furnished to the World by Correspondent Baxter of Sioux City." Lapeer stands strong and proud without the bodily contortions or facial exaggerations found in the adjacent images of Filipinos. He stands, in brief, like Kipling's *White Man* who understands his privileged place within the context of the savage landscape. To ensure our trust in this depiction of Lapeer, the image includes the ubiquitous words "From Photo," the cultural index of truth and documentation.[28]

Figure 29 "The Revenge of the Filipino," *World*, January 22, 1899. General Research Division, The New York Public Library, Astor, Lenox and Tilden Foundations.

The same media sources that attempted to evoke panic in relation to unhealthy blood in the colony often treated American military atrocities as permissible because the Oriental environment supposedly induced mind-altering states. In 1902, *McClure's Magazine* included a lengthy account of how an American soldier may become savage while serving in the Philippines. Dr. Henry Rowland, in his essay "Fighting Life in the Philippines," addressed rumors about American aggression against Filipino natives. Rowland assumed that executions had been carried out, that torture had been practiced, and that subordinate American soldiers had not questioned their superiors who demanded these actions. He asserted that American soldiers acted in ways incomprehensible to the typical American at home. Instead of apologizing for these war crimes, Rowland rendered these actions as acceptable by explaining the horrors of what it was like to fight on the other side of the Pacific Ocean.[29]

In his essay, Rowland, whom *McClure's* credits as having treated mentally ill soldiers, creates three "typical," yet fictive, American servicemen to explain his premise. He gives them the names Tom, Dick, and Harry and provides them with brief biographies that further their characterization as normative. For instance, "Harry is a clerk in his uncle's store, the only one in a middle Western village. He has watched the trainloads of troops rushing through on their way to the Pacific Coast, and being Anglo-Saxon, and therefore adventurous, he has been unable to resist the temptation of following them."[30] Rowland portrays Harry as vigorous and "high spirited" by describing the Anglo-Saxon race as "adventurous" and prepared for battle. Rowland also reveals the unpleasant realities of war. He details the mental anguish the American soldier must endure because of his distance from home. "Nostalgia," or homesickness, sets in, causing a variety of negative reactions that can remain undetected until it "finally bursts into a flame of suicidal, or homicidal, mania." In fact, he continues, homesickness "accounts for more dementia than sun or fever."[31] Rowland believes that being on Philippine soil leads to pathological behavior.

Eventually, Rowland explains, whether in "bursts" of murderous behavior or in the gradual form of psychological deterioration, the soldier expresses the malady of homesickness. Part of this melancholia is manifest in the Americans' disdain for native Filipinos. "They [the American soldiers] have long since ceased to look upon friendly natives with a kindly toleration; no longer do they play with the brown babies and chat with the soft-eyed mothers in the market-place. They have found comrades who had grown to trust these furtive islanders, cold and stark, hacked and dismembered in the bananas."[32] The American soldier loses his humanitarian interests in the quaint local culture and eventually the "sight of a trench full of dead insurgents awakens no more feeling than the wreck of a cattle train."[33] Mental anguish, stemming from homesickness and disingenuous natives, leads to an overall disregard for justice. Toward the end of his essay, Rowland gives an example of what this predicament of distance, coupled with being in the presence of savagery, does to soldiers. He describes a battalion that encounters a group of insurgents. According to Rowland, these Filipinos have already killed several American troops through decapitation. The insurgents are a swarm of life, "a foul festering life, such as only a tropic sun can spawn."[34] Once the Americans catch these Filipinos, one corporal disembowels a native and blows "his heart out." In short order, the Americans execute the entire Filipino group. The narrative builds to this cathartic moment of violence when the American soldier can no longer repress his anger and mental angst. But just in case we miss the point, Rowland summarizes the cause of the American soldier's lapse in sanity:

They have seen savage sights; they have eaten the food of the savages; they have thought savage thoughts; the cries of the savages are ringing in their brains. In all their surroundings there is not one single object to remind them that they belong to an era of civilization. Their lust of slaughter is reflected from the faces of those around them. They crave slaughter more than food and sleep.

Homesickness and fever, sun and treachery, have broken down their few centuries of civilization.[35]

The Philippine environment and its "savage sites" produced a type of behavior that Americans at home could never have comprehended. The same nation that the media constructed as a site of disease was also a place where maladies inherent to the native population could have infected innocent American soldiers. Savagery, in short, became contagious.

As in the "Revenge of the Filipino" article, there is a narrative about the victimization of Americans in Rowland's "Fighting Life" essay. In "Revenge," American soldiers face the horrors of Filipino savagery directly, while in "Fighting Life" we read about indirect American victimization that takes place as the result of a diseased and hostile climate. Even though the *World* and *McClure's* appear to be reporting on different issues, both ethnographically based representations worked because of their dual appeal to both imperialists and anti-imperialists. While one reader might have looked at the Filipino mind-set and bloodline as a cultural deformity that could be corrected through benevolent assimilation, others would have read about this faraway place and shuddered at the thought of American intervention. Imperialists projected onto these images fantasies about changing the Philippines, whereas anti-imperialists used this "evidence" to support the notion that the Philippines was too savage to think about civilizing under the auspices of colonial rule. The overt claim of savagery in the Philippines was not only a call for empire, but also a stern warning about where the United States was geographically expanding its borders through war. Americans became victims who could be idealized as martyrs, or victims who others thought should avoid further harm at all costs.

The US government did not ignore incidents of American military abuse. In April 1902, the *Evening Journal* reported that President McKinley "decided to appoint a commission to investigate the conduct of the war in the Philippines, particularly with reference to alleged atrocities inflicted by American soldiers upon the natives."[36] Above this article is a drawing with the headline "Water Cure's Horrors Stir Congressmen to Indignation." The "water cure," as the drawing illustrates, is a form of torture where large quantities of water are poured into the mouth and nose of a victim. In this image, three American soldiers hold down a Filipino insurgent leader, while another pumps water into the Filipino's mouth (fig. 30). In a visual reversal of the Lapeer image, the Filipino becomes the victim. What is so striking about this scene is that water, which often connotes notions of purity, is the substance forced into the native's body. One soldier testified before a Senate committee that the Filipino was "placed under a water tank and water [was] allowed to run into his mouth from a faucet to compel him to tell what he knew concerning the insurgents."[37] The drawing and written text function similarly to Rowland's description in his "Fighting Life" essay. In both cases, the American soldier enters the Philippines with a benevolent nature, but the savage landscape squelches his humanity; the soldier, according to the popular press, is unable to function rationally in diseased surroundings.

At the core of racially motivated discourse is often the cultural fear of miscegenation made visible through sexuality. Thus, one of the themes often repeated in the popular press was that the American soldier could catch the bug of infidelity while in the Philippines. An article in the *World* from 1903, entitled "A 'Madame Butterfly' of the Philippines," reports on a number of American officers who "have deserted their Filipino wives." The author, John Luther Long, who first published the Madame Butterfly narrative in 1887 in *Century Magazine*, asserts that this desertion of Philippine women is inconsequential because "in the Philippines and in Japan morality is not essential to good repute. What is grossly immoral on Broadway is quite correct in Tokio." The Filipino "girl" knows that her American soldier will be lost forever once his ship sets sail and she is not ashamed or morally condemned because of her decision to enter into a spurious marriage. Long claims that seen "from the moral standards of the Occident, this scheme of life is atrocious, barbaric, vile. The Oriental sees nothing but good in it. In some other respects the morals at Tokio are centuries ahead of New York. Don't storm; accept the fact."[38] Besides constructing the Orient as a geographic whole—the text collapses Japan and the Philippines into a monolithic representation of Oriental morality—the media forgives the American soldier's actions in lieu of his presence in the East.[39]

This article was the cover story for the *Sunday Magazine*, which was a weekly supplement to the *World*, and the cover includes the Madame Butterfly headline and a large drawing of an American soldier in full uniform kissing a native Filipina (fig. 31). In the background is a hut, and we can

Figure 30 "Soldiers Trying 'Water Cure' on Filipino," *New York Evening Journal*, April 15, 1902. General Research Division, The New York Public Library, Astor, Lenox and Tilden Foundations.

assume that this interracial couple will retire to this dwelling at the end of their intense embrace. Sex, and the possibility of more sex, is blatant. On the next page of the article is a Japanese geisha who strums on a stringed instrument as she gazes at the reader. These images can be compared to the sexually charged Tiffany menu cards and to Charles Longfellow's photographic collection discussed earlier. The imagery bolsters the turn-of-the-century notion of the Orient as exotic, visually rendering an overt form of sexuality that is so alluring that the typical American soldier may be unable to avoid its magnetism.

The drawing of the "water cure" and the images found in the Madame Butterfly article commodify the spectacle of empire. The sight of American soldiers administering torture to a helpless Filipino would have surprised a reader thumbing through these newspapers and this same reader would have been jolted by an image of an American soldier kissing a Filipina. Much like the decorative Orientalist interiors found in the *Art Amateur*, these visual scapes were agents in the intertwining matrices of consumerism and Orientalism. Readers were more apt to buy newspapers that caught their attention, and once the reader saw representations of torture, or an interracial kiss, the stage where these

Figure 31 "A 'Madame Butterfly' of the Philippines," *World*, June 7, 1903. General Research Division, The New York Public Library, Astor, Lenox and Tilden Foundations.

acts took place became even more exotic, more foreign, and ultimately, more Oriental.

Technology and Infrastructure

A turn-of-the-century novel about the Philippine-American War by the prolific Edward Stratemeyer of Nancy Drew and Hardy Boys fame describes US government efforts to introduce new technology into the Philippines. Stratemeyer's book, *The Campaign of the Jungle; or, Under Lawton through Luzon*, follows the plight of two brothers, Ben and Larry Russell, through their trying years of service in Asia.[40] Stratemeyer places his fiction within a historical framework by writing about "the Philippine Commission of the United States [that] issued a proclamation, translated into the Spanish and Tagalog languages, calling upon the insurgents to throw down their arms and promising them good local government, the immediate opening of schools and courts of law, the building of railroads, and a civil service administration in which the native should participate."[41] Stratemeyer understood how the commission facilitated and implemented American colonial policy. Building schools, paving roads, and creating rail lines—the act of redefining Philippine infrastructure—affected the daily lives of American troops in the Pacific, and Stratemeyer explains how taxing this was for the Russell brothers.[42] The effort was intense, and many of the grandest plans put forth by the colonial authorities never came to fruition.

The policy of restructuring the Philippines through technological advancement was integral to the American drive for total imperial control. Constructing new modes of transportation and other advances, in what the media already defined as a savage and diseased nation, helped the American public accept imperialism and satisfied the US government's policy of benevolent assimilation. In short, technology eased the colonization process by changing the Philippine landscape into a site that made American colonial officials comfortable. It was no longer necessary to understand the Philippines as a completely exotic location once engineers built railroads and other symbols of American innovation.

The press accused Filipino insurgents of destroying rail lines, roads, and other modes of transportation, thus inciting the United States rebuilding project. In June 1902, *Harper's Weekly* published a two-page article called "The United States Engineer Corps at Work in the Philippines." The brief essay reports how a group of insurgents "destroyed most of the bridges in their line of retreat" from American troops and wreaked havoc by demolishing rail bridges with dynamite.[43] In response to this devastation, the American military quickly reconstructed this property. *Harper's* concludes optimistically, "On looking back over the short time since the Americans have been in possession of these islands, it cannot be denied that the engineers have done their fair share toward their pacification and rehabilitation. It is a source of satisfaction to know that . . . our army . . . has brought order and system out of chaos."[44] A photographic essay enhances the article with six images illustrating the rebuilding process. Three of the photographs are grouped together and have text that explains the damage as a product of insurgent activity (fig. 32). All the photographs use very similar captions that adhere to a narrative about American improvements versus insurgent destruction. The bottom photograph of the three photos included here is particularly cogent and reads: "The Railroad Bridge near Naic, which was blown up by Filipinos in Retreat. This shows the preliminary and temporary method of our engineers in repairing it for pursuit."[45] The photograph depicts the bridge being rebuilt. Two men stand on the structure and five other men (two of whom have been cropped) prepare the ground for the next section of bridge.[46] The foliage surrounding the scene is raw and tropical, making

A Bamboo Ferry hastily Built by United States Engineers—Ferrying a Piece of Artillery across the River near San Fabian

Bamboo Bridge built by United States Engineers across the River near San Fabian for Troops and Wagons to Cross

The Railroad Bridge near Naic, which was blown up by Filipinos in Retreat
This shows the preliminary and temporary method of our engineers in repairing it for pursuit

THE UNITED STATES ENGINEER CORPS AT WORK IN THE PHILIPPINES

Figure 32 "The United States Engineer Corps at Work in the Philippines," *Harper's Weekly*, June 21, 1902. Courtesy of Vassar College Library.

technological intrusions seem out of place in the jungle-like environment. The media's juxtaposition of the uncivilized Philippine landscape with American technology enacts the fantastic project of American colonialism and the belief that the savage nature of this Oriental culture can be rebuilt and completely reconstituted with the help of American political dominion.

The popular press consistently lauded the technological aspects of benevolent assimilation, since it represented success to imperialists and a more acceptable form of authority to anti-imperialists. "Filipino Fireplaces," an article published in December 1900 in *Harper's Weekly*, includes two photographs that represent traditional Filipino cooking. William Dinwiddie, the same author who wrote about Aguinaldo for the *World*, writes here that the Spanish are to blame for the lack of cooking technology in the Philippines; Dinwiddie even quips with a reference to the Spanish-American War, "One does not wonder that the people of a so-called civilized nation [Spain] so far behind in modern progressive ideas should have had the stuffing knocked out of them in a naval engagement." He continues lampooning Spain: "Columbus discovered America and Magellan discovered the Philippines—for other countries to civilize."[47] Dinwiddie concludes with a prediction about what cooking might become in the newly Americanized islands. The native population may soon be cooking "hot baked biscuits and waffles for breakfast, broiled and baked meats for dinner, and a Welsh rarebit after the theatre at night."[48] The jocular passage evokes a vision of future Philippine domesticity. Dinwiddie hopes that American technology will soon lead to a civilized culture where the comforts of home, enacted in the making of a home-cooked Western meal, will soon be readily available.

The Philippine Commission facilitated technological control of the colony. The commission was a group sponsored by President McKinley to create a government for the colony and facilitate its implementation in Congress.[49] Part of this planning included the development of government infrastructure, such as city plans, transportation systems, and schools. The *World* described the Philippine Commission as "asking Congress to confer upon it powers such as were never before vested in a body of men." The commission wanted "the exclusive authority to grant street, railway, electric light, telephone and other municipal franchises in the towns of the island, subject only to the confirmation of the President."[50] Its technological incursions symbolized colonial authority through benevolent assimilation. Furthermore, infrastructure, put in place at the behest of the commission, allowed trade to expand as roads, railroads, and telegraphs permitted the easy flow of capital along systematic lines that were becoming the norm in American and European cities. Technology assisted in the creation of a colonial marketplace where goods could be produced and purchased through trade.

The Colonial Marketplace of Things

Advertisements in the popular American press evoked the conflict in the Philippines to sell products. Two days after New York newspapers reported commodore George Dewey's victory over the Spanish in Manila Bay, the *World* ran a Bloomingdales advertisement for flags (fig. 33). The text accompanying a rendering of a woman wearing a soldier's hat, with four American flags covering her body, connects the war effort abroad to commercial success at home: "Many retail concerns in and out of this city have issued strict orders to their buyers not to buy any merchandise during the war. We believe in an opposite policy. We have faith in this country and its ultimate triumph. Manila proves this."[51] Another advertisement, for the Mortimer G. Bloom Company, which ran from May to October 1898 in *McClure's,* sold a "Dewey" chair. A small photograph of the chair appears above copy that reads: "The famous Admiral's favorite chair, large, roomy, massive, handsome and comfortable. . . . You, your friends, and your purse will like it."[52] The chair's description reflects the ethic of American imperialism, which supported the expansion of US borders to make the country more "large, roomy, massive, handsome, and comfortable." The war became an advertising tool, and thus commercial goods were more desirable if they signified American global power.[53]

The popular press often praised the colonial incursion because these events signaled that American commercial interests were entering global markets. *Harper's Weekly,* for instance, endorsed the commercial potential of the Philippines. Three months after the invasion of Manila Bay, the magazine published an article giving an overview of "Manila and the Philippines." At the end of this lengthy piece by John Barrett, who was the "late United States Minister-Resident to Siam [Thailand]," the notion of the Philippines as a permanent colonial possession comes to the fore: "Were Manila permanently in our possession, or that of some enterprising European power, it could be made one of the most beautiful cities of the world, as well as a splendid commercial *entrepot* and great seaport."[54] Barrett, writing for *Harper's Weekly* two years after this first article, continues his presentation of the Philippines as a site for potential economic growth, arguing that "the Philippines, being the geographical

Figure 33 "Greater New York's Greatest Store," *World*, May 3, 1898. General Research Division, The New York Public Library, Astor, Lenox and Tilden Foundations.

and strategical centre by reason of physical location, will become under American influence the commercial centre of the transpacific coast, seas, and millions of people."[55] To ensure that the reader understood what Barrett meant by "commercial centre," the editors included a "Map of the Orient Showing Manila, P.I." The map depicts the East with three circular rings that represent the Philippines as, to use the words above the map's key, "the geographical centre of the Oriental commercial field" (fig. 34).[56]

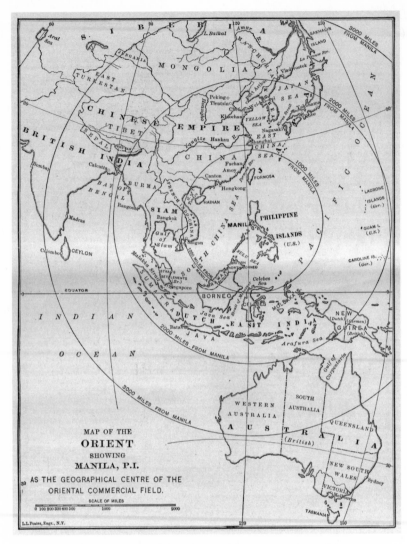

Figure 34 "Map of the Orient Showing Manila, P.I.," from John Barrett, "Manila and the Philippines," *Harper's Weekly*, August 6, 1898, 770. Courtesy of Vassar College Library.

Barrett concludes this article by describing the United States as the moral center of the globe:

Now that the Philippines are ours and will remain ours it is natural and logical that we should bend our energies to develop them commercially and materially as well as politically and morally. Never forgetting that we are a Christian as much as a commercial nation, we recognize that where moral and material interests labor to mutual advantage without the surrendering of the former to the latter, the greatest good can be accomplished. On this platform, it is fitting to study the map and remember what it teaches in regard to Manila's commanding location as the centre of the mighty Asian-Australian coast-line.[57]

At first glance, it appears as though Barrett deployed this map as a visual aide to represent the commercial advantages of colonization, but his discussion of empire also supported the popular notion that the United States could bring a necessary admixture of Christian values and commercialism to what the mass media depicted as the morally bankrupt Orient. Barrett wanted his reader to understand how the relationship between religion and capitalism enabled a sense of divine righteousness that justified the goals of benevolent assimilation.

Using the moral force of Christianity to extol imperial conquest became a heated topic (think back to McKinley's answered prayers about mapping the Philippines), and many took issue with arguments about the religious nature of colonial rhetoric. William Jennings Bryan—the frequent presidential candidate—wrote an editorial about the American presence in the Philippines in his newspaper the *Commoner*, in 1904, where he complained, "Every individual or group of individuals guilty of forcing any form of religion upon non-Christians or upon Christians holding to a different creed has done it under the firm conviction that the persons persecuted were being benefited." Bryan noted how this type of moral conversion deploys violence to supposedly benefit "the spiritual welfare of the persons tortured." While most Filipinos had already converted to Catholicism as a result of Spanish imperialism, many Americans believed they could "beat blessings" into those Filipinos who were non-Christians.[58]

Others critics of American empire, such as the cartoonist Charles Nelan, created images lampooning America's commercial venture in the Philippines. In his "William, You're Too Late," Nelan depicts the Philippine shoreline in a way that mocks America's awkward engagement with global trade (fig. 35). In the left foreground, Germany, embodied by a comical representation of emperor Wilhelm II, is armed with a sword and full military regalia. Behind him floats the bow of a boat with a box that reads "MADE IN GERMANY." Separating Wilhelm and the right background is a palm tree with a sign that declares, "PHILIPPINE ISLANDS. FOR PRIVILEGES SEE=UNCLE SAM. N.B. NO TRESSPASSING." On the sign hangs Uncle Sam's hat replete with stars denoting the American flag. The Germans were, as reported in the popular press, hostile to the American presence in the Pacific. Thus, the overtly antagonistic signage would have been

WILLIAM, YOU'RE TOO LATE.

Figure 35 "William, You're Too Late," from Charles Nelan, *Cartoons of Our War with Spain* (New York: Frederick A. Stokes Company, 1898). Milstein Division of United States History, Local History and Genealogy, The New York Public Library, Astor, Lenox and Tilden Foundations.

well understood. On the right, beyond the palm, Uncle Sam holds up a pair of pants for two Filipinos, one of whom wears a palm-leaf skirt. Both Filipinos have facial characteristics that have been exaggerated in a way that makes them appear like nineteenth-century representations of African American Sambo figures. Next to the two Filipinos and the stooping Uncle Sam is an open crate emblazoned with "AMERICAN GOODS," from where, the viewer assumes, other pairs of civilizing dress can be pulled. The entire cartoon visually renders the "privileges" associated with colonial trade, specifically referencing who has access—the Americans—and who does not—the Germans.

This image comes from Nelan's anti-imperialist book *Cartoons of Our War with Spain*, published in 1898, where he explains in his brief introduction, "I do not believe in the bitter, stinging cartoon. It's always best to produce a laugh with your argument; people seem to digest it better."[59] The book contains an array of drawings that poke fun at America's imperial hubris. As in many of the other images discussed in this chapter, Nelan stereotypes Filipinos. Here they are unwitting fools whose exaggerated features light up with the possibility of gaining access to the civilizing influence of American commercial goods, the ultimate symbol of imperial benevolence. However, Nelan's drawing also provides a sharp critique of the United States' expanding borders. The lone palm tree, with its hyperbolic no-trespassing sign, the exaggerated Uncle Sam, and the overall absurdity of the vignette belie the colonial effort. America is trading its "goods," but this commercial activity is happening with a savage race of men who wear little clothing, carry spears, and are oblivious—beyond their initial childlike excitement—to the wonders available in the box of American merchandise.

The Colonial Marketplace of Bodies

The commercialization of the Philippines for American use was inevitable after colonization; however, the commercialization of the Philippine people was also prevalent and far more complex. Five months after the invasion of Manila Bay, the *World* published an article in their *Sunday Magazine* titled "American Women in the Philippines: Picturesque Customs and Conditions They Will Meet in Our Probable Rich East." The article describes Filipino servants as one of the treasures Americans could find in the Philippines. The author, Grace Corneau, explains that "all natives are good servants if trained and looked after. It takes more of them to run a house. They are not expensive and attach themselves to their masters very much as do the Southern Negroes, ready to lay down their lives if necessary to save their master or his property."[60] The native Filipino becomes a slave-like commodity in this passage.[61] If the actual geography of the Philippines could be taken, then the next step could be the possession of people, especially if those people were inexpensive and could remind their American masters of the past wonders of slavery.

The *Evening Journal* mentioned the status connected with having an "Oriental Servant" four months after Grace Corneau wrote about the benefits of the Filipino servant in the *World*. The headline "Oriental Servants the Latest Fad of the 400" was the lead story in the February 1, 1899, edition of the "Household Magazine" section of the newspaper. While this article does not mention Filipinos (the article depicts images of Chinese, Indian, Japanese, and other Asian servants), the idea of those in the *Social Register,* referred to as the "400," owning Oriental servants is another instance of the American domestication of Asia. Included are drawings that show these Asian servants at work: nursing a baby, dressing a woman, making food, and performing as a butler.[62] These depictions of Asian subservience may have been new to American domestic life, yet the idea of commodifying the Oriental body is exactly what the *World* had scripted five months earlier in the context of the Philippines.

The domestic realm became the ideal setting for the enactment of fantasies about empire.[63] The carefully constructed world of domesticity was integral to American imperialism. Laura Wexler sees imaginings about the home as "a potent concatenation of ideas of scientific racism, social Darwinism, and economic pragmatism that could be used to orchestrate consent for expansionist practices," while "in the colonies . . . such ideals of domestic life were also disciplinary structures of the state."[64] Domesticity— that cocoon of sentimentality that flourished over the course of the nineteenth century—was not on the literal frontlines of America's march toward imperial conquest. Yet the home functioned as a powerful sign of global politics, where collecting objects that signified the world at large became entangled with the cultural logic of empire.

The mass media visually engaged with domesticity and empire in the "American Women in the Philippines" article from the *World*. Not only does Grace Corneau's essay mention Philippine servants, but she also gives advice about what clothing women should bring to the Philippines (she explains that it should be white in color, of course), what type of furniture should be acquired, and how important exercise is while in Manila. The imagery that surrounds the written text clarifies Wexler's insightful claim that the domestic sphere of the nineteenth century revealed a type of "tender violence," where veiled within sentimentality was "a compromise with or even a flirtation with the mechanics of racialized terror that kept a firm hold throughout the entire course of the . . . century."[65] Two representations found in the visual tableau that accompanies Corneau's advisory engage in a racially motivated discourse about domesticity (fig. 36). In the larger image, a woman in a long, white dress holds a fan while wearing a large hat. She sits comfortably in a cart that is being held up by a Filipino who looks at the viewer. The servant is only wearing pants; his arms relax, but he bears the load of the future weight of colonialism, which sits waiting to be taken to the home at the terminating perspective line created by the street. The Filipino is shown as turning the cart, thus posing for what the caption explains is an image derived from a photograph. He reveals the rhetoric of colonialism by displaying

Figure 36 Image from Grace Corneau, "American Women in the Philippines," *World*, October 23, 1898. General Research Division, The New York Public Library, Astor, Tilden and Lenox Foundations.

his own subservience enacted through the physical act of hauling this colonial freight. Unlike the attendant image of a Filipino woman holding an American child in her arms, which raises the notion of other types of domestic servitude found in the potential colony in 1898, the representation of "women [who] ride in carriages drawn by coolies" renders a not so subtle version of Wexler's concept of "tender violence." Race, clarified by the visual distinction between the woman in white and the brown man in very little clothing, adds complexity to the scene of colonial comfort that exposes the hypocrisy of benevolent assimilation. The formation of the American empire took place as the result of what was akin to slave labor furthered by the ideology of racial difference.

Let's return to the image of Aguinaldo on the couch (fig. 26). Again, as a brief reminder, the image of Aguinaldo captured places him in an interior space that Americans would have readily identified with. His domesticated and tamed body would have become fodder for imperialists and anti-imperialists. Those interested in expansion would have seen the insurrection thwarted, and the possibility of what benevolent assimilation could accomplish with its civilizing imperative. Anti-imperialists, however, would have decried the representation of Aguinaldo as exemplary of a problematic question endemic to imperial praxis: namely, why embark on colonial conquests by using duplicity and bloodshed to claim territory that was not rightfully America's to claim?[66] The popular press, and its creation of a mediascape where debates about empire could unfold, sold news to a demanding public by playing into that public's fractured political stance on turn-of-the-century American empire.

These popular newspapers and magazines created a catalog of America's new Oriental possession by inventing what Edward Said describes, through the words of André Malraux, as a "museum without walls, where everything gathered from huge distances and varieties of Oriental culture became categorically Oriental. It would be reconverted, restructured from the bundle of fragments brought back piecemeal by [reporters,] explorers, expeditions, commissions, armies, and merchants into lexicographical, bibliographical, departmentalized, and *textualized* Orientalist sense."[67] This ambiguous museum helped familiarize Americans with both the complicated machinations of empire and the striking differences that beset the archipelago. This mediascape often distorted the realities of military encounters, the promises of new technology, and the possibilities of commercialism to convey images of colonialism that were at times embraced by imperialists while at other moments lauded by anti-imperialists. The media reinvented and disseminated information, documenting what became a type of open-ended ethnographic display where knowledge about cultural customs and commerce could be deployed to sell newsprint through competing ideological tenets about American overseas power. This construction of knowledge through visual images and written text became the vehicle that helped Americans grapple with the idea of colonizing the Philippines.

FOUR

Mapping Empire

Cartography and American Imperialism in the Philippines

President McKinley's religious conviction about American empire in the Philippines putatively came after many nights of prayer. When "guidance" finally arrived, he realized that America needed "to help" the Filipinos, and his first order of business was to direct his head military cartographer "to put the Philippines on the map of the United States."[1] After McKinley went "down on [his] knees and prayed Almighty God for light and guidance," the mission became obvious and the imperative of mapping answered the president's entreaty.[2]

Maps facilitate the course of empire. By creating imagined landscapes, which, readers believe, arise out of a desire to represent the truth, maps epitomize an imperial logic. Cartographers distill the excesses of representation by judiciously redacting and making geography legible. Maps can be held in the hand, as if the world were available on a human scale; maps divide lands into tracts indicating possession, through the double act of naming and placing a rational grid of knowledge over the location depicted; maps edit out that which interferes with their supposed subject; maps enforce an ethos of total and complete perception through a visually mediated ideology of what the reader conceives of as an axiomatic understanding; and, finally, maps, as J. B. Harley has so astutely observed, envisage empire through their formulation of "myths which would assist in the maintenance of the territorial status quo."[3]

The flood of maps available to Americans that attended the imperial project in the Philippines is significant. Those created about the
Philippines during the early colonial period could be found in popular
newspapers, magazines, academic journals, government sources, and atlases. Historian Susan Schulten explains that the Spanish-American War
brought "critical changes" to American "cartographic culture."[4] These
documents appear to be innocent surfaces where the sole purpose is to
provide the reader with information about the Spanish-American War,
the Philippine-American War, or other facets of the early colonial period.
However, by assessing these maps, and the cartographic imperative that
incited their design and production, we can determine the role these images played in the creation of American empire. Maps were a cartographic
scape that helped instigate and further the objectives of American imperialism in the Pacific. By analyzing maps found in the popular press,
maps created by the United States military, and maps of Philippine bodies (done through photography, diagrams, and corporeal measurements)
this chapter details how the visual power of delineation allowed Americans to create a visually based assessment of the Philippine colony.

Philippine Legibility and the American Mass Media

In January 1900 the *World* ran an advertisement for a new edition of *The
Century Dictionary & Cyclopedia & Atlas* (fig. 37). The strength of this new
reference guide, according to the full-page advertisement, is the volume's
war maps. The copy explains how this presentation of battle cartography
"enable[s] one to trace *instantly* the movements of every important campaign on land or sea, the routes of invading armies, raids, etc., placing and
dating *on the maps* the battles, sieges and blockades not only of ancient
and medieval times, but also *those of the year just ended*—and this without
any complexity in the maps themselves."[5] In case the reader needed to
be reminded about recent wars, the advertisement has enormous graphic
representations of "Africa" and the "Philippine Is."[6] Thinking outside
the traditional borders of American nationhood became a selling point,
and an atlas—a cartographic guide to other places—became a desirable
resource; it rendered colonial locales by outlining their boundaries and
explaining their importance in relation to American empire.

The Century Dictionary & Cyclopedia & Atlas, published in 1899, is a ten-
volume set, and although this advertisement used the Philippines as a
hook, the enormous project devoted only a few pages to the archipelago.

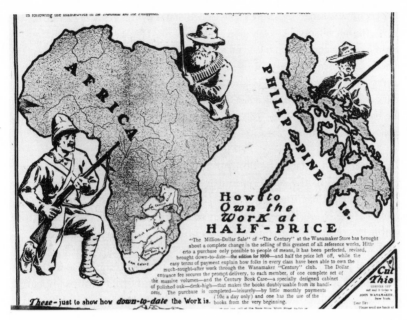

Figure 37 Advertisement for *The Century Dictionary & Cyclopedia & Atlas*, from *World*, January 3, 1900. General Research Division, The New York Public Library, Astor, Lenox and Tilden Foundations.

However, the need for atlases after the outbreak of the Spanish-American War was enormous, since many Americans finally realized, through the popular media, that there was a larger world to explore.[7] The oversized Century books promised to facilitate this encounter with the globe. Although it was an expensive reference guide, at $120 full price and $60 discounted at department stores such as Wanamaker's, the volume was advertised as an item for both personal and business use. Large advertisements in places such as the *New York Times* and the *World* speak to its marketing and availability.[8]

In volume 9 of the *Cyclopedia*, which contains *The Century Cyclopedia of Names*, the Philippines is described as "lying between the China Sea on the west and the Pacific Ocean on the east. Capital, Manila. It is situated on the east of the Annam and northeast of Borneo, and is separated from the Celebes on the south by the Celebes Sea." After providing the reader with a clear indication of where the islands could be found, the reference guide notes the "chief products" as "tobacco, hemp, coffee, sugar, cocoa, and rice." Only after establishing its economic viability do we read about the history and racial makeup of this contested place:

The group was ceded by Spain to the United States by the treaty of Paris, Dec. 10, 1898. The inhabitants are mostly different Malay tribes (Tagals, Visayas, etc.); there are also Chinese, Negritos, and mixed races. The nominal religion is Roman Catholic. The islands were discovered in 1521 by Magalhaes, who was killed there. Settlement was commenced in 1565. A native insurrection against the Spanish rule broke out in 1896, was quelled by Jan., 1898, but again broke out under the leadership of Aguinaldo after the battle of Manila, in May, 1898. In Feb., 1899, the insurgents turned their arms against the United States. Area 114,326 miles. Population, estimated, 7,000,000.[9]

The *Cyclopedia* redacts the Philippines into a single and simplified entry, giving details to the reader about its political, social, and economic viability. The Philippines is first given a geographic position, a place on the global stage. Next its marketable resources are listed, making its future viability come alive through its potential for commerce. Then its position within the history of empire is raised, followed by a discussion of its racial parameters and current political turmoil. Religion is defined as "nominal" in the colony, and "mixed races" and other groups appear to be members of a difficult insurgency that menaced Spain and now has rebelled against the United States.

Volume 10 of the *Cyclopedia* is the atlas, and the preface to this section introduces the importance of America's imperial expansion. Here we learn how "the results of the recent Spanish-American war have made it desirable that The Century Atlas should show with greater detail the regions affected by these events." Thus, the atlas includes a map of Hawaii and the Philippines, with additional maps that give details of Puerto Rico, the Lesser Antilles, and other recent colonial acquisitions.[10] Map number 118 in this volume is a standard representation of the Philippines from this period (fig. 38). It includes a representation of Hawaii and smaller, detailed maps of Manila and Honolulu. The overtly jingoistic tenor found in the popular press, where the *Cyclopedia* advertised, does not exist. The map, however, acknowledges the military victories that led to American interest in this part of the world. The upper-left quadrant contains this short history: "Note—The Spanish divisions of the Philippine Islands into 4 Governments, subdivided into 53 Provinces, are shown on this Map. During the Spanish-American War the Spanish fleet was destroyed in Manila Bay, May 1, 1898. The authorities at Manila capitulated to the United States, August 13, 1898." The same note further explains, "The Islands were ceded to the United States by the treaty at Paris, December 10, 1898."[11] Discussions of the Philippines were repeatedly found in the popular media during 1898, but not with the type of specificity provided in the *Cyclopedia*, where the editors included hundreds of town names and topographic information on

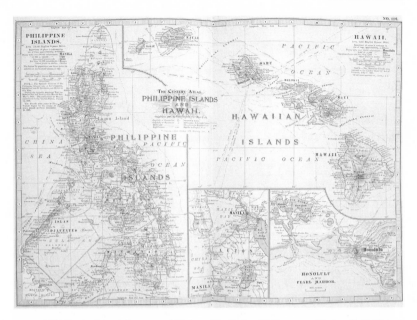

Figure 38 "Philippine Islands," map no. 118, from *The Century Dictionary and Cyclopedia & Atlas* (New York: Century Company, 1899), call #xspe1625.c4 1899, vol. 10, negative 831037D. Collection of the New-York Historical Society.

their map of the islands. The new technology of wax engraving allowed for details on this map that provided the viewer with astonishing amounts of information.[12] The *Cyclopedia* asserted a brief history of the Philippines and bolstered this narrative with geographic boundaries and minutia that defined this area that had been forfeited to American governance.[13]

Outside of the large expense of the Century guide, another way to capture the popular imagination was to create maps of military maneuvers in the mass media, where newspapers were inexpensive and plentiful. During 1899, Hearst's *Evening Journal* used several maps to depict battles from the Philippine-American War. One map from March 16 represents what the caption describes as a "Map Showing Scene of To-day's Battles," and another map from November 18 represents an American victory over the insurgent leader Aguinaldo with the caption "Aguinaldo Caught: Waited Too Long." The March map uses simple graphics with large black dots signifying battle sites (fig. 39), while the November map groups a circle of American flags (signifying American troops) surrounding a Filipino flag.[14] These maps permit a type of armchair travel that would give the reader the illusion of participation in an event that was taking place in a far-off locale. These military maps allowed the numerous readers of

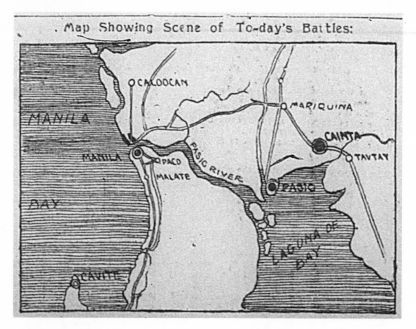

Figure 39 "Map Showing Scene of To-day's Battles," *New York Evening Journal,* March 16, 1899. Courtesy of Harry Ransom Humanities Research Center, The University of Texas at Austin.

the *Evening Journal* to be a part of the US colonization of the Philippines. Americans at home may not have actually been on the front fighting insurgents, but the press made this contested landscape accessible through a form of cartography that elided the realities of battle. Comparing these military maps with actual government maps from the period, and even *The Century Cyclopedia*'s map of the region, reveals how simplified representations of the islands were far more desirable in the pages of the popular press, where readers did not want to be taxed with details. Bold and crude graphics would have signified the travails of war without the burden of overly complex representations.

The press simplified maps of the Philippines, juxtaposed with jingoistic rhetoric, to excite the American public. A map from November 1898, in the *Evening Journal*, shows the Philippines with the caption: "The Islands We Demand in the East."[15] Another map, published five days later, includes the oceans surrounding the Philippines with the tag line, "Our New Sulu Islands."[16] Maps that showed the region beyond the Philippines were even more persuasive. In December 1898, the *Evening Journal* ran a small map of the world with circles around Puerto Rico, Hawaii, and the Philippines (fig. 40). Here the caption reads: "Map of the Greater United

States."[17] In May 1898, a few weeks after Dewey invaded Manila, the *World* published a brief column entitled "Facts about the Philippines," which informed readers about the size of the islands and statistics about natural resources. Underneath this article, at the bottom of the page, is a drawing of the globe (fig. 41). The words "THE SUN THIS DAY DOES NOT SET ON UNCLE SAM'S DOMAIN. BEFORE HIS SUNSET LIGHT FAILS THE PHILIPPINES; MAINE GLORIES IN THE DAWN" follow the curve of the earth's surface. Portions of the paragraph below this caption are even more jingoistic:

By a glimpse at the map it is readily seen that when the sun rises at Eastport, Me., it has not yet set at the Philippine Islands. And when it rises at the Philippines it has not set even on the coast of California. The possession of the great Asiatic group gives Uncle Sam his first equatorial territory, and places him in a position to enjoy any kind of climate he may desire, and to dwell among the most diverse races. If the climate of Washington, Denver, San Francisco or Alaska is not suitable to his state of health, he can sail for Manila, where the average native finds it comfortable to dwell the year round without clothes.[18]

The passage uses cartography, as well as an old adage about the British Empire, to carry out an imperialist fantasy predicated on the US presence in the Philippines, a location where the natives' predilection for uncivilized attire becomes an important highlight.[19] Images of maps and

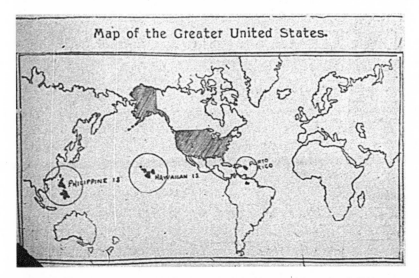

Figure 40 "Map of the Greater United States," *New York Evening Journal*, December 5, 1898. Courtesy of Harry Ransom Humanities Research Center, The University of Texas at Austin.

Figure 41 "The Sun This Day Does Not Set on Uncle Sam's Domain," *World*, May 15, 1898. General Research Division, The New York Public Library, Astor, Lenox and Tilden Foundations.

written text worked together to draw attention to the possibilities of empire.[20]

Returning to a map discussed in the previous chapter, titled "Map of the Orient Showing Manila, P.I.," (fig. 34) the imperialist ideology found in the popular press becomes more apparent. Recall that this map accompanied text that commanded the reader to remember America's primacy as a world leader and protector of capitalist virtue and Christian righteousness. This remarkable admixture of religious and financial wherewithal is, according to the article's author, John Barrett, critical in America's quest for the Philippines. Remember, Barrett commands us "to study the map and remember what it teaches in regard to Manila's commanding location as the centre of the mighty Asian-Australian coast-line." Heeding his call, we observe the concentric circles marking distances "from Manila." Each circle inscribes one thousand miles from the Philippine capital. As our eyes move outward, it becomes evident that to hold the Philippines was to possess an important part of Asia, and thus become a viable member of an elite group of nations that held colonies in this region, including, according to the map, the French, the Dutch, and, of course, the British. Each ring, with its mile marker, visually renders the critical importance of the Philippines as a geographic centerpiece of American hegemony in the Orient.

These maps from the popular press were guides to colonialism. After seeing a map of the Philippines and reading a caption that explained that this Oriental site was now in the protective hands of the United States, the reader would confidently assume a fund of knowledge. Seeing became believing, and this same ethos can be found in military maps from this period. Although more mission-oriented than the images found in the mainstream press, the military's maps also helped Americans visually navigate the colonial terrain.

Mapping Leyte

While the mass media disseminated maps to influence their enormous readership, the US military and government used cartography to facilitate colonial rule. These military maps of the Philippines do not overtly adhere to the jingoistic tenor of the popular maps from the period, but instead transform the Philippine landscape into a legible territory that could be readily controlled. These documents contain valuable information that helps us understand the extent to which visuality played a key role in establishing empire. Looking closely at a few of these government-sponsored cartographic exercises that focus on the Philippine province of Leyte makes it evident that the military and the colonial administration required maps to maintain the early colonial project.

The popular press commented on the government's interest in mapping America's new acquisition. A 1902 *Harper's Weekly* article relates, "With every expedition of any importance an officer of engineers, or another officer acting in his place, was sent, in compliance with existing orders, to map the country traversed, and other maps were made from time to time as the country became more pacified, covering the roads and principal trails." Cartography does not occur without training and so, "Engineer soldiers are given instructions in mapping-work, first in drawing conventional signs, then in making scales for plotting-work, and then in making reconnaissance sketches, first on foot and then mounted."[21]

These government-sponsored maps of the Philippines, created by groups such as the Engineer Corps, fit into three categories. First, there are reconnaissance maps that detail the Philippine landscape for military operations. Trails, densely overgrown fields, bridges, and other specifics fill the keys of these maps that provide the easiest and safest route from one location to the next. Many of these carefully drawn maps note that they were completed through observation and with reference to existing Spanish maps. Second, there are maps that provide details about warfare. Unlike the reconnaissance maps, which were carefully rendered on blueprint paper to allow for easy reproduction, these improvised maps are hand-drawn on paper and rendered in pencil. They are often signed by a witnessing officer and combine both typical cartographic markings and handwritten notations. Maps in these first two categories were, in the words of Warren Du Pré Smith, an early twentieth-century geographer, done by "primarily soldiers and professional topographers" and were "not so accurate" when compared to mapping done by American cartographers working outside the military. Regardless, during the early colonial period, the military mapped "an immense area throughout the islands" and were very "active" in the Visyan Islands, which are south of the capital island of Luzon and include the island of Leyte.[22] Finally, there are also government maps that detail American building projects in the Philippines. These efforts, which I will focus on in chapter 6, were not as numerous, but they were often completed with great care to show colonial officials projections of America's future in the colony.[23]

"Road Sketch from Tacloban to Carigara, Leyte, PI" is a typical blueprint military map of the Philippines from the first decade of the American occupation (fig. 42). The map is done in three sheets, and each is large, approximately twenty-four by thirty-four inches, to allow for ease of visibility and use. All three sheets include details of what Americans might find along the road in Leyte. The map's generous scale of three inches equaling each mile allows for details such as types of crops grown along the trail (hemp, coconuts, and rice) and whether or not bridges that cross streams and rivers are "safe" or "unsafe."[24] This oversized map could be copied multiple times, thanks to blueprint technology, and opened by infantries as they moved from Tacloban to Carigara. The map evokes a sense of clarity and order. The line of progress from Tacloban to Carigara is marked, and the intent here is to make certain that military units did not lose their way because of the hazardous diversions that dot the map's surface.

Other American cartographic endeavors from this period include copious notes about specific Philippine towns. In late 1902, second lieutenant Joseph Kay issued a lengthy description of Baybay, which is also in the province of Leyte. Kay starts with several typed pages that detail Baybay, including information about roads, houses, and churches. On the third page of the report, after he estimates the population of Baybay at twenty thousand, Kay claims that the town's "inhabitants are very untrustworthy and during insurrectionary times were fairly respectful to Americans, But are now very indifferent." This group is so devious they "seem to enjoy any trouble or misfortune which comes to an American." They also take advantage of their position economically and sell goods "at exorbitant prices" when they can. Finally, he notes, "They are very lazy and unfriendly."[25] Kay's qualifying language about the people of Baybay was typical. Stereotypes about Philippine behavior became another factor in the larger configuration of the landscape that Kay wanted his superiors to keep in mind while they were in Leyte. Not only does the unknown landscape need to be carefully described, but the people in that landscape also must be mapped in a way that explicates their faults and potential menace.[26]

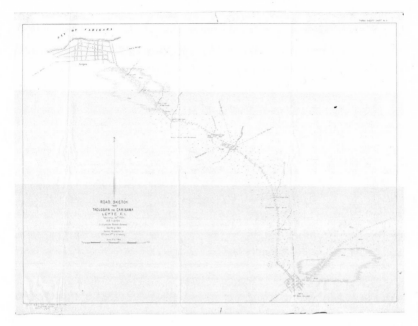

Figure 42 "Road Sketch from Tacloban to Carigara, Leyte, PI," 1904. Cartographic and Architectural Records, Record Group 395, National Archives II, College Park, Maryland.

Kay includes two small maps in his report. One details a river (maybe the Tigbauan) crossing from Baybay to Tigbauau (fig. 43) and the other shows a crossing from Baybay to St. Augustin (fig. 44). The first map represents a river where there is a "ford for ponies, but very difficult for American horses." The other map includes a notation about how "native boats (canoes) are easily obtained[.] Only adaptable for light load, seldom having ferrying capacity beyond 600 lbs." Earlier in the report Kay also claims, "Native boats can be procured without difficulty." For all their supposed lazy and troubling behavior, it is peculiar to encounter ways in which the local population can be helpful, especially when it comes to moving American troops through a route that Kay describes as being "very poor."

Kay's commentary brings together the cartographic and the ethnographic into an official account. He maps the region of Baybay by deploying the charged Orientalist language that repeatedly surfaced during the American colonization of the Philippines. Kay's discourse follows a well-trodden strategy where the landscape and the people of the Philippines need to be mapped and analyzed to ensure American mastery over their new colony. In fact, given the December 1902 date of this report, Kay's

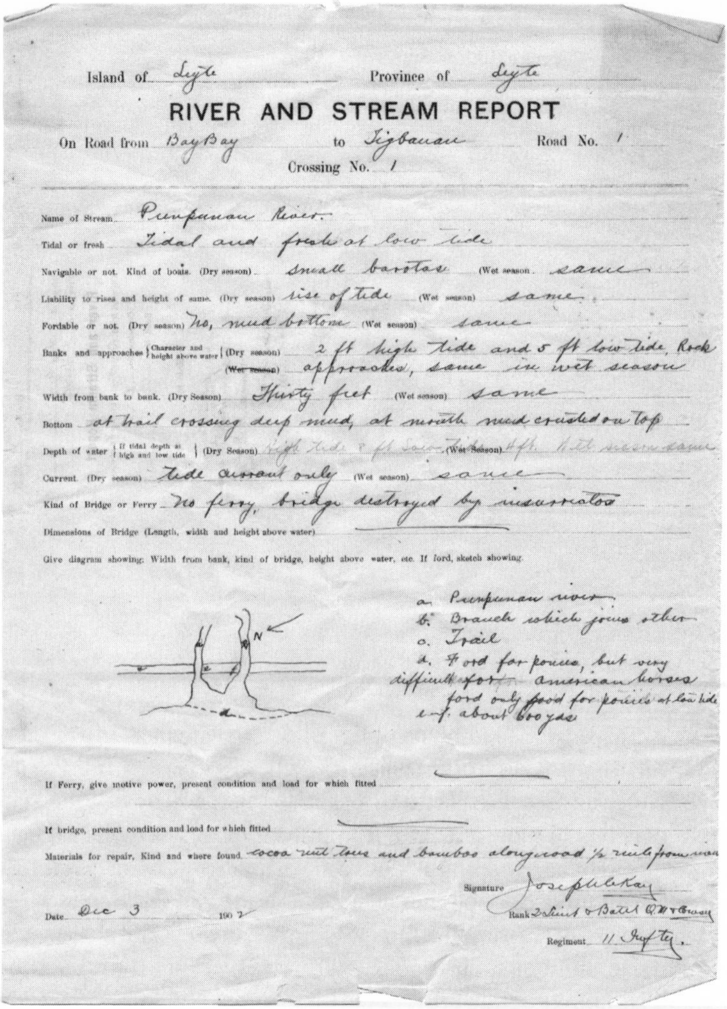

Island of *Leyte*   Province of *Leyte*

RIVER AND STREAM REPORT

On Road from *BayBay* to *Tigbauau*   Road No. *1*

Crossing No. *1*

Name of Stream *Puupunau River.*

Tidal or fresh *Tidal and fresh at low tide*

Navigable or not. Kind of boats. (Dry season) *small barotos* (Wet season) *same*

Liability to rises and height of same. (Dry season) *rise of tide* (Wet season) *same.*

Fordable or not. (Dry season) *no, mud bottom* (Wet season) *same*

Banks and approaches {Character and height above water} (Dry) *2 ft high tide and 5 ft low tide, Rock* (Wet) *approaches, same in wet season*

Width from bank to bank. (Dry Season) *Thirty feet* (Wet season) *same*

Bottom *at trail crossing deep mud, at mouth mud crusted on top*

Depth of water {if tidal depth at high and low tide} (Dry Season) ... (Wet Season) ...

Current. (Dry season) *tide current only* (Wet season) *same.*

Kind of Bridge or Ferry *No ferry, bridge destroyed by insurrectos*

Dimensions of Bridge (Length, width and height above water)

Give diagram showing: Width from bank, kind of bridge, height above water, etc. If ford, sketch showing.

a. *Puupunau river*
b. *Branch which joins other*
c. *Trail*
d. *Ford for ponies, but very difficult for american horses ford only good for ponies at low tide*
e-f. *about 600 yds*

If Ferry, give motive power, present condition and load for which fitted

If bridge, present condition and load for which fitted

Materials for repair, Kind and where found *cocoa nut trees and bamboo along road ½ mile from river*

Signature *Joseph Kay*

Date *Dec 3* 190 *2*

Rank *2 Lieut & Battl Quartermaster*

Regiment *11 Inf'ty.*

Figure 43 Joseph Kay, "BayBay to Tigbauau," December 3, 1902. Cartographic and Architectural Records, Record Group 395, National Archives II, College Park, Maryland.

thoroughness—his obsessive documentation of what he visualizes—is not surprising. Recall that in July 1902, President Roosevelt claimed the Philippine-American War complete, but the conflict continued regardless of this presidential pronouncement.

A hand-drawn map submitted to the American military command in the Philippines, from 1906, reveals the protracted nature of the colonial conflict. Underneath the map's key we read that this is the "Route of expedition from Abuyog leaving Nov. 7th 1906." Additionally, the "arrow[s] indicate route of troops by 1st Leiut R.G. Rutherford Jr. 24th U.S. Infantry" (fig. 45). Rutherford's handwriting is different from the cartographer's, but his signature shows that this was seen as an official document meant to serve as evidence of a series of skirmishes. The map is approximately twenty-four by twenty-seven inches, and it represents a rough outline of the area near Abuyog, which like Baybay, Tacloban, and

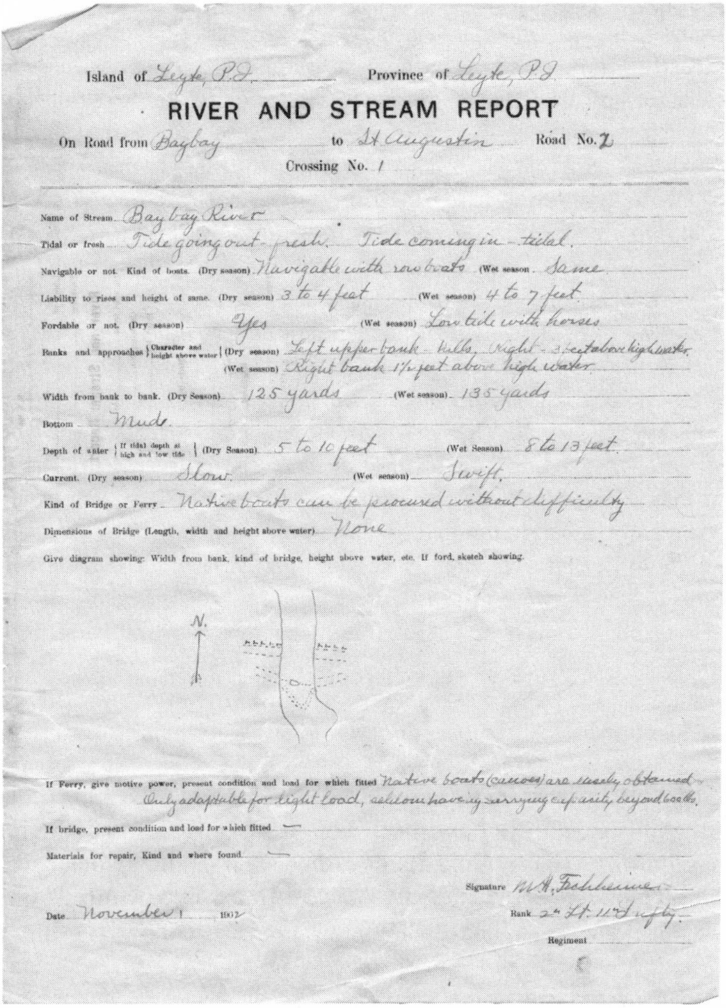

Figure 44 Joseph Kay, "BayBay to St. Augustin," November 1, 1902. Cartographic and Architectural Records, Record Group 395, National Archives II, College Park, Maryland.

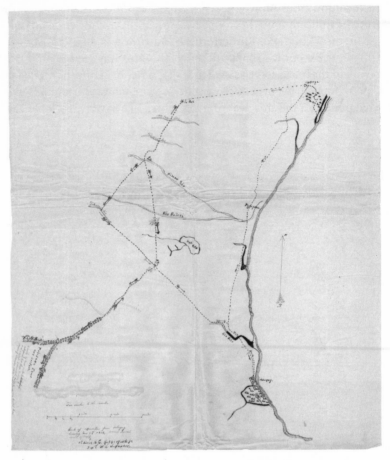

Figure 45 "Route of Expedition from Abuyog Leaving Nov. 7th 1906." By R. G. Rutherford. Cartographic and Architectural Records, Record Group 395, National Archives II, College Park, Maryland.

Carigara is in Leyte. Trails, rivers, route arrows, and what may be lakes are the only clear markings on the map. In the lower-left quadrant the trail is drawn in thicker ink and the arrows are more numerous, indicating a high level of activity. In the angle vector created by two diverging trails is text:

Pulajane Camp and Outposts.
Struck by troops under Lt. Rutherford
Pulajanes hit three times

One 1 killed 5 wounded, later
Report of Volunteer States Pablo Vsodo was killed here.[27]

The Pulajanes were a supposedly insurgent tribe on Leyte.[28] The map details an attack that happened to the 24th Infantry, but Rutherford and his men struck back and were victorious. There is no mention of American deaths, and the military must have wanted Vsodo dead, since his full name is included.

Each of these maps suppresses the conflict of war through a dramatic exercise in visual editing. These mapping efforts highlight what the military deemed as necessary information, such as facts about the terrain, quick judgments about Filipino character, and details about insurgent deaths. One of the most dramatic aspects of these maps is the empty space that dominates these documents. Were people living in these un- filled areas? Was it simply vegetation? What was there? Additionally, unlike the maps found in the popular media, these examples focus on a very specific region of the Philippines that most Americans from this period would not have been aware of. Some ethnographic accounts of the colony mention Leyte, but it is not given the attention that Luzon (the capital island) receives. In short, these maps outline what the military might find on Leyte and the events that transpired while US troops were there. Once the military began the process of charting the colonial land- scape, these records provided a type of comfort couched in visuality, or the ability to discern America's new colony. An important part of these possessions, of course, included the people of the Philippines who were now under American dominion. Thus, the final section of this chapter turns to American interest in mapping Philippine bodies, a project initi- ated during the early colonial period.

Mapping the Philippine Body

On April 5, 1909, the physician and anthropologist Robert Bennett Bean ordered that a Kodak Brownie camera be used to capture a remarkable sight at his medical clinic in the town of Taytay in the Philippines. Bean explained that a man entered the dispensary and "was treated for sexual neurasthenia. The man disappeared as quietly as he came, and I was un- able to find him again." The man, according to Bean's physical assess- ment, resembled nothing less than a Neanderthal, an earlier form of man long thought connected to modern man by a chain of evolutionary change. To document the case, Bean "endeavored to obtain a photograph, but unfortunately the Government photographer was absent that day, and the only camera available was a No. 2 A Brownie pocket Kodak. This was utilized, and the resulting photographs are reproduced here for the first time."[29] We can imagine Bean, or perhaps one of his Filipino workers, rushing to get the camera out to snap the images that would provide visual evidence of the "missing link."

Bean's main purpose in the Philippines was to map the bodies of different types of Filipinos and group their forms into racial categories. As he declares in the preface to his book *The Racial Anatomy of the Philippine Islanders*, "This book . . . represents a new departure in anthropology, and the term racial anatomy of the living is not inappropriate as a title."[30] Using a variety of measurement techniques, Bean offered clear delineations between Filipino types. Head sizes, limb measurements, and assessment of stature led him to conclusions about Filipinos and their place within the evolutionary hierarchy that was popular within anthropology in the early years of the twentieth century. Bean mapped the Philippine body as an exercise in colonial knowledge that could help his American readership better understand the physical attributes of their new subjects.

Bean must have seen detailed maps of the Philippine landscape in the popular press, and, perhaps, in the more rarified context of government publications that he would have been privy to as an American working in the new colony. He took the idea of mapping to its next logical conclusion: if the landscape could be surveyed and redacted into the form of a map, then certainly the Philippine body—the corporeal enigma encountered in the colonial zone—could also be surveyed, represented, and visually mapped for an American audience. In a scientifically motivated act similar to Charley Longfellow's amateur quest for visual souvenirs of Asia, Bean investigated the body of the Other to explicate and catalog the people of the Philippines.

Bean came to this work because of his background as an anthropologist and physician. Born in Virginia in 1874, Bean received his undergraduate degree from Virginia Polytechnic Institute (now called Virginia Tech) and then went on to receive his MD from Johns Hopkins University in 1904. In 1907, he went to the Philippines to work in anatomy at the Philippines Medical School. It was undoubtedly his interest in mapping the human system that fostered his obsession with measuring and detailing specific differences between Philippine racial types.[31]

To accomplish his task of understanding the "racial anatomy" of Filipinos, Bean compared several groups of Filipinos with racial types from the United States. He explained that he "measured a few negroes in Baltimore at the Anatomical Laboratory of the Johns Hopkins University." To make the study as exhaustive as possible he also "added the measurements of about 100 negroes in the Free Dispensary" at Hopkins and "more than 1,000 students at the University of Michigan, and the measurements of 1,500 school children of Ann Arbor, Michigan, in 1905–07." He compared this American cohort to about "800 students of the Trade and Normal Schools of Manila, more than 100 Igorots, 500 individuals of Taytay and Cainta, and about 200 subjects of Malecon Morgue."[32] Although his measuring criteria were inconsistent throughout the book, Bean assessed these groups based on head measurements (what he refers to as the Cephalic Index), stature (height), eye color, limb measurements, and even ear dimensions. In the first chapter of *The Racial Anatomy of the Philippine Islanders*, which focuses on Filipino students, Bean described how racial characteristics can be imparted through generations. In fact, he made specific references to Mendelism and revealed that like the characteristics of plants in Gregor Mendel's experiments, Filipino racial categories get passed down through generations of offspring.[33]

To highlight these differences in racial typology, Bean includes visual charts that map the bodies of Filipinos and their Euro-American counterparts. He provides clear diagrams that demarcate bodies using lines. For instance, one diagram has dotted lines on the right side that represent the "average Taytayan" and on the left side a solid line that represents the "average European" (fig. 46). In this image the Taytayan is shorter in stature than the European and Bean indicates exactly how this difference in body height measures along the entire length of both bodies. The diagram combines the Philippine and the European statures into one whole, abstracting the form of legs, torso, and head. The melding of corporeality into one single form—a body that is part Filipino and part European—is precisely Bean's point. His study often references connections between racial groups whose geographic point of origin are disparate. For instance, in his discussion of the Igorots, who were, as discussed in the previous chapter, a major focal point for ethnographic studies of the Philippines, Bean claims that "in a few individuals a tinge of red may be seen, or the face appears bronzed, some Igorots strikingly resembling the North American Indian."[34] There are also numerous places where Bean describes how migration patterns led to new racial types "as the recent infusion of Spanish in the Filipino during the past few hundred years may be suggested" as an important development.[35] Thus, visual schematics that diagrammed the divide between the East and the West with a single body visually render Bean's contention about the range of racial types living in the colony.

The graphic representation of the Taytayan man is similar to the geographic maps of the Philippines that filled the pages of the popular press

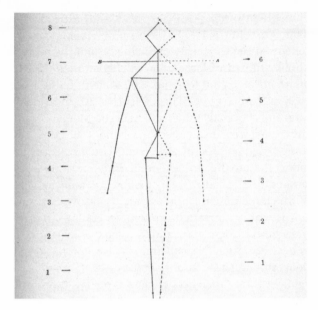

Figure 46 Diagram from Robert Bennett Bean, *The Racial Anatomy of the Philippine Islanders* (Philadelphia: J. B. Lippincott Company, 1910), 113.

and the folders of American military commanders. Bean redacted the body into straight lines that abstract human form, allowing his audience to project fantasies about the physicality of this Taytayan onto the drawing. Arms, legs, torso, and head are marked to provide a sense of stature, but the Taytayan's particular physical features are absent. In a rendering that imitates the manner in which cartography reduces the landscape to a set of mere lines, Bean's drawing permits the viewer to imagine this Filipino's attributes. This lack of characteristics is further heightened since straight lines signify the European's stature, while dotted lines, which have a greater sense of absence because of gaps and periodic spaces, signify the Filipino. Thus, the myriad readings that turn-of-the-century Americans would bring to this seemingly underdetermined Taytayan man are significant. Bean utilized photography in other sections of his book, but, in this instance, the simplicity of the dotted line renders a man whose mapped body manifests Bean's racialized understanding of the archipelago.

The single-body forms depicted in these line diagrams, which unite Filipino, Western, and Southern-hemisphere types, also suggest a history of racial progress, an anthropological obsession from the turn of the century that connected notions of racial hierarchy with a survey of races from around the world. "The three types represent the three fundamental units of mankind, the Iberian being the fundamental European type, the Primitive being the type of the Orient, and the Australoid the primary Negroid element." Bean continues, "The other types, such as the Cro-Magnon, Alpine and B.B.B., are modifications and combinations of the three fundamental types."[36] Bean concludes by revealing that the Philippines has people "derived principally from East Indian sources, the southern Pacific Islands, China, and Japan, and Europe."[37]

One of Bean's important contributions to early twentieth-century anthropology was, as one contemporary reviewer of his book explained, that he "invented in this work a racial anatomy of the living."[38] Rather than rely on cadavers, Bean took his work into the field and measured live humans to assess the racial makeup of America's new colony. Given the ongoing media attention that the Philippines received during this era, the notion of getting a better understanding of the colony through a careful study of live "specimens" is not surprising. Bean divulged information about the island nation that would have been seen by his academic audience as current and fresh. His diagrams and photographs would have been understood as documentary evidence that presented not a dated representation of the empire, but a place filled with living potentialities.

Let us return to Bean's use of the Brownie camera that he mentions in his book's appendix. Included in this final chapter, which declares that earlier forms of man exist in the Philippines, are photographs supposedly taken with the Brownie. As the title of the appendix notes, Bean calls this man "Paleolithic Man in the Philippines: *Homo Philippinensis*." Opposite the first page of this chapter is the man standing barefoot in front of a thatched hut. He wears light-colored pants and a collarless tunic type of shirt over his very thin body, where the bones of his ribcage create ridges in the shirt's opening (fig. 47). The "*Homo Philippinensis*. A Hillman from near Taytay of the Australoid Type," as the caption posits, stares at us with his right hand behind his back and his left hand at his side. A set of four photographs of the same man appears on a plate three pages later (fig. 48). Here the photographer who manned the Brownie took two images straight on, and two images that depict the man's profile. Reminiscent of other photographs in Bean's text, these images represent the man from different angles to ease the process of identification. The man, whose name, Alejandro Mesa, is at the top of a chart that details his specific body measurements from his lip width to the distance from his chin to nose, is shown from a variety of angles to reveal Bean's estimation that this is "the primordial form of man. Europeans are modified products of various forms that have evolved from the primordial. It is conceivable

Figure 47 Photograph from Robert Bennett Bean, *The Racial Anatomy of the Philippine Islanders* (Philadelphia: J. B. Lippincott Company, 1910).

that a form similar to this primordial type produced *Homo Philippinensis.*"[39] Bean claims that this earlier version of man, the Neanderthal type, perhaps left Europe during the ice age in the hopes of finding a better climate, hence creating a geographic distinction between the disparate races of man.

In all the photographs that Bean includes, *Homo philippinensis* stares at the camera in a manner reminiscent of a police mug shot. The intent here is to create a sense of scientific accuracy—a map of the human form—so the camera depicts the "Philippine Man" from multiple angles: head-on, left profile, and right profile. In fact, two of the images appear to be the same (figures 22 and 25 in Bean), but the first image, on the upper left (22), gives us a close-up to make certain we can assess the man's Neanderthal traits; additionally, Bean may have altered this photo with a pen or pencil to make *Homo philippinensis*'s features more pronounced. Bean notes, "The features of this man are large and heavy, the lower jaw is heavy, long, square, narrow. . . . The brow ridges protrude, the cheeks are large and prominent, the nose is massive, wide, straight, and depressed at the nasion, and the lips are full and thick."[40] The photos function as a form of Foucauldian power, where the body is on display for the viewer's surveillance. John Tagg describes a group of nineteenth-century identification photos where there is "a repetitive pattern: the body isolated;

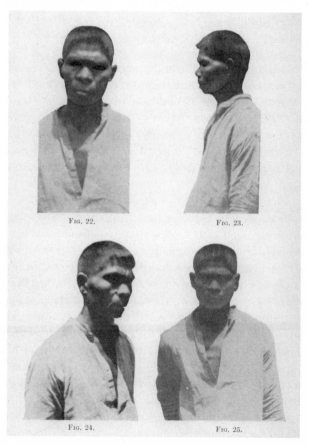

Fig. 22.

Fig. 23.

Fig. 24.

Fig. 25.

Figure 48 Photographs from Robert Bennett Bean, *The Racial Anatomy of the Philippine Islanders* (Philadelphia: J. B. Lippincott Company, 1910).

the narrow space; the subjection to an unreturnable gaze; the scrutiny of gestures, faces and features; the clarity of illumination and sharpness of focus; the names and number boards."[41] In Bean's plates the focus is not there, after all a Brownie camera had been grabbed to capture this man's unique physical presence, but, otherwise, there are "traces of power" within the visual field. The photos of the Philippine Neanderthal type manifest the American colonial policy. Indeed, they represent the diminished evolutionary state of America's new geographic possession. The man looks at the camera and clearly, but unwittingly, calls out for benevolent assimilation.[42]

Like many of his colleagues in anthropology, Bean understood Europeans as having progressed from primordial man.[43] However, *Homo philippinensis* is a form stuck in time, a leftover specimen that signifies an earlier type of man. Bean describes recent discoveries in places such as Heidelberg and La Chapelle-aux-Saints, the original locations where Neanderthals were found, to the measurements of several men he has seen in the Philippines. "In the Philippines to-day men of similar form [to the Neanderthal] may be seen, rarely, it is true, but the close observer who lives among the people of different parts of the archipelago for years can hardly fail to notice such types."[44] Enmeshed in Philippine culture and able to observe individuals at close range, Bean identified a new classification of human that the camera documents as conclusively linked to an earlier period, a time when man's physical form was nascent and not evolved.

Since its discovery in the mid-nineteenth century, the idea of a Neanderthal has been a contested topic in anthropology. In the early twentieth century it was seen as axiomatic that the Neanderthal was an early form of man descended from simians. Anthropologists spent ample time mapping the geographic regions and "races" that descended from Neanderthals, arguing how different continents could be linked to variations of early man. For instance, John Gray created a speculative diagram tracing the Neanderthal, which eventually arrived in Europe and evolved into modern man (fig. 49).[45] One of the racially charged visual clues that Gray included in his chart of arrows is that while the Neanderthal crossed with Chimpansoids, and closely followed the path of Gorilloids, its line of evolutionary ascent went directly to Europe in an upward motion away from Africa. However, the chimp and gorilla family continued downward toward Africa, marking the ancestry of the Southern hemisphere as simian and distinctly separate from the European past. On the other hand, anthropologist Gustaf Retzius explained to his readers in 1909 "that there does not exist anything like enough material for definite conclusions

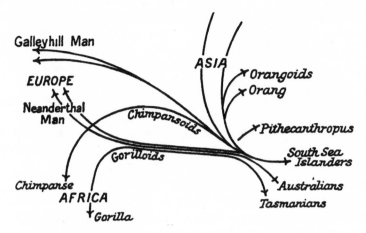

Figure 49 Chart from John Gray, "The Differences and Affinities of Paleolithic Man and the Anthropoid Ape," *Man* 11 (1911): 120.

to be drawn concerning" the Neanderthal.[46] Regardless of the myriad theories that filled the pages of anthropological journals during the early years of the twentieth century, well-regarded scholars accepted that there were early forms of man who were considered less evolved and inferior to modern man.

Erik Trinkaus and Pat Shiplan have traced the nineteenth- and twentieth-century academic approaches to the study of the Neanderthal. They reveal how the Neanderthal was thought to be a missing link to man's current state and how it was understood as uncivilized, devoid of modern man's refined sensibilities.[47] One theme that recurs in early twentieth-century descriptions of Neanderthals was their supposed cannibalistic practices. Because of nineteenth-century claims that surfaced shortly after the first discovery of Neanderthal bones, it became accepted that Neanderthals practiced cannibalism. Trinkaus and Shipman note that this practice "is one of the most universal taboos, one of the most repellent and uncivilized behaviors."[48] Since many writers in anthropological journals stressed the connection between Neanderthals and the continued existence of primitive man throughout the world, especially in those regions understood as in need of colonial intervention, it became de rigueur to mention this distressing ritual as a way of separating modern man—Western man—from the abhorrent custom of cannibalism.[49] And, of course, scholars often singled out the Philippines as a site where cannibalistic practices could be found. While speaking to the American Geographic Society in 1901, George Becker claimed the Manobos, a Philippine tribe that could be found in Mindanao, "practice ceremonial cannibal- ism and offer to their gods human sacrifices."[50] Granted, Bean did not suggest that *Homo philippinensis* engaged in anthropophagous behavior, but these types of sensational characteristics about Neanderthals and Fili- pinos were prevalent. Bean's subject must have been frightening to an American audience, since *Homo philippinensis* qualified as both a savage Filipino and a modern-day Neanderthal.

Bean's photographic plates, his desire to use a camera, and his obses- sive physical mapping of Philippine bodies reveal a quest to label the Philippines as uncivilized for his American audience. His work, and other scientific inquiries into the archipelago described in the previous chapter, purported stereotyped mythologies about the Philippines that adhered to the colonial rhetoric of the early twentieth century. Bean's theory that the Neanderthal still existed in all its physical glory supported both his own belief in the notion of early forms of man, and his and the wider colonial project's contention that the Philippines was the home of a less evolved human form. Ultimately, Bean's desire to map the corporeality of the Philippine citizenry was not unique, and many other Americans looked at the Philippines as a place where reading the colonized—the sizes, shapes, and dimensions of Filipinos—could lead to knowledge, al- though dubious, about America's subjects.

These cartographic conceptions of bodies and places fostered Amer- ican visions of empire. While the intrigues of empire often remained distant and physically removed from the everyday, these maps and pho- tographs authorized Americans to create a "place-image" that would ad- here to turn-of-the-century fantasies about imperial conquest.[51] These representations established a duality of both distance and proximity in relation to the colonial zone. On the one hand, the armchair traveler, the soldier, and the ethnographer could have the sense that the Philip- pines was a knowable terrain, a cartographic scape where the movement of empire could be delineated and understood. On the other hand, these maps—both in their corporeal and geographic manifestation—allowed for a type of distancing where the colony could be magnified and easily seen, but from the safety of a detached position. Even in the case of the soldier, who would have utilized the hand-drawn maps while in the colony and in the heat of battle, the rendering of the landscape permitted a type of disassociation from the actual bloodshed and complexities of war. The place-image formed by these maps facilitated empire through a visually mediated cartographic scape where the agents of empire—the popular press, the military, and the anthropologist—defined boundaries of meaning that established the American colony in the Philippines.

FIVE

Celebrating Empire

New York City's Victory Party for Naval Hero
George Dewey

In September 1899 an advertisement for Pears' Soap appeared in *Harper's Weekly* that depicted admiral George Dewey washing his hands at a small sink aboard his famous ship, the *Olympia* (fig. 50). Because this is an advertisement for soap, it is not surprising that Dewey wears all white and seems intent on getting his hands clean. His dress enhances the power of the image, as the uniform pays tribute to naval pride and the importance of presenting one's honor while "wearing whites." The oval-shaped portrait imitates the form of the ship's porthole that is open in front of the naval hero, and surrounding the central drawing are four smaller vignettes. On the upper left and right are representations of ships at sea; in the lower-left quadrant, boxes of Pears' Soap are being loaded off a ship; and at the lower right, in the most charged representation of the four, a white man offers Pears' Soap to a supplicating native. The text beneath these images explains how "the first step towards lightening The White Man's Burden is through teaching the virtues of cleanliness." The pedantic tenor of the copy continues, "Pears' Soap is a potent factor in brightening the dark corners of the earth as civilization advances."[1] Pears' promotes its soap as the agent that will clean up those parts of the world shrouded in savagery.

The year before this advertisement appeared in *Harper's*, Dewey led the American navy to a swift defeat over the Spanish in Manila Bay; thus his appearance would have alerted

The first step towards lightening

The White Man's Burden

is through teaching the virtues of cleanliness.

Pears' Soap

is a potent factor in brightening the dark corners of the earth as civilization advances, while amongst the cultured of all nations it holds the highest place—it is the ideal toilet soap.

Figure 50 Pears' Soap advertisement featuring Admiral Dewey, *Harper's Weekly*, September 30, 1899. Courtesy of Vassar College Library.

the turn-of-the-century reader to the issue of colonialism. Indeed, it was the admiral's actions that enabled Americans to think about the potential of building an empire. The representations of colonial subjugation and commerce further enhance the imperial context of the Pears' image. The title of Rudyard Kipling's famous poem "The White Man's Burden," which first appeared in *McClure's Magazine,* declares in this advertisement the magnitude of the American colonial project.[2] In this poem, Kipling deems civilization's most important function—its "burden"—as the delivery of culture to those "savage" parts of the globe that need to be cleansed.

Why would a product made for the American home use the politically charged issue of empire to promote sales? As we have seen, Americans often brought violence into their homes through surprisingly subtle cultural machinations. Rather than an isolated domestic sphere, which we usually associate with the nineteenth century, the turn-of-the-century home was the stage on which acts of connoted violence took place.[3] The Pears' ad does not make an overt reference to the violence that attended the American colonial project, but it overtly signifies imperialism. *Harper's* readers could bring empire into their homes via the associations with imperialism that the soap company explicitly rendered in this striking advertisement.[4]

The year this ad appeared, images and writing about the recently promoted Admiral Dewey flooded the New York press on the days preceding his famous homecoming in New York City. Articles in enormously popular newspapers, such as the *World* and the *Evening Journal,* focused on everything from Dewey's physiognomy to his recent naval victory over the Spanish in the Philippines. Dewey's humility in the face of celebratory fervor is the ongoing refrain in these hagiographic puff pieces, where he explains his victory with a modest tone that seems to ignore the building tension around the party that was soon to commence in his honor. Two days before his official return to New York, the *World* quoted the admiral at length about his experiences in Asia. Even though Dewey was hypervigilant about not sounding too haughty in this interview, he was more than willing to share his opinions about American colonialism. Dewey explained, "The Filipinos are not fit for self-government just now. They are a queer people—much mixed. But I think they can be capable of self-government in time."[5] By calling attention to the peculiarity of the racially hybridic Filipinos, Dewey cast doubt on their ability to govern based on stereotypes. His explication of racial queerness was no doubt even more believable to readers who had learned about Dewey's reportedly unpretentious character. For instance, the article suggests that Dewey was unwilling to accept calls for his presidential run because he insisted, "I am not a Politician, but a Sailor." However, the "sailor's" willingness to talk about the Philippines and the potential role for outside governance in the island nation speaks to a not-so-subtle recognition of what Dewey must have been experiencing as the United States embraced his quick victory over the Spanish in Manila Bay.

To glorify the US presence on the other side of the Pacific Ocean, and proffer support for the Philippine-American War that followed the Spanish-American conflict, turn-of-the-century Americans created public spectacles in support of empire. By the latter part of 1898 it was a well-recognized fact that Dewey's orchestration of the naval defeat over the Spanish helped the US military set up a colonial stronghold in the Philippines. Citizens of the United States immediately grasped the significance of Dewey's military action and began to canonize him as a heroic figure. It was with a desire to play a part in the creation of a new national hero that New York City sponsored a celebration held in Dewey's honor on September 29 and 30, 1899. This event included a naval parade, a land parade, fireworks, street decorations, swarms of visitors, the construction of the monumental Dewey Arch, and a range of other cultural productions designed to praise America's naval idol. The centerpiece of the celebration was the enormous Dewey Arch. According to Kirk Savage, monumental works of sculpture from the nineteenth century represented "not just a rhetorical space where people debated image and symbol, but . . . a real physical space where publics could gather and define themselves at ceremonies and rallies."[6] The Dewey festivities were a mass celebration devised to define American empire.

Since the advent of the Spanish-American War, the media had constructed the Philippines as an "Oriental" site, a visual scape that could be understood, categorized, and possessed, given the right combination of intellectual knowledge and military power. This chapter reads the Dewey festivities in New York as a visual scape mediated through the complex machinations of a public spectacle attended by militarism and a hyperbolic form of masculinity. These festivities did not exoticize the Orient like the material in the previous four chapters, but the parade and public spectacles examined here enacted the obsession with empire that swelled the jingoistic rhetoric found in the United States in the months proceeding the Spanish-American War. The visual discourse that enabled these outrageous events fostered enthusiasm toward Dewey's naval triumph and, ultimately, helped Americans decipher the state of late nineteenth-century American empire. The Dewey phenomenon reveals that the cultural logic of empire does not always occur in the colony, away from the metropole. In this instance, events that transpired in New York shaped American perceptions about empire building in a distant location, a site where wild speculation and fantastic conjecture incited the public's imaginings.

Preshow Hype

The immense scale of the Dewey festivities required marketing. Selling the idea of the celebration would accomplish two goals, satisfying both corporate and government interests: first, celebrating Dewey meant an increase in commerce through sales of everything from newspapers, which would construct Dewey's celebrity, to hotel rooms, which would house New York's visitors; second, promoting Dewey also meant acclimating Americans to their new imperialist venture. Imperialism was more difficult to define than Dewey's biography as a military hero, but it was a narrative that ran throughout this advance publicity. Celebrating Dewey became another way of creating interest for the potential of American colonialism.

Before the Dewey celebration could become a possibility, its financing had to be approved by New York's city government. In early June 1899, the *World* reported that "four members of the Board of Aldermen and one member of the council opposed the appropriation of $150,000 for the Dewey celebration at the meeting of the Municipal Assembly yesterday. . . . The appropriation finally was passed." Several members of the Board of Aldermen could not justify spending money on an ephemeral moment. Alderman Okie, for example, "wanted the $150,000 spent for a Dewey School in New York."[7] Even after granting this initial sum, the Board of Aldermen refused to listen to Okie's complaints and made room for further financial liabilities.[8]

Aside from the fiscal logistics of planning these festivities, other types of pre-event narratives, such as the cottage industry of creating a Dewey hagiography, promoted the growing mania. To construct Dewey as a perfect, deserving, and masculine hero, he first had to be described as modest in character. The *World* quoted the admiral: "I do not desire fetes or demonstrations at home. It is enough for me that my country knows I did my duty as a soldier."[9] Other newspaper articles and period books reported on Dewey's past and represented his military character as overtly masculine, which appeased the turn-of-the-century American public. An article titled "Dewey the Boy," from the *World*, details the admiral's training at the Naval Academy in Annapolis and proclaims, "His characteristics as a student, as shown by his final examinations, were proficiency in Spanish, in steam, in the practice of gunnery and in navigation. These by a curious coincidence were the very things of which he required the most expert knowledge at Manila."[10] The same article describes a fight at the Naval Academy where Dewey gave his opponent "a swinging right-hand blow on the chest that spun him around, and then instantly kicked him into the Severn River."[11] Immediately following this story about Dewey's strength is a physical description that further inscribes his masculinity: "Dewey was registered as sixteen years and eleven months old when he entered the Naval Academy. He wore a heavy beard and mustache and looked much older than he was. Nearly all of his classmates were beardless youths."[12]

A children's book from 1899, titled *The Story of George Dewey for Young Readers,* continues this masculinist narrative by describing Dewey as a physically imposing youth. Mabel Beebe writes that when Dewey entered the academy he "was a strong, active boy, and fond of outdoor sports. He was also a lad with whom no one could trifle."[13] This heroizing of Dewey through the assistance of a hypermasculine chronicle is similar to the biographic style deployed in the *World.*[14] In fact, Beebe writes about a fight Dewey allegedly engaged in while at the academy, where he gave his classmate a "thrashing." Various manifestations of popular culture repeatedly describe Dewey as a capable military man whose experiences as a youth edified his masculine and militaristic character. Whether fact or pure fiction, the accounts' enthusiastic tenor enhanced their subject's bravado.

In addition to celebrating Dewey's physical strength and masculine features, the press linked his other corporeal attributes to this heroic characterization. The *World,* the day before the Dewey festivities began, assessed the admiral's physiognomy. Along with close-ups of Dewey's right hand, eyes, nose, ear, chin, and mustache (fig. 51) is text that gives "minute" details about each aspect of his physical appearance. Dewey's hands, according to the article, "show the Admiral's high-strung spirited nature best of all. They move constantly; but they are not the gestures of an excitable nature. They are not dramatic; they are serious and emphatic." The article describes Dewey's face as inherited from a cultured, or "Civilized" and "Western," past: "His face might be called classical. It is just a trifle too heavy, perhaps, for an Apollo Belvedere, but it would be a mighty good face to trust."[15] Dramatic close-ups of Dewey's body, along with descriptive words such as "classical," would have helped an American audience construct Dewey as a hero who naturally carried the "white man's burden" of racial superiority.

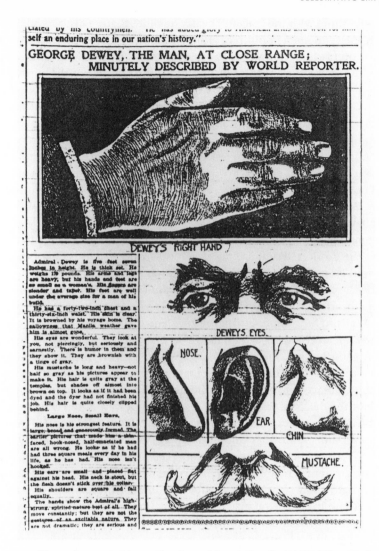

Figure 51 "George Dewey, the Man, at Close Range; Minutely Described by World Reporter," *World*, September 28, 1899. General Research Division, The New York Public Library, Astor, Lenox and Tilden Foundations.

On September 27, in an editorial in the *New York Evening Journal*, William Randolph Hearst, the newspaper's famous owner and editor, furthered this theory about Dewey's racial excellence. Hearst wrote that Dewey embodied "the highest physical and moral expression of the characteristic, kindly, frank, vigorous type of American manhood. He simply shines with the graceful, hearty qualities that we like to associate with the gentlemen of our race and our nation."[16] Hearst predicated his praise on his characterization of Dewey as a racially advanced man who manifested the turn-of-the-century masculinist virtues of the superior American race. Selling the notion of American imperialist control over the inferior Philippines became easier while lauding Dewey with the help of social Darwinism. Hearst's understanding of Dewey as racially exceptional incited him to conclude, "The only thing which could prevent the Admiral from becoming President of the United States is his absolute refusal to be a candidate."[17]

Praise for Dewey became so prevalent that the press compared him with George Washington, America's favorite presidential hero. In September, a front-page political cartoon from the *World* (fig. 52) depicted a woman hanging a portrait of Dewey next to an image of Washington with the caption "Dame Democracy—'A Second George.'" The Dewey portrait is smaller in size than the Washington image and does not include the celebratory inscription of "First in war, first in peace, and first in the hearts of his countrymen," which is part of the lower portion of the Washington frame. Furthermore, Dame Democracy has removed her democratic bonnet, which hangs on the wall below both frames. In place of the bonnet, she wears what may be a Spanish hairpiece; perhaps this is a signal that America's democratic ideals are being ignored, as the nation embraces the perils of empire signified through her donning the garb of the defeated Spanish empire. Placing Dewey, a minor figure as implied by the scale of his portrait, next to the larger anticolonial Washington, Dame Democracy questions the hazards of empire that may lie ahead.[18] Thus, the implications behind Dame Democracy's actions are not so apparent: a new American hero is being cultivated, and the iconic Washington may soon have a partner within the pantheon of American history, but the consequences of including this new hero are uncertain. Both imperialists and anti-imperialists could have attached their own set of meanings to this image. Moreover, the rendering of this cartoon of Dame Democracy in a domestic environment would have impacted a range of readers. As insinuated in the Pears' Soap ad, Dewey becomes part of the domestic realm in this fictitious parlor. Constructing Dewey as a heroic figure was becoming such a dominant cultural obsession that articulating his popularity within the confines of the American home—the material space that staged a carefully contrived notion of domesticity—became a way to make the admiral more universal and familiar. He was a hero for all spheres, not "separate spheres."[19] By en-

Figure 52 "Dame Democracy—'A Second George,'" *World*, September 18, 1899. General Research Division, The New York Public Library, Astor, Lenox and Tilden Foundations.

visioning Dewey in the mythic parlor of American heroes, newspaper readers could bring the imperial project into their own homes through an imaginary framework of domesticity that obfuscated the militaristic realities of colonialism while both celebrating and questioning its supposed success.

The popular press frequently depicted Dewey in domestic settings. In August 1899, the *World* published an image titled "Dewey Playing with His Pet Dog Bob" (fig. 53).[20] Here Dewey, dressed in white, reaches out to pet his dog. Dewey is not in a militaristic venue in this scene "taken at Miramar, near Triest, Austria"; instead he is at ease with his pet. The inclusion of Dewey's dog could have incited imaginings about Dewey in a domestic context. This representation would have led the *World*'s

THE WORLD; MON

DEWEY PLAYING WITH HIS PET DOG BOB.

(Taken at Miramar, near Triest, Austria.)

Figure 53 "Dewey Playing with His Pet Dog Bob," *World*, August 21, 1899. General Research Division, The New York Public Library, Astor, Lenox and Tilden Foundations.

audience to believe that they had personal knowledge of Dewey's everyday experiences outside the navy. This familiarity, although based on the media's careful construction of a biographic narrative, would have helped the American public create a fantasy about an accessible and domesticated hero. This familiarity would have also aroused a fictional understanding of empire, as imperialism could be brought into the home through the safety of a domestic vignette.

Dewey's "progress" away from Asia and toward the United States also became a popular subject in newspaper imagery. A small drawing of the world with a line charting Dewey's route from the Philippines to New York exemplifies this obsession with his geographic location during the month preceding the New York celebration (fig. 54). Above this map from the *Evening Journal* are lines marking chronological time and a small ship representing Dewey's current location. The geographic form of the world demarcates Africa, Europe, and Asia, and New York is a skyline with fireworks exploding overhead. The excitement over Dewey's imminent arrival is vivid in this small cartographic rendering that permits the newspaper reader to become more familiar with Dewey in the context of the *miniaturized* world of news, a microcosm of knowledge held in the reader's hands. In fact, this mapping of Dewey's progress depicts the world as a negotiable territory navigated with ease. What more could the armchair traveler have wanted, within the confines of his or her own domestic safety, than visual reassurance that places like the Philippines could be mapped and understood? The Philippines was so accessible in these small maps that now the enterprise of American colonialism would have appeared even more viable.[21]

Why is the cartographic outline of New York replaced with a skyline engulfed in a pyrotechnic display? Part of the preparatory excitement about the Dewey celebration focused on fantasies of what the spectacle would look like, and the use of fireworks was one way to promote the upcoming events. The New York City Board of Aldermen praised this fascination with illuminating the city sky in honor of Dewey. Minutes from their September 5 meeting conflate pyrotechnic displays with jingoistic candor: "Resolved, that the ordinance relating to the discharge of fireworks

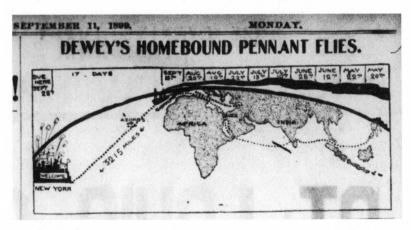

Figure 54 "Dewey's Homebound Pennant Flies," *New York Evening Journal,* September 11, 1899. Courtesy of Harry Ransom Humanities Research Center, The University of Texas at Austin.

in The City of New York be, and the same is hereby suspended from September 25 to October 1, 1899, in order that our citizens and residents may, by displays, add their share to the splendid arrangements being made officially in the name of our City to welcome home the hero of our Navy, Admiral George Dewey."[22] The brief suspension of law promoted excitement, asked for citizen involvement, and permitted the Board of Aldermen to record their own patriotism.

The city government and the popular press generated a tremendous level of support for Dewey's homecoming. By late July, the Dewey Reception Committee predicted that a million out-of-town visitors would descend on the city in the admiral's honor. That estimate would rise as expectations of the spectacle became increasingly hyperbolic.[23]

Entering the Public Spectacle

The efficacy of a parade is dependent on giving the public a vantage point from where they can watch proceedings without visual obstruction. In early September 1899, the Board of Aldermen voted to allow "citizens and residents of the City of New York, to place trucks and wagons, along the curblines of streets intersecting and adjacent to the line of march of the parade in honor of Admiral George Dewey . . . for the one and only purpose of affording people opportunity to witness said parade."[24] This resolution formulated the Dewey celebration as a parade through its call for spatial order. One can imagine a row of small trucks lining the streets of New York with parade witnesses standing both on and in their vehicles to get a glimpse of the Dewey-inspired festivities. The very language of the government's decree, however, demonstrates that citizens could act in a manner that would be reprimanded under everyday circumstances. For a brief period of time, the law could be broken without consequence.[25]

The celebration for Dewey took place on the last two days of September in 1899. The water parade, starting at a point north of Manhattan proceeding down the East River, occurred on Friday, September 29, and a land parade, beginning on the Upper West Side moving down to Washington Square, followed on Saturday, September 30. Three days before the official start of the events, the media met Dewey's September 26 arrival in New York City with a call for further viewer participation. A map of greater New York printed in the September 26 edition of the *Evening Journal* points to the specific geographic location of Dewey with the phrase "Olympia [Dewey's ship] at Anchor." The caption "You Can Go See Dewey" above the map explains the purpose of this cartographic depiction. Since his arrival in New York, Dewey had been anchored at a predetermined site, which was "one and a half miles from the Government pier at Sandy Hook, four miles northeast of Atlantic Highlands and eighteen miles from the Battery." Following this detailed explanation of Dewey's location, the text concludes, "You can get there by tug, yacht, sloop, rowboat, or any old boat."[26] Dewey and his ship may have been cordoned off to allow viewing from a distance, but the press told citizens that they could become active participants in these events by searching for Dewey's naval entourage.

While Dewey revelers could participate, the *Official Programme* of the Dewey celebration and published maps of the processional route separate the viewer and the viewed through regulatory language. Under the heading of twelve noon for the September 29 naval parade, the program guide states, "Naval parade starts up North River from Government anchorage off Tompkinsville. The Olympia will be in the lead, followed by the squadron, in the following order: Armored cruiser New York, Rear-Admiral Sampson's flagship, Capt. Chadwick commanding; armored cruiser Brooklyn, Capt. Jewell."[27] The notations about the Saturday land parade use similar language, and the final page of this official pamphlet is titled "Detailed order of march: The Programme for the big land parade." A street map representing the "Official Route of the Dewey Land Parade," found in the *World*, also conveys a message of processional rigor. The text beneath the rectangular sketch of the parade path describes this rendering as the official "route of the land parade on Saturday Sept. 30, as finally fixed by the Dewey Plan and Scope Committee."[28] Words such as "fixed," "detailed," and "order" all programmed the event as a closed narrative that would not permit disorder within its boundaries.

A book of photographs compiled by Moses King depicts the land parade. King captions one image the "New England Women's Grand Stand, Sixty-first Street and Central Park West, Northern Part of Durland's Riding Academy" (fig. 55). In this photograph, rows of viewers line the curb and a few policemen stand in the street containing the crowd. This well-dressed and orderly group of bystanders exhibits the ideal characteristics that constitute the model parade: order, symmetry, and discipline.[29] The architecture behind the curb continues this display of pride in Dewey's honor. Decorations (note the image of Dewey on the right side of the structure) and viewers on the roof, in the windows, and flowing out from risers highlight the celebratory atmosphere.[30]

The photograph of "The New England Women's Grand Stand" answers a list of gender-related questions from the August 30 edition of the *Evening Journal*:

NEW ENGLAND WOMEN'S GRAND STAND, SIXTY-FIRST STREET AND CENTRAL PARK WEST
NORTHERN PART OF DURLAND'S RIDING ACADEMY

Figure 55 "New England Women's Grand Stand, Sixty-First Street and Central Park West, Northern part of Durland's Riding Academy," from Moses King, *The Dewey Reception: New York* (New York: Chasmar-Winchell, 1899). Courtesy of the Library of Congress.

How are the women going to celebrate Dewey's return?

What preparations have the wives and sweethearts of the men who fought under Admiral Dewey made to welcome him home?

Are they not to be included in the general thanksgiving for the return of Admiral Dewey? Is the hour of celebration to be solely a man's hour?[31]

The presence of women fostered the leitmotif of masculinity that dominated Dewey's return, while concomitantly negating the role of the New Woman. During the late nineteenth century, the New Woman had become a contested source of cultural anxiety. Carroll Smith-Rosenberg has identified this group as those educated, middle-class women who "sought to use male myths to repudiate male power—to turn the male world upside down."[32] Suffrage, the right to education, and freer sexuality were issues this group brought to the attention of turn-of-the-century Americans. Constructing Dewey as a cultural hero who would stop these and other transgressions against gender identity required the production of an overtly gender-prejudiced biography, which included, for instance, moments from Dewey's childhood that accentuated his masculine character.[33] Fireworks, military ships, men in uniform parading in synchronic fashion, and the celebration of brute militaristic force facilitated the production of this masculine narrative.

The inclusion of women bolstered the event's masculine bias. The article in the *Evening Journal*, which offers queries about women's participation, gives several examples of how this issue surfaced. In fact, one section declares that "Dewey's namesakes will parade before him," and a small image of a child in a carriage illustrates the article's claim that "every mother with a son named Dewey will carry or wheel in his carriage the fortunate youth, beside others of equal good luck."[34] Here the media predicates the inclusion of women on the understanding that women are only to be given visibility if their presence reinforces the masculinity that enveloped Dewey's heroic return. After all, what could be more stereotypically masculine than the fantasy of excessive procreation represented by a vast number of children bearing Dewey's name? A fantasy of studlike reproduction enhanced Dewey's masculine character through this parade of children.

The water parade, on Friday, September 29, received some media attention, but the press saved most of its coverage for the land spectacle. The front page of the *World,* on the day of the land parade, represented the visual spectacle that attended these events. The headline exclaims: "New York a Volcano of Fire for Dewey; 5,000,000 Will See To-Day's Parade." Below this headline appear Dewey's remarkable comments: "I feel as if it were a dream, that I am spectator, not the object of this ovation. How the people exaggerate what I have done! The scene to-day was tremendous." Dewey's own visually determined object-spectator confusion becomes understandable after looking at the image that frames the article at the center of the front page. Fireworks explode in the sky, beacons of light crisscross, and a "Welcome Dewey" sign is on the left horizon line. As all this activity takes place, the recently erected head of the Statue of Liberty looks over the scene in the right foreground (fig. 56).[35] This visual conflagration teems with conflicting spectacles vying for the viewer's attention.

The press focused on events beyond the gloss of the illuminated cityscape. An abundance of Dewey-inspired consumer activity took place on the city's streets. The *Evening Journal* from September 25 reiterates the trope of firelike imagery of other articles with the headline "City Ablaze with Flags to Welcome Admiral Dewey." Several of the subheadings beneath this headline examine the Dewey craze in relation to conspicuous consumption. One subsection, for instance, uses both sketches and text to describe a "Harvest for Street Fakirs [vendors]."[36] According to the article, "There are armies of them [*fakirs*] all over the city, and they are doing a rushing business selling all sorts of souvenirs for Dewey day. The stock on hand includes everything from buttons to alleged oil paintings, and the visitors from out of town are large purchasers."[37] Three small sketches of men selling their Dewey wares accompany this article, and an awkward map depicting the "line of march of fakirs" is included.

Department stores also sold Dewey decorations to fill the urban landscape. Wanamaker's ran an advertisement for Dewey paraphernalia

Figure 56 "New York a Volcano of Fire for Dewey," *World*, September 30, 1899. General Research Division, The New York Public Library, Astor, Lenox and Tilden Foundations.

framed by an arch constructed with two Corinthian columns and a ribbon of flag (fig. 57). The columns are wrapped in cloth printed with the names of the ships Dewey successfully navigated in Manila Bay, and perched on the columns and over the center medallion, which announces Dewey's name, are three eagles. Anchors, stars, and the inclusion of the Vermont (Dewey's birthplace) and New York state insignia all add to the jingoistic aesthetic. The notice mentions that "Decorations and Attractions" can be found at the store to enhance the celebration.[38] Other advertisements (think back to the Pears' ad and the Dewey chair from chapter 3) used Dewey's fame to attract business. The Siegel Cooper Company included fireworks imagery in its large advertisement for the "Dewey Dollar Dinner"; Hunter Baltimore Rye mentioned that its beverage should be enjoyed while welcoming home the "Conquering Hero"; and the George Childs Cigar Company depicted Dewey's face as a way to offer "cheers" for the admiral in the hope that New Yorkers and New York's visitors would buy its cigars.[39] All these companies used the excitement of Dewey's return to promote business.[40] In September 1899, the media asked an entire city and its visitors to join in the festivities and bring Dewey into their lives through consumerism.

The utilization of the arch in the Wanamaker advertisement held special meaning for those involved with the Dewey homecoming. The first line of the ad's small text hints at the genesis of this arch form: "The Sculptors have given our Public large, artistic and pleasing private decorations for the Dewey Occasion."[41] The mention of sculptors and artwork is a direct reference to the National Sculpture Society, whose members were busy finishing the Dewey Arch, a sculptural group built in New York City in honor of the hero's return. The debate about the construction of the arch, the structure itself, and how revelers construed the arch during the Dewey celebration and in its aftermath reinforced several of the prevalent themes that surrounded Dewey's return. The arch was a material

Figure 57 Advertisement for Wanamaker's department store, from *World*, September 28, 1899. General Research Division, The New York Public Library, Astor, Lenox and Tilden Foundations.

manifestation of America's newfound interest in displaying the vast possibilities of empire.

Building a Centerpiece

The Dewey Arch was a symbol of triumph and heroism. Recall that the *Art Amateur* reported on the death of two workers who were constructing the arch in September 1899. The magazine noted "the patriotism of the sculptors who volunteered to decorate the Dewey Arch has unfortunately resulted in the death of two of their number, and the prostration, through an attack of paralysis, of a third."[42] The terrible accident must have created quite a spectacle of horror on the streets of New York. As the monument continued to rise, even in the wake of this incident, the fallen bodies of artisans who were busy finishing the arch would have been a shock. Like the soldiers' deaths that continued to accompany America's new war venture, this incident would have reminded onlookers that even the business of celebrating empire could become tinged with death. Thus, the arch symbolized the possibility of America's expansion, but also connoted the violence of war.

The Dewey Arch became the centerpiece of the land parade and functioned as a static contrast to the animated revelers (fig. 24). In August 1899, the editors of *Harper's Weekly* declared:

Silence is often as eloquent as words. While thousands of citizens along the line of the Dewey parade will be roaring themselves hoarse in welcome to the Admiral and in excess of patriotism, there will be a number of figures in Madison Square, standing singly and in groups, with dumb mouths, motionless. Yet they will be no less eloquent. I speak of the statuary which will adorn the triumphal arch and its approaches.

It is not only that the individual figures represent famous seamen of the past, men whose names conjure up a host of patriotic memories and recall the great crises through which the republic has passed; not only that the groups portray symbolically such stirring episodes . . . but behind all these are the patriotism and civic pride of the sculptors who planned them.[43]

"Silence" becomes the ironic noun that explains the significance of both the arch and the artists who built this monument. The arch spoke to New Yorkers at the turn of the century by signifying the public's experience with the possibilities of imperialism.[44] The *silence* of the arch offered a powerful utterance of jingoistic pride and was, moreover, a symbol of imperialism that could be traced to the glory of Rome. In short, it provided the Dewey festivities with a focal point that framed the parade's fervor.

Charles Lamb, the architect, suggested the idea for a naval arch at a special meeting of the National Sculpture Society. As Michele Bogart points out, the society was founded in the late nineteenth century as a way to create a professional guild for sculptors. The society was part of a larger turn-of-the-century movement to create organizations that would validate various fields of work as viable professions.[45] Lamb related in his scrapbook that the "suggestion [to his fellow sculptors] was received with great enthusiasm, and a committee appointed to discuss the matter with the city authorities—The first informal meetings of this committee were held on the Veranda of 'Falcon Lodge' on the Palisades in early summer of 1899."[46] By late July, the press began to cover the progress and planning of the arch. The *World* reported in July 1899 that the National Sculpture Society had submitted a plan for the arch before the Committee on Plan and Scope of the Dewey Celebration and approximated the arch's cost at $10,000. The committee "referred the design back to the sculptors for further consideration" because of this high price.[47]

Work on the arch began on July 29.[48] Seven days later the *New York Journal* noted that "the Dewey celebration . . . is likely to prove a fizzle unless the force of public opinion can be brought to bear upon the Board of Aldermen" to spend more money.[49] On August 9, the Board of Aldermen received a letter from Randolph Guggenheimer, the mayor of New York, who pleaded with the municipal government to allocate funds for the arch.[50] By late August, the city and private donors provided money, and work on the arch was moving forward. The National Sculpture Society promised to donate its members' time and charge the city only for the cost of building materials to stop the aldermen's financial balking.[51]

The sculptors' patriotic act of work, mourned in the pages of *Art Amateur*, became a source of entertainment and civic pride in other publications. Numerous images represented the glorification of the artists' labor. In mid-September, the *Evening Journal* published an engraving from a photograph titled "Progress of the Dewey Arch." According to the engraving's caption, "The work on the magnificent arch is being pushed rapidly." Indeed, "Many workmen are busy on the arch this morning, the sculptors being hidden by big curtains from the curious crowd."[52] The performance of patriotic work became such a crowd pleaser that a few days before the land parade an article in the *Evening Journal* declared, "The crowds about it [the arch] all the time are tremendous, and it seems to be the magnet which draws all strangers as soon as they reach New York."[53]

Figure 58 "The Great Dewey Arch, the Most Artistic Structure Ever Reared to Welcome a Hero—And Other Striking Features of the Celebration," *World,* September 24, 1899. General Research Division, The New York Public Library, Astor, Lenox and Tilden Foundations.

Part of the struggle the National Sculpture Society confronted was the fight for artistic originality. An unusual article entitled "New York's Stolen Arch" revealed that "Chicago architects claim to have discovered an artistic steal in the design for a 'Dewey arch' made by the New York Sculpture Society. . . . It is said that the design has been copied from the arch of Titus at Rome, some figures being added to symbolize Dewey's victory at Manila."[54] If the arch was built to glorify American imperialism, why did the young empire need to borrow an architectural template from another culture?

The press raised questions about the ingenuity of the sculptors, yet most newspapers posited the connection between the Dewey Arch and the Arch of Titus as a patriotic pairing that made the arch a Beaux-Arts success rendered "invincingly pure."[55] A September 24 drawing published in the *World*, with the caption "The Great Dewey Arch, the Most Artistic Structure Ever Reared to Welcome a Hero—And Other Striking Features of the Celebration" (fig. 58), exemplifies the media's praise for the arch. This representation is pure fantasy; none of the events pictured had transpired. Here images of the future parade, its viewers, and, of course, the ubiquitous fireworks going off overhead surround the arch. Although the arch was still in the final stages of construction on September 24, it had become a target for projected fantasies about the way the city would soon be visually transformed in honor of Dewey's victory. The media's fantastic conjectures about the arch, however, eventually came to an end. One day before the land parade, on September 29, "There was a yell of triumph from 25,000 throats in Madison Sq at 5 pm today, when the last plank of scaffolding fell to the ground and exposed to view for the first time the Dewey arch in all its white, imposing beauty."[56] This audience size is probably exaggerated, yet there were undoubtedly a number of people present for the dramatic unveiling. Questions about what these bystanders saw on September 29 still remain. What, in short, was beneath the scaffolding?

The National Sculpture Society built the Dewey Arch in Madison Square along an axis on Twenty-fourth Street at Fifth Avenue. The society decided to cast the monument out of staff, the impermanent building material first used at the World's Columbian Exposition in 1893.[57] The artists hoped that the public, after seeing the beauty of the arch, would demand it be rebuilt as a permanent fixture. The arch was "seventy feet long, thirty feet wide, and eighty-five feet high." It opened onto Fifth Avenue at the intersection of Broadway. Bogart notes that the arch was "the focal point of a vista that extended from several radiating avenues, it was visible from Washington Square to Central Park on Fifth Avenue, from Herald Square to 10th Street on Broadway, and from the East River to the Hudson on 24th Street."[58] The Dewey Arch commanded a prime piece of real estate in the midst of Manhattan's commercial activity. Moving away from the arch, a sculptural group consisting of a procession of double columns on plinths, except for the end units, which were made up of four grouped columns on plinths, stretched northward to Twenty-sixth Street and southward to Twenty-third Street. Artists decorated the end members of the group and adorned the other double columns with winged victories, a motif that appeared throughout the sculptural project.

Both sides of the arch extolled American expansionism by depicting what the National Sculpture Society described as the four patriotic steps. Bogart relates, "To the northeast stood *The Call to Arms* (Patriotism) by Philip Martiny; at the southeast was *The Combat* (War) by Karl Bitter; at the southwest was *The Victors Returning* (Triumph) [also referred to as *The Triumphal Return*] by Charles Niehaus; and at the northwest *The Warriors Resuming Their Occupations* (Peace) by Daniel Chester French."[59] The entire surface of the arch continued this decorative schema of praising

Figure 59 Dewey Arch, southwest pier. Image from *Art Amateur* (October 1899): 91.

American imperialism with imagery relating to both US naval history and the importance of America's new role in international politics. By looking closely at two specific sculptural groups from photographs, it is possible to explain how the monument represented the nation's new imperialist mind-set.

Against the southwest pier of the arch was Charles Niehaus's work celebrating the return of the American military (fig. 59). Niehaus centered this group of modeled figures with a statue of winged victory, who towers over the crowded ensemble holding a sword in her right hand and a wreath, representing peace, in her left hand. The most classicizing aspect of Niehaus's work is Victory's enormous wings, a clear reference to the

Hellenistic work of Greek sculpture *Nike of Samothrace* (190 BCE). A group of soldiers surrounds Victory and marches toward the homecoming festivities, while families greet the two soldiers in the foreground. Admiral Dewey stands at the center, stepping out of the sculptural space and saluting the crowds who would walk by the arch. In Niehaus's work, Dewey embodies victory coupled with the promise of a domestic homecoming. Contemporary discussions about this sculptural group placed Niehaus's depiction in a liminal state between masculine victory and domestic peace. The famous critic Charles Caffin explained, "We are not a nation of fighters, but men who can fight. When the occasion arises and the summons comes, American manhood springs forward to the call, is eager to reach the fighting line, but just as eager for return to home and civil life."[60] Niehaus captured the challenge of manhood followed by the glory of return.

On the west face of the arch was Johannes Gelert's low relief representing *Progress of Civilization* (fig. 60). Here two figures sit in the bow of a boat, while a woman stands beneath the furled sail of the vessel. Gelert depicts these figures moving forward carrying pride and progress with their travels; this is a representation of empire expanding. There is no fighting in Gelert's work and all signs of military life are absent. "Progress" takes place without bloodshed. This sculptor shows the underlining confidence and assumptions that provoke imperialism, or what he terms the "Progress of Civilization."

The logic of this narrative repeated the cultural understanding held by many turn-of-the-century Americans. The popular media reported that Dewey brought American dominion into the Orient, but that dominion was culturally understood as an effortless act requiring little more than the mind-set of "progress." Again, the notion that the United States was "not a nation of fighters, but of men who can fight" articulated what the National Sculpture Society wanted the public to believe after seeing the arch. The sculptors needed to depict success, but their representations obfuscated militarism. Showing progress without violence mitigated the experience of visually encountering the realities that attended manifest destiny. The project of colonialism would be more readily accepted if it could transpire without the loss of American lives.

The sculptural group became an architectural hub for the processional march on September 30, providing a gateway through which military units passed on their way to the parade's endpoint at Washington Square. Photographs and film, taken to document the patriotism of the parade, show regiments marching through the colonnade and arch on their way downtown.[61] The press reported that Dewey reviewed the parade at the

Figure 60 Johannes Gelert's low relief representing *Progress of Civilization*. Image from Charles Schenk, *The Dewey Arch and Its Details* (New York: P. Wenzel, 1899), 8. Courtesy of Art and Architecture Collection, Miriam and Ira D. Wallach Division of Art, Prints and Photographs, The New York Public Library, Astor, Lenox and Tilden Foundations.

arch but, much to the dismay of the National Sculpture Society, he never actually passed through the structure.[62]

Soon after the Dewey celebration ended, the arch began to lose its cultural appeal. A private group of citizens became alarmed over the arch's fate and tried to raise money to build a permanent structure. This project never came to fruition, however, because Dewey decided to run for president in 1900, which meant that building a permanent arch would become too overtly politicized. Part of this disregard for the arch can be traced to the rise of an anti-imperialist sentiment.[63] Voices of dissent against empire did not favor a monument advocating American expansionist activity.

Before the city government dismantled the arch, the press reported a strange series of incidents: citizens began hacking away at the once celebrated work of art. Were these acts of destruction undertaken by vandals who had no regard for Dewey as a heroic figure? Or, could those who "ruined" the arch be described as radical anti-imperialists who wanted to destroy any signs of American pro-imperialist sentiment? These explanations seem unlikely. This vandalism did not surface because of a lack of respect for the Dewey celebration, but was instead a desire to domesticate and take home souvenirs of the monument that materially displayed zeal for empire.

The popular press called those who destroyed the arch vandals, but vandals who wanted reminders of Dewey. Two days after the land parade, the *World* declared that "in their mad desire to get Dewey souvenirs yesterday hundreds of people hacked at the columns along Fifth avenue and even at the figures in the triumphal arch itself. They would have ruined it had not the police interfered. . . . Women helped small boys to climb onto the pedestals of the statues and help in the work of destruction."[64] Other reports in the press continued to posit those who were ruining the arch as hounds engaged in a pursuit of souvenirs. The *New York Telegraph* noted that soon fragments from the arch would appear "on the whatnots [nineteenth-century display cabinets] of Oshkosh, Kalamazoo and other rural villages along with the plush album and the bullets from Gettysburg."[65] Mentioning the possibility that this sculptural debris would soon be honored next to Civil War memorabilia and the all-important photographic album clarified the significance of these remarkable keepsakes.[66]

Souvenirs help us formulate narratives of events in place of the actual happenstances of an event. They allow us to fabricate and recreate experiences.[67] Breaking pieces off a work of art that showcased American imperialism allowed Dewey revelers to take a piece of the action home. One could have left the two-day Dewey affair with a reminder, an artifact that activated the memory of the Dewey mania that had enveloped New York. Additionally, these remnants could have triggered a more significant memory that the Dewey phenomenon often elided, the culturally inculcated memory of America's first experience with overseas imperialism. For these relic gatherers, the narrative of imperialism could be distilled into a scrap of sculptural trash.

Part of the narrative of imperialism inscribed on the work of pilfered art was related to violence. W. J. T. Mitchell insightfully reveals that "public art has served as a kind of monumentalizing of violence and never more powerfully than when it presents the conqueror as a man of peace imposing a Napoleonic Code or a *pax Romana* on the world."[68] The Dewey Arch played an active role in the narrative creation of a type of artistic violence predicated on colonial policy, which became obvious with each mark of the sculptors' tools. While the National Sculpture Society tried to obscure these matters using a classically inspired veneer of peace, the imperial mind-set that incited the construction of the arch was obvious. Thus, the act of gathering and collecting pieces of the monument can also be read as a type of participatory violence. By tearing off portions of the National Sculpture Society's work in staff, and bringing these remnants into their homes, parade participants were displaying fragmented representations of the violence that attended the creation of empire.

A small souvenir booklet about the Dewey Arch evokes the manner in which New Yorkers became enraptured with the Dewey craze in 1899. The anonymous author writes:

IN THE TRIUMPHAL ARCH erected in honor of Admiral Dewey, New York has achieved a triumph as complete and remarkable in its way as the brilliant victory is meant to commemorate. This imposing and stately structure not only expresses the admiration of the people for the bravery and genius of the great Admiral, but also marks what has been aptly termed the beginning of time.[69]

A new era had commenced, and its genesis could be traced to the American invasion of the Philippine Islands. Accordingly, imperialism needed to be lauded because it marked the inception of a new epoch. The last two days of September in 1899 inscribed this "beginning of time" in a grand manner. Millions of participants celebrated the military prowess of Admiral Dewey, whose success on the other side of the Pacific set a precedent for the future of American colonialism.

The Dewey festivities became a way for New Yorkers to celebrate empire through the visual scape of a public spectacle. Before Dewey landed in the Philippines, America did not possess a colony, and by 1899 a three-year war to ensure the future of an American presence in the Pacific was well under way. Thus, the celebration for Dewey distilled the cultural imperatives that formulated America's ongoing colonial effort in Asia. For instance, arguments about how much to pay for the Dewey affair were similar to the political fighting over money to support the war effort in the Philippines. And the importance of masculinity in the descriptions of Dewey was never absent from discussions about American troops in the colonial zone.[70] Finally, the idea of using art and design to mark the landscape in honor of imperialism became an important part of the larger American effort to transform the Philippines, an idea the next chapter will explore.

The Dewey homecoming may have taken place over a short period of time, but this moment encapsulated the powerful fantasy of a lasting commitment to American imperialism through the experience of a wildly popular visual spectacle. Citizens of New York could not stop their frenzy for embracing this initial foray into colonialism. For over a century, Americans had watched Europeans pursue their colonial projects, and Dewey's success represented America's chance to further its position on the world stage, where imperialist adventures were always popular attractions. These events on the last days of September in 1899 were less about Dewey's naval ability and more about a new phase of America's ongoing presence on the proscenium of empire. There were debates about America's overseas conquest—remember that Dame Democracy removes her "democratic" bonnet, relinquishing America's own historic affiliation to anti-imperialism—but the fervor that animated the streets and waterways of New York in September 1899 was overwhelmingly in favor of colonialism. Once the experience of colonialism had been discussed, analyzed, represented, and, in the case of Dewey, feted, America turned its attention to altering the Philippine landscape.

SIX

Building Empire

Architecture and American Imperialism in the Philippines

Throughout the Spanish-American and Philippine-American Wars, the US government and the American media used architecture to inscribe the Philippines as a geographic locale where the primitive population could not be trusted. An 1899 article from the *World*, for example, titled "The Revenge of the Filipino," reports on the unfortunate American soldier injected with leprosy by a group of Filipino insurgents (fig. 29). The illustration that shows where the American soldier, Private Lapeer, became infected with leprosy has the following caption: "In such a hut as this the incident happened."[1] The tradition of using a hut to mark the savagery of its inhabitants was not lost on those trying to advance American empire; thus another image of huts (fig. 61), this one taken from a jingoistic book published in 1898 titled *History of the Spanish-American War*, is on the page before an anthropologic claim that the "fiercest and most primitive savages inhabit the scattered [Philippine] islands, sometimes two or more antipathetic races occupying the same island and ceaselessly waging war against each other and the government alike."[2] The primitive dwellings, like the hut in the *World* article, provide a visual depiction enhancing ethnographic language about the uncivilized Philippines.

Two years after the United States claimed victory over the Philippines, the government hired Daniel Burnham, the famous architect who orchestrated the layout of the 1893

Figure 61 Photograph from Henry Watterson, *History of the Spanish-American War* (New York: Western W. Wilson, 1898).

World's Columbian Exposition in Chicago and who played an integral role in the development of the tall building, to redesign Manila as the capital city of its new geographic possession and to plan a summer capital in a rural area called Baguio. Although Burnham was in the Philippines for only a brief period in 1904 and 1905, his plans set a precedent for future colonial construction. Burnham's vision was part of a larger turn-of-the-century project of conceptualizing the Philippine landscape as a place without a history, a savage nation devoid of civilization. Additionally, Burnham's plans for taking Western city planning abroad manifested the American project of bringing Occidental fantasies about design appropriateness into the Orient. Burnham and his fellow designers hoped to navigate the conflicting forces between what Amy Kaplan describes as the desire for American empire with the reality of imperialism taking place in locations perceived of as foreign and threatening.[3] Thus, at the turn of the century, the visual scape of the built environment played a significant role in the expression of Orientalist discourse and the defense of imperialist action.

This discourse about the design deficiencies found in the Philippines could be found in two world's fairs before the government sent Burnham into the colonial zone. Both the 1901 Pan-American Exposition in Buffalo and the 1904 Louisiana Purchase Exposition in St. Louis contained Filipino villages that staged Philippine culture for millions of visitors. I will focus on the 1904 fair, which had a village of forty-seven acres compared to the eleven acres found at the 1901 exposition. By 1904, the fair's organizers had more of a vested interest in expanding their representation of the Philippines by encompassing a greater landmass, since the Philippines was now an official American colony.

At the Fairgrounds

The 1904 fairgrounds in St. Louis covered a twelve-hundred-acre expanse, nearly doubling the landmass of the 1893 fair in Chicago. The fair's theme was the Louisiana Purchase, hence it explicitly celebrated the expansion of America's borders. The grounds resembled a rectangle of two miles by one mile. Most of the large exhibit buildings could be found in an area named Forest Park, where structures such as the Art Palace, the Horticultural Building, and the Festival Hall formed the central element of the fairgrounds in the shape of a fan. These buildings were ivory white with dashes of color accenting their roofs. They were mostly Classical Revival buildings that highlighted how the progress of Western design had helped create an unprecedented civilization on American soil. Architects from all over the country came to St. Louis to design these edifices, including Cass Gilbert, John Carrère, and Thomas Hastings.[4]

West of Forest Park was an area referred to as the Skinner Tract where, like the Midway at the 1893 Chicago fair, non-Western cultures were the focal point. Out of the 422 acres forming the Skinner Tract, 47 acres became the Philippine Exposition. Next to the Philippine Exposition was the Native American exhibit. One book, declaring itself *The Official History of the Fair*, notes that the "red man of America and the brown man of Oceanica, both races the ward of Uncle Sam, both including many tribes, were almost side by side, each on a forty-acre tract. One pathetic difference between the red man and the brown was brought out at this twin exhibition, and that is the Indian is a disappearing race, while the Filipino appears to be just on the eve of a substantial and lasting development."[5] Although there are debates about how effective the Philippine exhibit was in convincing the fair's visitors of the efficacy of American colonial policy, there is little doubt that the $1 million exhibition space—funded by the Bureau of Insular Affairs, the Philippine Commission, and the World's Fair management—projected the central tenet behind American colonial policy in the Far East.[6] After all, 1904 was two years after America declared victory in the Philippine-American War, and this was also a period when anti-imperialist sentiment swept the political landscape. The Philippine Exposition would, it was expected, provide the proper message about the importance of the American presence on the other side of the Pacific Ocean to Filipinos, Americans, and the rest of the world.

A visitor entered the Philippine Reservation through a model of the Spanish walls that could be found in Manila. Inside this walled-in area was an exhibit displaying war relics procured by the US military during its engagement in the Philippines. Passing through the walled section of the exposition, one encountered over a dozen buildings and several native villages. This part of the reservation held three separate spheres of culture: one focused on the Spanish influence found in the Philippines, one centered on the current ethnographic state of the Philippines, and one detailed how US imperialism could further the cause of civilizing Filipinos.[7]

The fair's organizers brought approximately twelve hundred Filipinos to participate in the exhibits; some of these men and women performed cultural activities in the supposedly indigenous villages, others attended a "typical" Filipino school, and many took part in the construction of native architecture. One exposition guidebook relates that beginning "in October, 1903, the first Filipino carpenters and builders began to arrive, and commenced the work of building their native houses and camps."[8] Images found in *Jackson's Famous Photographs of the Louisiana Purchase Exposition* explicate the importance of architecture in this artificially constructed colonial tableau. Photographs show a group of Igorot tribe members "constructing their dwellings in the Philippine Reservation."[9] In these representations, a group of native Filipinos wears very little clothing while using antiquated tools to build. The entire scene of construction is overly staged; these are not candid shots capturing craftsmanship, but posed photographs. In one image, two Igorots move a handsaw back and forth on a piece of timber (fig. 62). The two workers and two of their fellow tribesmen wear only loincloths. Their upper bodies and feet are bare. Other pieces of sewn timber lay next to their unprotected feet, and their hair is long, straight, and pulled back in ponytails. The caption beneath the image notes that these workers are building a dwelling, but the written paragraph that follows the main caption explains that the fair's management insisted that the Filipinos wear more complete clothing and that the state of undress captured on film was no longer an acceptable practice.[10] In short, there was the promise of more generous apparel if the armchair tourist traveled to the fair after viewing Jackson's risqué—yet compelling—images.[11]

The US government, along with the fair's organizers, hoped that the Philippine Reservation would incite Americans to, and I quote from

IGORROTES CONSTRUCTING THEIR DWELLINGS IN THE PHILIPPINE RESERVATION.
The above picture shows a few of the natives of the Island of Mindano, now within
the World's Fair grounds at St. Louis. This picture was taken after the Fair was formally
opened, but the management insisted upon the adoption of a more generous use of wearing apparel, so that today shirts and trousers, or a sacque and skirt, if it be a woman,
are worn.

Figure 62 Image from C. S. Jackson and Charles Walter Brown, *Jackson's Famous Photographs of the Louisiana Purchase Exposition*, 1904. Warshaw Collection, Archives Center, National Museum of American History, Smithsonian Institution, Washington D.C.

Rudyard Kipling, whose words act as an epigraph in one of the guide book-
lets to the Philippine Exposition, "Take up the White Man's Burden."[12]
Jackson's photographs depict this imperialist mind-set by creating visual
evidence of the Westerner's "unique claim to civilization."[13] Furthermore, the expectation of architecturally altering the Philippine landscape
became a cornerstone of the American colonial project in Asia, and his
images reveal native Filipino architectural traditions as uncivilized. These
photographs do not represent white men wearing work clothes laboring
away at Classical Revival structures that were the cultural rage at the
time of the fair, but here we witness, through the putative confirmation
of photography, scantily clothed, dark-skinned natives working on huts.
The thatched roofs, the native bodies, and the primitive tools enhanced
the popular notion that the Philippines was a savage state in need of a
civilizing force. The architectural performance, put on by the natives at
the fair's organizers' behest, staged the imperative of modifying the Philippine landscape with Western architecture. Indeed, fair visitors could
marvel at the wonders of Forest Park and visually compare the design

deficits staged on the Philippine Reservation with the spectacle of the fair's classical centerpiece.

The popular US sentiment at the turn of the century was one of fear toward the Philippines. This anxious trepidation could be found in both imperialist and anti-imperialist arguments. Proponents of imperialism wanted to quell their fear with military action that would help pacify the savagery they found in the Pacific, and those against imperialism often contended that Americans would not be safe in the colony. Think back to Private Lapeer and his distressing, yet fictive, encounter with leprosy in the primitive hut (fig. 29). In this drawing the fear is palpable. Lapeer crouches on the ground, a desperate victim of tainted blood and the terrors associated with what Americans repeatedly described as a dreadful place. Thus, projects such as the one staged in 1904 in St. Louis were attempts at a solution to the Philippine problem. Many Americans believed that the primitive culture found in the colonial zone was inferior and in need of a civilizing influence. The US government wanted to change the Philippines through a kind and helpful hand, which could counter the colony's savagery.[14] Architecture, a visual scape of design that fostered fantasies of economic growth and civilizing influence, became an important component of benevolent assimilation. Philippine attempts at design represented a cultural shortcoming that needed (in the eyes of the American colonial administration) to be fixed with Western ingenuity.

Several souvenir books from the 1904 fair share this interest in native Filipino architecture. One "official publication" from the fair, titled *The Universal Exposition Beautifully Illustrated* by Robert Reid, notes that Filipinos "have no fixed habitation but wander around at their pleasure, erecting small huts where they tarry. Intellectually they are a feeble people, and possessed of the full share of savage vanity."[15] The hut, once again, becomes the cultural marker of the primitive. The sentence on architecture precedes the sentence on intellectual capacity and demonstrates, through the presence of huts, the Filipinos' "full share of savage vanity." Nothing could be more egregious and in need of repair to the colonizer's eye than an infantile approach to life that manifests as wandering the landscape with a vane sense of self-worth, a seemingly empty existence where Western conceptions about permanence are nonexistent. *The Official History of the Fair: St. Louis, 1904* also devotes several pages to the primitive Philippine architecture found on the fairgrounds. The book's author, John Wesley Hanson, writes that the houses in the village "were built by Filipinos, of native materials, bamboo, nipa and other island products."[16] Later Hanson explains that it was quite a "sight to witness the savage islanders constructing their huts upon their arrival at the fair. The Igorrote band worked faithfully—faithfully for Igorrotes—and completed two grass-roofed huts, a big one and a little one, in as many days." To ensure that the reader understands who is doing all this construction, he continues, "All the work on each was done by the savages. Woodwork for all the huts had been brought along, but parts had been lost on the way, and it was necessary to hew timbers anew."[17] Hanson calls attention to the Filipino act of construction. The work of sawing, framing, and raising these native homes becomes a spectacular sight for the American audience. Even in moments of escaping work through the act of song, these Filipino craftsmen perform as a spectacle of curiosity. Hanson reports that close to "the entrance to the stockade the women were reveling in a great mound of native grass, tieing it into wisps and chanting wierd [*sic*] songs as they worked."[18] The racist notion of happy Filipinos "chanting" as they work is striking in this descriptive sentence that posits a link between the author's ears tuned to native song while his sight focuses on the framing of a hut.

Ironically, the exposition ended in failure. As a result of tension between the fair's conflicting motives, advocating education and uplift for Filipinos while at the same time creating a racially based spectacle of hyperbolic stereotype, the message of the 1904 fair became a morass of conflict. While the events in St. Louis expose an important historic moment related to American empire, the fair was a chaotic enterprise that led to colossal expenses and unrealized expectations.[19] Regardless of these difficulties, the colonial administration continued to plan other ventures that would improve America's imperial position. Indeed, later in 1904 the architect Daniel Burnham would be sent to the Philippines to begin the massive project of refashioning the landscape into a Western image. Burnham's work, like the 1904 fair, did not have the effect the colonial administration desired. The fantasy behind his architectural vision clearly found its impetus in previously staged cultural venues, such as the Louisiana Purchase Exposition, but many of his dreams never came to fruition. Burnham's architectural plans were an attempt at finding a design panacea to the Filipino dilemma.

The Plans

Daniel Burnham's selection as the official colonial architect in the Philippines was contingent on his reputation as a city planner and his previously established relationship with the head of the Philippine Commission, William Cameron Forbes. In an April 1904 letter to Forbes, Burnham relates that this type of work "is the sort of thing a man might well make personal sacrifice for, because it surely will offer an opportunity to do work of great beauty and consequently of great interest. If I could see my way to general charge of it I would jump at the opportunity." Burnham becomes so fervent in this letter that at one point he adds "there can be no monetary profit in this work but it would be a door to happiness to men who care to improve opportunity for the sake of the poetic thing itself."[20] This notion of self-sacrifice and the need to bring a type of architectural poetry into the new colony exemplifies Burnham's belief in his own work, his sense of a great architectural opportunity, and his conviction about imperialist activity. Burnham wrote Forbes a follow-up letter nine days later and reaffirmed that the "Luzon [the island where Manila and Baguio are located] work should have a man's whole heart. Dreams will not come for pay. Whoever does this should go in because he can't keep out."[21]

Burnham was not the Philippine Commission's first choice for redeveloping Manila as a colonial capital. In October 1903, the Municipal Board of the City of Manila issued a statement explaining "that an effort should be made to secure the services of Mr. [Frederick Law] Olmsted [Jr.] or a man of the same class, with the idea of having an expert come to Manila for six or eight months, or a year, if necessary, for the purpose of making a thorough study of the best disposition of [the existing city] . . . and prepare plans for a system of parks and boulevards and recommending the location and varieties of shade trees."[22] The US government did not want to hire one of its military engineers for this position, so Olmsted Jr. was the obvious choice because he was the child of the most famous landscape architect in nineteenth-century America, Frederick Law Olmsted Senior. Frederick Sr. educated his son in an apprenticeship that ended when his health began to fail rapidly.[23] In late March 1904, Olmsted Jr. sent his regrets to secretary of war William Howard Taft explaining that he would not be able to help with the American colonial project because of previous commitments. The tenor of his letter is unusual in that it goes beyond a mere apology; Olmsted appears mournful: "but turn which way I will, I cannot see my way open to go."[24] The next day Forbes wrote to Taft that he would work with Olmsted to find another capable architect.[25] After some deliberation with Taft, Forbes asked his old friend Burnham if he had any interest in working for the US government.[26]

Burnham and Forbes's writing from this period reveals how eager they were to alter the colonial landscape, a visual scape seen as lacking civilization. Writing to his wife Margaret on his first day in the island nation,

Burnham connects the Philippines to American naval might and notes that Manila "is against the sea; we can look out over the grounds where Dewey fought. . . . I am in white, as everyone else is, and am attended by lots of silent Chinese servants."[27] Burnham's enthusiasm during his trip continues throughout his journal entries, which are brief, yet filled with curious anecdotes. He especially admired Baguio, where he "saw far away over the mountains the langayen Gulf out at sea, a most magnificent sight."[28] Forbes wrote more than Burnham, and his extensive comments help us understand how "it is new, strange, and delightful, this laying out a city [Baguio] on this rolling land. We [Forbes and Burnham] have about thirty things to provide sites for and we want to distribute them beautifully, conveniently and expediently."[29] Forbes clarifies the types of infrastructure he and Burnham are planning by noting the soon to be built "hotels, official buildings, official residences, court house, schools, colleges, sanitariums, playgrounds, railroad terminals, business section, markets, churches, residence section, country club, etc. The problems are great fun."[30]

Burnham left the Philippines on January 16, 1905, forty days after his arrival, but his writing about American imperialism became even more pointed after his departure. Perhaps the most extraordinary example of Burnham's post-trip enthusiasm can be found in a letter from March 1905 to his friend and future biographer Charles Moore. Burnham confesses:

The dive into the Orient has been like a dream. The lands, the people, and their customs are all very strange and of absorbing interest. It surprises me to find how much this trip has modified my views, not only regarding the extreme East, but regarding ourselves and all our European precedents. It will take time to get a true perspective of it all in my mind.

[. . .]

The Manila scheme is very good. The Baguio scheme is emerging and begins to warrant hope of something unusual among cities.[31]

Burnham's experiences had, he believed, changed his preconceptions. But how were these perceptions altered? How did Burnham's official plans for Manila and Baguio manifest these changed insights about the Orient? Or, did Burnham's short trip to the Philippines simply further established notions about the uncivilized colony?

To promote his colonial vision to a wider audience, Burnham asked his partner Peirce Anderson to present their plans for Manila and Baguio before the annual convention of the American Institute of Architects held in January 1906 in Washington D.C. Burnham also submitted an abstract of this presentation to the *Western Architect*, an important professional journal, to further explain the Philippine project. His article focused on the urban changes these plans devise. Burnham opened his discussion by summarizing his imperialist convictions, contending that Manila, under the Spanish, "was an old walled city, situated on the shores of Manila Bay at the mouth of the Pasig River. There was no plan by which the city was built and as a result, the place was ill suited for the abode of white men. The plans for the development of the city should make it, not only healthful but beautiful as well."[32]

Burnham understood his work in the Philippines as a type of architecture that would improve the built environment for colonists, and this, in turn, would provide the landscape with a history, a newly conceptualized colonial sense of place. His plans illustrate an imperialist desire to make the Philippines into a colony where white Americans can feel at home. He took an active role in what geographer David Lowenthal describes as "seeing the past in our own terms." Lowenthal asserts that Western cultures posit their own constructed sense of the past onto landscapes in order to "reshape artifacts and memories accordingly."[33] Since Spanish colonial architecture was insufficient in supplying the instant gratification of an established American colonial present—a form of faux history that would find credence in previous building ventures—an American colonial architecture had to be devised. Not only was Spanish precedent unacceptable, but the landscape of the Philippines had been deemed anachronistic and lacking civility. The American colonizers viewed the Philippines as, it is critical to remember, savage, primitive, and in dire need of change. The discourse of architecture furthered this imperialist mind-set.

Burnham's "Report on Proposed Improvements at Manila," submitted to Taft in June 1905, uses both word and image to detail the history of imperialism in the Philippines. After critiquing the presence of Spanish architecture in Manila, Burnham notes that this Spanish influence "could be profitable taken as examples of future structures."[34] However, Burnham found problems with the state of urban design in Manila after he considered that the city's population would grow rapidly due "to the probable active development of industry and agriculture in the near future."[35]

Burnham's plan conflates colonial expansion with the City Beautiful methodology of urban design that he began experimenting with at the World's Columbian Exposition of 1893 in Chicago. Parks, symmetrical pathways for traversing the city, and the importance of classical motifs are all integral to the total experience of the City Beautiful.[36] After the Chicago fair, Burnham brought the City Beautiful to other locations, including Washington, D.C., Cleveland, and San Francisco. Burnham's notion of changing the urban landscape by including design elements that would quell fears about the expanding city, through the presence of parkland and motifs from the history of architecture, became the focus of his driving ambition.

Burnham's street system for Manila exemplifies his reliance on the City Beautiful. He started with the streets at the center of Manila, which he insisted should be left unchanged because of their Spanish design. Except in areas where traffic was so congested that "new street lines" could be established without affecting present property lines, Burnham believed that the city's kinship to its imperial history should be unaltered. In dire cases where property had to be destroyed to help further his plans, it could occur slowly over time "as is done in Paris."[37] He felt that the outer districts, however, where no street system had been approved, should receive different treatment. There he proposed that new buildings should all be oriented in the same direction, streets should radiate outward from a central point in the shape of a fan, and diagonal boulevards should permit direct movement between each city district.[38]

In Burnham's plan, waterways, like streets, would facilitate transportation. He approached these waterways in a hybridic manner, as in his work with Manila's street system. He contended that certain elements of the waterways, which were a product of Manila's history, should be left intact, but other aspects of the waterway system should be expanded. For example, Burnham noted that a system of existing narrow canals, called *esteros*, unified the city and was a viable way to transport goods. He admitted that these canals might not be aesthetically pleasing, but an *estero*, "it should be remembered, is not only an economical vehicle for the transaction of public business; it can become as in Venice, an element of beauty. Both beauty and convenience dictate a very liberal policy toward the development of these valuable waterways."[39]

Burnham's discussion of the *esteros* in relation to US commercial interests reveals his desire to bring the City Beautiful to Manila under the auspices of American imperial expansion. In fact, Burnham addresses these commercial issues as part of a larger capitalist enterprise. "Large manufacturing houses," he notes, "can serve their own interests without inconvenience to the public by building river slips or branches of the *estero* system on their own ground."[40] The visual plans Burnham submitted along with his written plan accentuate the connection between commerce and water transportation in Manila. They depict the city divided into a grid of individually numbered plots (fig. 63). Burnham's cartographic rendering also shows the orientation of existing and future

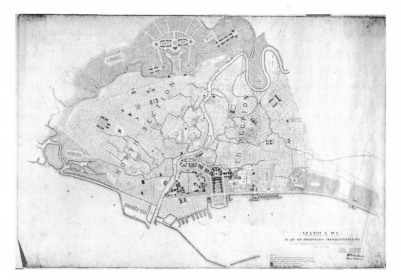

Figure 63 Manila, P.I., *Plan of Proposed Improvements*, Daniel Burnham and Peirce Anderson. Courtesy of Avery Architectural and Fine Arts Library, Columbia University.

buildings and the location of waterways. Manila Bay, as these plans detail, would include several boat slips built into the shoreline. Near these slips and the shore of the Pasig River, Burnham marked one structure as a customhouse and another as the chamber of commerce. The short distance between the customhouse and the quay would have facilitated the clearing of goods imported from other countries, while the proximity of water to the chamber of commerce exemplified the architect's commitment to improving Manila's commercial interests via waterways.

A separate plan submitted to the Philippine Commission in September 1906 details Burnham's vision for a vast transportation system in Manila that would support commerce. In his "Report on Proposed Passenger Station and Track Connections at Manila, P.I.," he proposes that a rail system be linked with Manila's waterways to further mercantile success. He contends that the "section north of the Pasig [River], stretching from Santa Cruz, Binondo and San Nicholas northward to the Vitas Channel could be converted into a splendid machine for handling freight and doing business on a large scale with the most modern methods."[41] Burnham asserts the need to use waterways and railways in the context of one transportation system. Furthermore, and analogically striking, he posits the city of Manila as a machine, a type of urban engine, which, through good planning, can cope with the business of America's newfound commercial entrepôt.

In October 1905, Burnham submitted his "Report on the Proposed Plan of the City of Baguio Province of Benguet, P.I." While the visual plan for Baguio does not contain the divided map of landownership that dominates the Manila map, city blocks with two central streetways dissecting the town cordon off the "future community" of Baguio in a grid-like fashion (fig. 64).[42] Burnham stressed that Baguio was nothing more than "abrupt and hilly country" when the Philippine Commission decided to build there, so the rural landscape provided the perfect space for the enactment of imperialist building on an anachronistic stage; it was a new city completely unencumbered by an imperial past.[43]

The first portion of the Baguio plan addresses the street system. How these streets would work in such a hilly environment concerned Burnham, so he used Western examples to explain that unconventional land can be molded into functional terrain. To Burnham, of course, "one of the most notable examples of this admirable system of street planning is the Capital [sic] at Washington as approached from Pennsylvania Avenue, Maryland Avenue, and the Mall." He noted that the "steep grade at Washington prevent[s] the carrying of these streets directly up to the Capital, but . . . the line of vision is kept open permitting the buildings to command the vista down these streets."[44] Burnham had completed plans to redesign the nation's capital in 1902 and here the City Beautiful schema for Washington served as a template for what could be accomplished in Baguio.[45] He assured his bureaucratic audience that he would use the same problem-solving techniques in Baguio that Americans found in Washington.

Burnham discusses the health of Baguio's future residents by exploring the directional orientation of streets. He contends that all future homes can receive direct sunlight on each of their four sides if streets are not placed in north-south or east-west configurations. According to Burnham, this residential positioning facilitates "a condition of very great value in the point of view of ventilation and sanitation."[46] Here Burnham indicates how the progressive reform architecture of the turn of the century informed his planning ethos. During this period, architects used the built environment as a way to regulate what they perceived as a dangerous housing situation in sections of cities, specifically those geographic regions of the city housing immigrants or colonists. Reformers wanted to improve sanitation, ventilation, lighting, and a wide range of other urban ills by passing laws that would normalize those areas that strayed from culturally perceived ideals.[47] In short, Burnham's concerns in the colonial setting were the concerns of an entire generation of architects who defined themselves as urban activists.[48] In Burnham's economy of

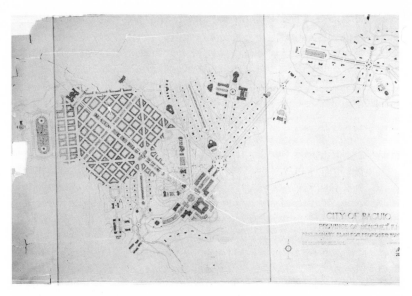

Figure 64 City of Baguio, *Preliminary Plan for Proposed Town*, Daniel Burnham and Peirce Anderson. Courtesy of Avery Architectural and Fine Arts Library, Columbia University.

imperialist architecture, the Philippines was an Oriental site that, like the immigrant-filled cities in the United States, needed safe airflow and sanitary conditions.

Colonial officials understood Baguio's location as a site where health could flourish away from the heat, humidity, and oppressive weather found in Manila. Secretary of War Taft, in 1908, commented in an official report to president Theodore Roosevelt how Baguio is "within easy distance of Manila" and offers "an opportunity where the same kind of revitalizing atmosphere may be found as in a temperate climate."[49] There was a widely held belief that Americans in the Philippines were susceptible to a variety of ailments because of the intemperate landscape. Baguio was ideal, since temperatures did not soar to the far reaches of the thermometer, as they did in Manila and other places in the archipelago. Thus, Baguio became an outpost that served as not only the summer capital, but also a place where recreation and rest could become a curative to the maladies that purportedly thrived in the tropical Philippines.[50] In fact, the belief that Baguio's climate could help restore the health of Western colonials was also integral during Spanish colonialism. An area called La Trinidad, near the future American outpost in Baguio, was home to sanitariums where members of the Spanish army and Filipino elites could recuperate.[51] The American extension of this initial colonial use for the northern island of Luzon could be found in the United States' investment in sanitariums, military camps, and country club–like venues brought to the area after portions of Burnham's plan became reality. As Taft related, "With the construction of a railroad, transportation to Baguio may be made exceedingly reasonable and sanitariums built which will furnish for very moderate cost a healthful regimen and diet." He concluded, the area is integral to "the system of government sanitation."[52]

A *Manila Times* article headlined "Fence Thrown Round Baguio" reported in late 1904 that soon land would be sold in this cordoned-off area. This article from the American press in Manila continued by explaining that there would be a limit on the sale of lots and "not more than two business and two private lots . . . [would] be sold to any person" in the ten-square-mile zone.[53] In a letter to Burnham from 1905, Forbes writes, "The first sale of lots in Baguio took place. I succeeded in buying the hill which I have named 'Topside,' that . . . I chose for my future Baguio home. . . . The sale was a tremendous success, Americans, Englishmen, Spaniards and Filipinos all united in buying and 89 lots in all were disposed of for residence purposes."[54] That Forbes was going to build his own summer home in Baguio is indicative of the status connected with this new resort city. The lots were sold only to wealthy individuals who held political power, financial security, and a clear position of status within the American colonial milieu.[55]

Burnham's plans created a model of imperial design that others could follow. He marked his fantastical visual scape with everything from government infrastructure to entertainment venues, giving colonial administrators a clearly designed template of the built environment that would solidify and further the goals of the American imperial project. However, like the hopes that attended the construction of the 1904 fair in St. Louis, many of Burnham's intentions never came to fruition. Although Baguio was built, and large tracts of Manila underwent enormous change, there were other parts of his proposals that were left untouched. The fiscal and historical realities of running a colonial outpost ensured that many of Burnham's loftiest plans would remain unrealized fantasies, relegated to the frustrating confines of paper architecture.

Realizing Burnham's Architectural Fantasy

Burnham helped hire the architect who would carry out his work in the Philippines. After interviewing several candidates, he eventually selected William Parsons, a Yale BA, Columbia MS in architecture, and École des

Beaux-Arts graduate committed to the vision proposed in the Manila and Baguio plans.[56] In a letter to Parsons from October 1905, Forbes summarizes the new consulting architect's duties in the Philippines by explaining "our intention is to compel the construction of buildings of a design to be approved by you whenever a semi-public building is contemplated or one which would have intimate relation through the scheme of beautifying the city and which has been laid out by Mr. Burnham."[57] The other members of the Philippine Commission realized the importance of passing an ordinance to enforce the powers given to Parsons. Act 1495, voted into law by the commission in May 1906, dictated that the consulting architect would advise the American colonial government in the Philippines "on all matters pertaining to the architectural features of construction, repair, or alteration of a material nature of public buildings." Section 4 of this law asserted that Burnham's plans were "hereby adopted as bases for the future development of the said places [Manila and Baguio]."[58] Parsons now had his own responsibilities, but these obligations were contingent on the sovereignty of Burnham's vision; the primacy of Burnham's plans was law.

Parsons's work immediately pleased Forbes. In a journal entry from March 1906, Forbes claims that "Parsons is a real artist. . . . Parsons considers this job an 'architect's dream' and is enthusiastic over some of the old buildings, the Burnham plan, and Baguio."[59] A letter to Burnham a month later continues the narrative of Forbes's praise for the new consulting architect. Parsons, Forbes contends, "has proved an excellent choice. He is quiet, tactful and apparently very efficient and practical."[60] Burnham, impressed by this acclamation for Parsons, wrote to his protégé: "If you have the time I should be very glad to receive a general outline of the Philippine work as you see it."[61] In late August 1906, Burnham received Parsons's first annual report as consulting architect. Burnham felt that Parsons had "done a great deal already—more than expected—and I congratulate you upon the work. I am very glad indeed that the government has your services and I hope they will continue."[62]

Parsons's first annual report indicates how he perceived his post and became committed to specific building materials while in the Philippines. The report covers the period from November 1905 to June 1906. He opens by quoting from Act 1495, suggesting to Forbes, whom Parsons addressed the report to, the importance of the consulting architect. Parsons then continues by citing specific examples of buildings where he served as the principal in the colony. He also mentions his connection to the Burnham plans with a caveat by explaining that Burnham's "plan should be accepted as offering suggestions, rather than as showing exact locations, since in many cases a close study of conditions on accurate maps shows that deviations from his plan are not only advisable but necessary."[63] After revealing that Burnham's plans cannot always be taken as axiomatic, Parsons discusses specific issues in reference to supervising colonial construction. First, he addresses the topic of native architecture and claims that if structures do not require massive funding, then local authorities can oversee their design. Second, Parsons consults with his reader on the ramifications of different types of building materials. He asserts that native timber is sufficient for small structures, but "a construction of masonry or reinforced concrete is urged for buildings containing government offices, where valuable records are liable to destruction by fire." Parsons concludes, "A higher standard of design and construction in public buildings is not only essential to the dignity and permanency of their purpose," but using high-quality building techniques also "may tend to elevate the standard in private constructions."[64] Public architecture became a way to preserve the colonial infrastructure through the use of concrete that would also establish a didactic model for vernacular building throughout the archipelago.

The use of concrete in the Philippines emphasized the importance of sanitary conditions in the colonial setting.[65] An article from the *Architectural Record*, written by A. N. Rebori, details how Parsons and his staff utilized concrete as an easily cleaned and supposedly germ-free building material. While discussing the construction of markets throughout the Philippines, Rebori notes that Americans made the floors of these markets out of concrete "so that the place may be washed down with a hose daily, allowing no food waste to remain over night to rot."[66] Remember that popular American conceptions of the Philippines often represented the new colony as a disease-laden site. Imagery related to tainted blood— think back to Private Lapeer, for instance—appeared frequently in the American press. Thus, deploying concrete as a hygienic way to build in the "contaminated" colony became an architectural imperative.

The peculiar conflict between creating infrastructure that would promote visions of sanitary colonial living and anxieties about the contaminated colony further incited political discourse about health.[67] In his official 1908 report to President Roosevelt, Taft connected the importance of sanitation with the design of infrastructure. After describing the prevalence of a variety of diseases in the colony, Taft notes that dysentery is "spread" because Filipinos are imbibing "impure water." "With a view to the removal of this difficulty, new waterworks are in the process of building at a cost to the city of Manila of about two millions of dollars."[68]

The search to thwart the potential pitfalls of empire was ongoing, and infrastructure could help quell this phobia about unsanitary conditions.

Even with the political and fiscal attention that the Philippines received after its annexation, Parsons had very little opportunity to build Burnham's imaginary grid of architectural power in Manila. One of the few areas of the Burnham plan that Parsons executed in Manila was for a district called the "New Luneta." Burnham positioned this parkland on Manila Bay with a casino on one side and a hotel on the opposite end; this, along with the construction of a new port, a grade school, a university, and a hospital, was one of the few sections of Manila that the American government physically altered.

An assessment of the Manila Hotel, a specific project completed by Parsons on the transformed space of the New Luneta, provides a better understanding of his role and American architecture in the colony. The *Manila Times* reported that a local official set the cornerstone for the Manila Hotel in August 1910 and that this construction project would allow "residents of the Philippines as well as tourists from the United States and the China Coast . . . [to] have every convenience which a modern hotel in any part of the world affords."[69] The following day, the *Manila Times* commented that the hotel "will serve as a striking introduction to Manila for all incoming tourists."[70] Parsons finished the hotel in 1912. Still standing, the structure is five stories high flanked by two wings. While the ground floor is made up of an arcade of arched windows and Doric columns, the other floors have a horizontal line of windows that do not continue the Classical Revival motif found in the arcade. The upper floors of the hotel appear boxy with flattened-out surfaces accentuating the building's horizontality (fig. 65). Floor plans depict guestrooms facing the bay only in the central part of the hotel and in the smaller wing, yet the larger wing has rooms extending all the way around its perimeter.[71] The larger wing of the lobby contained a gift shop, a ladies' parlor, and toilet rooms. The smaller wing, or east wing, housed the men's smoking room, a men's clothing shop, and a grill room. To the back of this gender-divided lobby was the main dining room, which Parsons designed in the shape of a semicircle to provide spectacular views of Manila Bay.[72] Parsons designed the entire structure with concerns about ventilation, resulting in large windows, placement of rooms in relation to sea breezes, and open verandas circulating air through the extravagant lobby.[73] He and his staff included Western luxuries that the American visitor wanted while in the Philippines. Ample space, Western food, clothing, and public areas for social smoking made tourists feel at home.

Figure 65 Manila Hotel, 1912. Photo by author.

Parsons's work in Baguio was similar to his efforts in Manila, but in Baguio the transformation was more dramatic. Baguio was not a metropolitan center like Manila, and it lacked connections to Spanish imperialism. Thus, the city today looks a great deal like Burnham's preliminary design. The streets adhere to his regulated grid and a park space (called Burnham Park) is at the center of the city. One of the structures Parsons built in Baguio is the Brent School, which he completed in 1909. Even though Parsons's efforts in Manila stressed classicized forms molded in concrete, such as running arcades and pilasters, this school building is simple and made of wood. It deploys classicized elements using local materials. A Classical Revival back porch, for instance, with Doric columns carved out of wood, leads students in and out of what is called Ogilby Hall (fig. 66). Other sites, like the now rebuilt Mansion House, which Parsons designed in 1908 for the governor-general of Baguio, utilize concrete and have the same flat facade with arcading effects found in his Manila projects.[74]

Although the US colonial government executed very little of the Burnham plans outside of Baguio and a small area of Manila, the fantasy of colonial architecture continued to resonate well after the turn of the century. In 1919, Ralph Doane, a consulting architect who worked for the Philippine Commission after Parsons's departure, posited that Philippine architectural history lacked a distinctive style. In an essay from the *Ar-*

chitectural Review, Doane claims that this dearth of a "characteristically Philippine architecture is not necessarily a reflection upon the Filipinos." He notes, "There are many critics who contend, with some degree of justification, that America has no distinct architecture and who accuse American architects of plagiarizing the ancient Greek and Roman and Renaissance architectural forms."[75] Doane further relates that it is the "duty" of the Philippine government to recognize the value of bringing fine art to the people, because a nation that does not genuflect to the power of fine art "is no true democracy."[76] His musings on Philippine architectural history, or what he constructs as a lack of that history, were typical for an American colonial official who supported the mantra of benevolent assimilation. Like education, architecture could be introduced as a civilizing influence that would bolster the Philippine Commission's projected goals about how to improve the colony. Doane renders Western culture as a necessity that introduces art into a cultural void.

Doane's plea for classical art could be understood as an argument that merely attempts to delineate a distinction between classically built forms and a vernacular style, but later in this same article his language becomes racially charged while he examines the indigenous culture of the Philippines. Doane insists, "Filipino artistic attainments are most unsatisfying. They are insubstantial and, in short, amount to little more than tinseled clap-trap. The quality of permanency, while a strong element in the great arts of the world, receives little consideration in Filipino art which is

Figure 66 Ogilby Hall, at the Brent School, Baguio, Philippines, 1909. Photo by author.

absolutely devoid of the element of substantiality."[77] Doane does not discuss specific Philippine buildings, but his notion about Filipino art and its lack of "permanency" supports his contention that Filipinos have no distinct architectural style. Like many of his fellow critics, Doane believed that a nation possesses no stylistic uniqueness when its attempts at artistic competence are ephemeral. Since Doane and others saw Filipino architecture as impermanent, it could only be described as inferior, primitive, and ahistoric.

Anne McClintock comments on the Western practice of excising history from colonial subjects. McClintock examines the colonizer's erasure of the colonial subject's past through a discussion about "anachronistic space." "According to the colonial version of this trope, imperial progress across the space of empire is figured as a journey backward in time to an anachronistic moment of prehistory. By extension, the return journey to Europe is seen as rehearsing the evolutionary logic of historical progress, forward and upward to the apogee of the Enlightenment in the European metropolis."[78] McClintock's subject is the British Empire, but the movement she identifies between the colonized site as a location of "prehistory" and the imperialist nation as a location of "enlightenment" is the narrative thrust that unfolds in Doane's article. In fact, this same narrative was an implicit part of the American building project in the Philippines. Doane contends that the Philippines has no "distinct" architectural history, and then he supports his theory by claiming that virtuous architecture can be developed only under the auspices of a Western economy of fine art. Again, he notes that America lacked a true architectural history, yet through the use of classical forms the United States developed a style, a history, and, ultimately, an enlightened relationship with architecture. Conceptualizing the Philippines as an "anachronistic space," a geographic locale without the benefits of a civilized past, was a theme American colonialism continuously secured and reinvented through the construction and planning of an artificial scape of architectural design.

Burnham never returned to the Philippines after his initial trip, and he died in 1912. The following year Parsons left the colony. Before leaving, Parsons wanted to construct a memorial in Burnham's honor, and in a letter to Forbes from February 1913 Parsons explained his idea of placing a flag mast on a marble base at the center of the New Luneta (the area of the Manila plan that saw the most dramatic transformation as a result of Burnham's plans). The base would measure "nine feet across taking the form of a low seat, then there might be a second marble base about four or five feet across bearing the appropriate inscription." Parsons claimed that the New Luneta would be the ideal location for the monument because it "was the first definite step taken in carrying out the Burnham plan, and this [the flag mast] would come nearly at the exact center."[79]

Two weeks after Parsons proposed this design for the New Luneta, Forbes wrote to anthropologist Edward Ayer in Chicago about how "Baguio has taken action and named a boulevard after Mr. Burnham right in the center of the main axis of his plan."[80] Although there is no indication that the Burnham monument in Manila ever existed, or that a Burnham Boulevard ever traversed Baguio, there is a large park in the center of contemporary Baguio called Burnham Park. The location of this green space is in keeping with the esplanade as marked on Burnham's original plans for the summer capital. The park has a small pond at its center, and regimented rows of grass and sidewalks accentuate the small-scale, City Beautiful–influenced design of this heavily used public space.

An enormous bust of Burnham sits at the top of a row of steps at the west end of Burnham Park (fig. 67). The inscription on the plaque below the sculpture reads:

IN RESPECT

The message of Love, Amity, and Mutual respect was the touchstone in the construction of this memorial marker as a lasting tribute to Daniel Hudson Burnham. A world renowned American architect from Chicago, United States of America who at the turn of the nineteenth century designed the land use patterns of the city of Baguio, specifically the city's main park which bears his name Burnham Park. His vision, dedication and industry helped build the reputation of this mountain resort [as] a lasting premier travel destination in the country, a significant episode in the passage of an act by the Philippine Commission which established the City of Baguio as the "Summer Capital of the Philippines." The construction of this memorabilium was initiated and coordinated by the National Correspondents club of Baguio (NCCB), for and in behalf of the people of the city with the invaluable cooperation and support of the people of the Department of Tourism (DOT), the Philippine Tourism Authority (PTA) and the National Parks Development Committee (NPDC) and other friends of the NCCB media aggrupation.
Inaugurated December 27, 1992

This inscription mitigates a tumultuous history that included the bloodshed, loss, and cultural trauma that accompanied the Philippine-American War and other events that characterized American influence in the island nation. Here the Philippine government and local authorities laud

Figure 67 Burnham Memorial, Baguio, Philippines, 1992. Photo by Virgilio C. Fuerte.

Burnham for making their city into a site of touristic pleasure that continues to thrive.[81] Indeed, Burnham's giant head, which sits above these
words, has a symbolic view of the park that has been named in his honor;
his stone eyes gaze upon the landscape that he helped devise. The placement of the monument permits the continuation of a colonial gaze in a
postcolonial setting as Burnham's specter watches over the built environment in the Philippines.

This colonial gaze furthered the hubris associated with redesigning
the Philippines so that the colony's physical scape could reflect American
ingenuity. Represented at American world's fairs as a landscape devoid of
civilization, the Philippines required an intervention. Thus, Burnham's
vision promised change on a massive scale where the City Beautiful could

help develop an American colonial outpost. Here trade could flourish and subjects would follow American law while having to contend with the gridlike rigidity demanded by the reconfiguration of Manila and Baguio. Although Burnham's full intentions never completely materialized, his fantastical ambition promoted the conceit of empire.

Taft Decorates the White House

One of the chief characteristics of the Orientals—indeed, one of the chief characteristics of all nations that are ignorant—is suspicion and distrust, and the primary rule of policy in dealing with them is absolute honesty and straightforwardness.
WILLIAM HOWARD TAFT, 1905[1]

In 1900, president William McKinley appointed William Howard Taft as the head of the Philippine Commission. Taft arrived to a tumultuous scene. The three-year Philippine-American War was already under way, and Taft's first priority was quelling insurgent activity. A year later, Taft became the civil governor of the Philippines. After his initial involvement with America's new colony, Taft became president Theodore Roosevelt's secretary of war. One of Taft's accomplishments as a member of Roosevelt's cabinet was hiring Daniel Burnham to redesign the landscape in Manila and Baguio. Taft's commitment to the Philippines was evident. Indeed, he ascended through the ranks of government by way of his direct experience with American empire. He was the personality that ran American colonial policy in the Pacific, and he consistently encouraged the future of Philippine-American relations through military action and economic expansion.[2] After Taft became president in 1909, the Philippines was still a pressing concern, but other matters, such as the political struggles between government and American corporations, became more urgent to his beleaguered one-term administration.

As secretary of war, Taft repeatedly insisted that colonization would make life better for Filipinos. This was, he contended, the ultimate aim of US policy in the archipelago. The American presence in the Pacific was not a selfish act, but, according to Taft's well-documented logic, a way of bringing the Philippines into the civilized world through political, medical, infrastructural, and commercial aid. The soon-to-be-elected president focused his reasoned argument about the Philippines on several key themes that have surfaced throughout my book, premises that directed American colonial policy at the turn of the century.

First, Taft followed President McKinley's edict for benevolent assimilation. The claim that America was in the Philippines for the benefit of Filipinos was a narrative that Taft frequently gestured toward in his support of American colonial efforts. In his 1908 *Special Report of William Howard Taft Secretary of War to the President on the Philippines*, he frames the American presence in the Philippines as a kind act, set up to help with the "development of the lower classes and preservation of their rights."[3] He claims that it is for the safety of Filipinos that America controls the islands. Taft hypothetically relates:

If the American government can only remain in the islands long enough to educate the entire people, to give them a language which enables them to come into contact with modern civilization, and to extend to them from time to time additional political rights so that by the exercise of them they shall learn the use and responsibilities necessary to their proper exercise, independence can be granted with entire safety to the people.[4]

The Philippines, according to Taft, cannot determine what is best for its own well-being; thus the United States must provide guidance in the form of colonial rule that will assimilate its colonial subjects into a civilized existence that purportedly extols liberty.

A large portion of the "for their own good" edict that fell under the heading of benevolent assimilation could be traced to the American claim that diseases ravaged the Philippines and spread thanks to unsanitary conditions. A lack of health led to what colonial officials construed as an absence of sound government that could provide adequate oversight. Taft, in his 1908 report, noted that too many critics had derided the colony because of its deficient sanitation and, in fact, "the Philippines is exceptionally comfortable and healthful."[5] Regardless of this disclaimer, Taft described the numbers of deaths that occurred in the Philippines as a result of tropical diseases. The refrain of diseased blood and infectious potentiality was rampant in the popular press (recall the image of Private

Lapeer crouched down in horror after being injected with leprosy, fig. 29). According to Taft, the numbers of deaths in the islands from various diseases had dropped precipitously as a result of American intervention. He contended that Spanish imperialism only made matters worse, but that since "the decade of our stay in the islands, the conditions of life for Americans have steadily bettered." Furthermore, the reported incidents of diseases, such as leprosy and malaria, had decreased in number. From 1905 to 1907 the "number of known lepers in the archipelago" declined from 3,580 to 2,826.[6] Taft fostered the larger cultural fears that inscribed the Philippines as a diseased location in need of either American assistance (a refrain repeated by imperialists) or evasion (a theme that anti-imperialists stressed).

Not only was the corporeality of the Filipino seen as in need of attention, but the physical infrastructure of the colony was also understood as suffering and requiring aid. As witnessed in everything from Burnham's plans (chapter 6) to the American army's focus on bridge building (chapter 3), the importance of creating networks of communication and transportation was critical to the larger colonial project. Indeed, the obsession with mapping the colony, as related in chapter 4, was also part of this impulse to gain insight into what colonial officials understood as the threatening Philippine landscape. Taft recognized the imperative for infrastructure and understood that more work had to be done to improve the colony. In a turn of phrase that linked the immaturity of the people with transportation systems, he predicted, "The truth is that good roads will develop as the people develop, because the people can keep up the roads if they will, and it is not until they have a large sense of political responsibility that they are likely to sacrifice much to maintain them."[7]

Taft was also very enthusiastic about the economics of American colonial policy. He encouraged mining, even though he understood its speculative nature, and even went so far as to request that the Philippine Commission allow corporations to hold larger tracts of land to increase the potential for profits from mining. Taft's report provided the president with specifics about trade, and although many American farmers protested against the importation of Philippine crops, for their own protective interests, Taft was "still strongly of the opinion that justice requires that the United States should open her sugar and tobacco markets to the Philippines."[8] He believed that trade could become a very beneficial product of empire.

Taft's ultimate quest for the Philippines was order. In a published speech he gave before the Chamber of Commerce in New York, in 1904, he explained, "The Object of War has been accomplished. Tranquility and good order prevail in the Islands." He continued, "The number of white troops in the Islands has been reduced from 75,000 to 15,000 men."[9] Later in the same speech, Taft returned to the theme of order and declared, "The first requisite of prosperity in the Philippine Islands is tranquility, and this should be evidenced by a well ordered government. The Filipinos must be taught the advantages of such a government."[10] To Taft, order was the consequence of lessons, and the central goal of the United States in the Philippines should be to confer didactically upon our "little brown brothers" the importance of order by imparting this instruction. This paternalistic quest for order in the Philippines would continue after Taft became the president of the United States.[11] Indeed, it was within the interior design of the White House that Taft's acquisition of specific pieces of Filipino furniture exposed his desire to display and arrange the colony within the framework of the most famous of American domestic spaces.

Furnishing Order

A photograph of the Yellow Oval Room in the White House, taken during Taft's presidency (1909–1913), reveals a number of items one would expect: two Federal-period chairs (one on a rocker) are on the right side of the image, another rocking chair is in the left foreground, and a classically inspired fireplace framed with paneling is at the back wall (fig. 68).[12] The Colonial Revival's prescription for revitalizing the American past would have dictated the inclusion of this predictable décor during the early years of the twentieth century. Scattered throughout the Yellow Oval Room are a surprising number of Filipino objects. Note the draperies around the window, the embroidery covering the round table in the middle of the room, the wall hanging to the right of the back door, and the matching chair (on the right edge of the image) and side table beneath the wall hanging. All these furnishings are from the Philippines; they are objects the Tafts procured during their time in Asia.[13]

Other rooms in the Taft White House contained decorative references to the American colony. During his first year in office, Taft orchestrated the expansion of the White House's executive offices. The new suite of rooms was described as "convenient and comfortable," while not overly ostentatious. One of the more impressive features, included in what we now refer to as the Oval Office, was a floor made of indigenous wood

Figure 68 Yellow Oval Room of the White House during the Taft administration. Courtesy of the Library of Congress: 8759.

from the Philippines. The *New York Times* reported that "visitors to the President's private office" would be "sure to have their attention arrested by the handsome floor of Philippine wood."[14] Another article from Taft's first year as president mentions other signs of Filipino décor. After explaining how the cabinet room "makes impossible any sentimental suggestion," the author reveals how "Mr. Taft's long service in the Philippines is symbolized in the coverings of carabao [*sic*] skin—the white buffalo of the archipelago." The article's author explicitly links Taft's sentiment to the Philippine furnishings used in this interior. These rooms may have been almost void of the president's feelings and emotions, but the caribou covering was there to connote a distinctly tender connection.[15] We can imagine Taft walking on his floor, a type of symbolic allusion to the imperial landscape that was underfoot and now under American imperial control, and thinking about how other types of raw material could be removed from the colony. Then while contemplating this potential economic boondoggle, he would have looked at his Philippine décor with a sense of longing and admiration toward the American colony. In short, Taft inscribed his imperialist sensibilities onto the newly renovated White House.

The President's Nostalgia

Taft's souvenirs from the Philippines manifest the results of an aggressive nation taking its military competence abroad, finding another nation to control through both commercial and political means, and removing resources. The drapery, wall panel, embroidery work, chair, side table, caribou skin, and flooring functioned as a miniaturized museum; these objects were a small collection that signified the colonial experience. Much like Charles Longfellow's obsession with gathering material culture related to his time in Asia, Taft also wanted to bring together various objects that would reflect his experiences in the Philippines. To many unknowing people who walked through these rooms during Taft's presidency, these objects probably meant nothing. But to those who knew about the complex history and provenance of these furnishings, here was verification that America had colonized the Orient and begun the process of replacing disorder with the harmonious promise of benevolent assimilation.

While serving as governor in the Philippines, Taft completed a census of the colony. Predicated on Western notions of race, the 1903 census, as Vicente Rafael describes it, was a panoptic counting system that helped the American government manage its new acquisition. The lengthy text divides the Philippine population into categories based on racial typologies. Nevertheless, numbers and typology were not enough, so Taft included his own description of Filipino characteristics in the introductory section: "Like all Orientals, [Filipinos] are a suspicious people, but when their confidence is won, they follow with a trust that is complete."[16] How, Taft implicitly asked, do you order a "suspicious" people who for three years led a war against American empire? His remarks are not only descriptive, but also prescriptive, replete with details about how to get Oriental subjects to accept the American colonial project.

One way to allay fears about the Other was to place objects produced by that group within the confines of a space clearly marked Western. The West relentlessly tried to define the East through curatorial efforts that classified the Orient by cataloging it, making artistic judgments about it, and situating its artifacts throughout the domestic realm. Moreover, no space could be more culturally sanctified for this type of exhibition than the ceremonial confines of the White House. Thus, Taft's decorating schema was analogous to what readers of *Art Amateur* did to their homes. As my second chapter detailed, during the nineteenth century the American home became a place where household décor reflected the status and values of middle-class families. *Art Amateur* reported that many of the items that filled a typical middle-class home should be Oriental in nature. Japanese screens, Chinese vases, and other items from the East acclimated Americans to the idea of gaining cultural knowledge about the Orient. Taft's placement of Filipino items in the White House was also unlike what the pages of *Art Amateur* prescribed. Remember that the consumers of Oriental culture twenty years before Taft entered the White House collected Asian goods without knowledge of the impending expansion of America's political domain, while Taft was acutely aware of the recent US incursion into the Philippines. The inclusion of Filipino furniture created a space within the White House that could function as a type of trophy for Taft. He could enter this room, see these Filipino objects, and be reminded that he had helped America become what he defined as a well-ordered global empire. Reminiscent of the revelers who looked at the Dewey Arch as a centerpiece to their celebration of conquest, Taft turned to the visually mediated power of objects to commemorate empire.

Taft's Filipino furniture also evokes what anthropologist Renato Rosaldo refers to as "imperialist nostalgia." This form of nostalgia occurs when "agents of colonialism," such as Taft, "display nostalgia for the colonized culture as it was 'traditionally' (that is, when they first encountered it)."[17] Reviewing the American colonization of the Philippines, Rosaldo shows how anthropologists, military personnel, and others often return to the scene of colonization and experience a type of melancholia at the loss of native culture. "When the so-called civilizing process destabilizes forms of life, the agents of change experience transformations of other cultures as if they were personal losses."[18] These emotional states allow the colonizer to obscure the fact that he has created these changes. In the case of Taft, his Philippine décor made his yearning for indigenous Filipino culture apparent.

Was Taft having second thoughts about the changes he and others brought to the Philippines during the early years of the American colonial period? By placing these objects in the White House, Taft elevated their status while suggesting both his longing for his colonial post and, ironically, his lament for a disappearing culture that he himself had altered. Taft had been in the Philippines at the height of the Philippine-American War in 1900. By 1909, when he became president, the American colonization of the Philippines was well under way. Recall, as he described in his official statements from the period, that schools had been built, forms of commerce had been established, and the physical landscape had been refashioned to accommodate American needs; benevolent assimilation had had a dramatic influence on Philippine culture. Taft's collection of native Philippine material culture brought the colony into ethnographic focus. These furnishings made that "native" ethnicity come to life and permitted Taft, at a very safe and comfortable distance, to yearn for remnants of an unadulterated Filipino past.

This craving for the purity of the Philippines was not an ideal fit with Taft's quest for order. Remember, Taft and others had spent years trying to argue that the Philippines had to be remolded into a type of facsimile of the United States that would permit the Pacific nation to thrive. Thus, the ambiguity between American order and an untainted Philippine past must not have been easy for Taft to negotiate as he deployed the visual scape of the White House interior to enact a miniaturized vignette displaying American colonialism. This uncertainty, which harkens back to the friction between the Colonial Revival and the exoticism of the nineteenth century we witnessed in the pages of *Art Amateur*, reveals the continuing tensions that would plague American empire well into the twentieth century and beyond.

Acknowledgments

This book started at Boston University where a very active and engaging intellectual environment made for a remarkable graduate school experience. My mentors and teachers, including Regina Blaszczyk, Richard Candee, Carolyn Jones, Leland Monk, Kim Sichel, Nina Silber, and Shirley Wajda (who also gave me significant last-minute editorial advice) all provided feedback, critique, and kindness. Additionally, Keith Morgan was a calming presence and he got me to rethink my approach to the built environment. My advisor at BU, Patricia Hills, continues to offer extraordinary insight. Without Pat this book would never have happened, as she celebrated its central premise from its inception and made sure I stayed on task (even asking me how "the book was going" at my wedding). Pat took me into her classroom when I was a junior in college and I continue to cherish her friendship twenty-two years later. I also had the camaraderie of fellow students at BU who helped advance this project. Cheryl Boots, Thomas Denenberg, Lori Kenschaft, and Erica Martin were always available to share ideas. Erica has continued to bless me with her terrific husband and her beautiful children.

Several institutions supported this work. While at the University of Delaware I received funding to give papers related to this project at a variety of conferences. My colleagues at UD, including Martin Brueckner (the map guru!), Ann Gibson, Jodi Hauptman, Bernie Herman, Larry Nees, and Damie Stillman, all provided advice. Additionally, West Chester University gave me funds to pay for images and also provided money to attend conferences. I continue to miss my friends and support system in Pennsylvania. John Baker, Richard Blake, Virginia daCosta, Belle Hollon, Henry Loustau, Nancy Rumfield, Peggy Schiff-Hill, Gus Sermas, Donna Usher, Linwood White, and Sally Van Orden were phenomenal colleagues.

My colleagues at Parsons The New School for Design have also contributed to this project. Laura Auricchio has helped me write my way out of a number of frightening corners. Hazel Clark has been a very supportive chair and dean. The dean's office at Parsons has been generous with money for the images that appear here. Additionally, Parsons and the New School gave me a sabbatical so that I could finish the book, and Saraleah Fordyce relieved me of teaching Introduction to Design Studies during my sabbatical. And, being a part of the NSSR/Parsons visual culture reading group (Visual Culture Lab), which includes Margot Bouman, Clive Dilnot, Oz Frankel, Orit Halpern, Vicky Hattam, Janet Kraynak, and Ken Wark, has improved this project. I also received research assistance at Parsons from Neeve Kelly, who has been a sensational student and a very funny friend.

Scholars at other institutions were also wonderfully supportive. Michele Bogart, Donna Cassidy, Amy Gilman Srebnick, Kristin Hoganson, John Howard, Patricia Johnston, Karen Lucic, Richard Meyer, Steven Nelson, Vicente Rafael, Walter Srebnick, and Christopher Vernon all provided essential comments on my work. John Davis has been a consistent source of intellectual inspiration and a very kind friend. And Diana Linden has listened to me kvetch endlessly and gave me quick feedback during critical moments. She also made me a part of her beautiful family (Alex and Emily rock!), and I love her for that.

I have been able to use some of the most amazing archives and libraries in the world. The Avery Architectural and Fine Arts Library at Columbia University, the Boston Public Library, the Haughton Library at Harvard, the Library of Congress, the Longfellow National Historic Site (thank you Anita Israel), the National Library of the Philippines, the New York Historical Society, the Ryerson and Burnham Libraries at the Art Institute of Chicago, the Smithsonian Institution Libraries, Vassar College Library, Winterthur, and other institutions have been extraordinary resources with knowledgeable staff who helped me find those things I never would have been able to locate on my own.

The ideas here were first aired at a number of conferences, including the American Studies Association, the Popular Culture Association, and the International Communication Association. Additionally, the University of Delaware and Winterthur provided venues where I could share my ideas with a larger forum. Two journals published different versions of chapter 5 and chapter 6: *Prospects: An Annual of American Cultural Studies* 25(2000): 391–424 (© Cambridge University Press; reprinted with permission) and the *Journal of Asian American Studies* 4(2001): 123–45. Jack Salzman at *Prospects* was an excellent editor who helped me develop my thinking about Dewey; and Gary Okihiro, at *JAAS*, helped me explore the theoretical implications of Daniel Burnham's architectural designs.

This project would never have been published without the amazing guidance and sage advice of Douglas Mitchell. I will never forget the first coffee I had with Doug at an ASA conference and his immediate enthusiasm for *Visualizing American Empire*. Others at the University of Chicago Press have also been wonderful guides. Timothy McGovern was very helpful with details, and Carol Saller's copyediting made my language more readable. Chicago sent my work to several anonymous readers who only made this book stronger. And, of course, John Howard introduced me to Doug and the Chicago family; I consider myself fortunate to have met John early in the 1990s at an American Studies graduate student conference held at Boston University.

My friends and family have been patient and enormously generous. I especially want to thank my Boston family (Tas Steiner, John Mahler, Kevin Steen, Eric Orner, Steve Parks, and Chris Sullivan). Additionally, Sean Haley and Josh Srebnick (my wonderful friend and patient editor!) have been ideal sounding boards during this lengthy journey. A special thanks, as well, to my New York family: Paul Aferiat, Andrew Arrick, Fred Bateman, Todd Bishop, Michael Hofemann, Peter Kozuch, Robert O'Leary, Maurice Sahar, Amy Sagan Srebnick, Peter Stamberg, and Greg Weithman.

My parents thought I was crazy when I first embarked into academia, but once I jumped onboard they stood with me every step of the way. They helped me through graduate school, and their love and unyielding enthusiasm are a gift. My brother, Jonathan, is a true scholar. I continue to marvel at and get inspiration from his intellectual passion. Jonathan is also an extraordinary best friend.

Finally, there is James. James has been there when the chips have been down and James was there to celebrate as I revised this project into a book. He learned to live with my rather bizarre work habits and his presence makes my life easier, comfortable, and filled with "love love."

Notes

INTRODUCTION

1. William McKinley quoted in John Bancroft Devins, *An Observer in the Philippines; Or, Life in Our New Possessions* (Boston: American Tract Society, 1905), 70.
2. Ibid., 70–71.
3. Ibid., 71.
4. I am very thankful to the anonymous reader who suggested that I look at the idea of "scapes" to reframe my project. For Arjun Appadurai's explication of scapes, see his book *Modernity at Large: Cultural Dimensions of Globalization* (Minneapolis: University of Minnesota Press, 1996), esp. 33.
5. Edward Said, *Orientalism* (New York: Vintage Books, 1978), 3.
6. See Homi Bhabha, *The Location of Culture* (New York: Routledge, 1994); Aijaz Ahmad, *In Theory: Classes, Nations, Literatures* (London: Verso, 1992); Reina Lewis, *Gendering Orientalism: Race, Femininity, and Representation* (London: Routledge, 1995); Meyda Yeğenoğlu, *Colonial Fantasies: Towards a Feminist Reading of Orientalism* (Cambridge: Cambridge University Press, 1998); and Anne McClintock, *Imperial Leather: Race, Gender, and Sexuality in the Colonial Contest* (New York: Routledge, 1995).

    There are several other excellent critiques of Said. See James Clifford's essay "On *Orientalism*" in his *The Predicament of Culture: Twentieth-Century Ethnography, Literature, and Art* (Cambridge, Mass.: Harvard University Press, 1988), 255–76, which takes Said to task for blending antithetical methodological approaches. Clifford views Said's writing as problematic because it constantly shifts between that of a humanist searching for "truths" to that of a Foucauldian genealogist who debunks the entire notion of truth. Robert

Young traces the way Western theory positions history as a discipline in *White Mythologies: Writing History and the West* (London: Routledge, 1990). Young devotes an entire chapter to Said and evokes many of the same criticisms that can be found in Clifford. Young's study is particularly useful because he places Said in the context of a larger theoretical tradition.

7. "The Revenge of the Filipino," *World*, January 22, 1899.

8. Paul Kramer, *The Blood of Government: Race, Empire, the United States, and the Philippines* (Chapel Hill: University of North Carolina Press, 2006), 117.

9. For other helpful sources on anti-imperialism, see Michael Salman's *The Embarrassment of Slavery: Controversies over Bondage and Nationalism in the American Colonial Philippines* (Berkeley: University of California Press, 2001); and Victor Bascara's *Model-Minority Imperialism* (Minneapolis: University of Minnesota Press, 2006). Salman reveals how the idea of slavery created fractures in American politics over the role of colonialism in the Philippines, and Bascara makes insightful links between debates about American economic policy and anti-imperialist rhetoric.

10. See Clifford; Linda Nochlin, *The Politics of Vision: Essays on Nineteenth-Century Art and Society* (New York: Harper & Row, 1989); Todd Porterfield, *The Allure of Empire: Art in the Service of French Imperialism, 1798–1836* (Princeton: Princeton University Press, 1998); Darcy Grimaldo Grigsby, *Extremities: Painting Empire in Post-Revolutionary France* (New Haven: Yale University Press, 2002); Beth Fowkes Tobin, *Picturing Imperial Power: Colonial Subjects in Eighteenth-Century British Painting* (Durham: Duke University Press, 1999); Zeynep Çelik, *Displaying the Orient: Architecture of Islam at Nineteenth-Century World's Fairs* (Berkeley: University of California Press, 1988); Robert Rydell, *All the World's a Fair: Visions of Empire at American International Expositions, 1876–1916* (Chicago: University of Chicago Press, 1985); Benito Vergara, *Displaying Filipinos: Photography and Colonialism in Early Twentieth-Century Philippines* (Quezon City: University of Philippines Press, 1996); Amy Kaplan, *The Anarchy of Empire in the Making of U.S. Culture* (Cambridge, Mass.: Harvard University Press, 2002); Vicente Rafael, *White Love and Other Events in Filipino History* (Durham: Duke University Press, 2000); and Laura Wexler, *Tender Violence: Domestic Visions in an Age of U.S. Imperialism* (Chapel Hill: University of North Carolina Press, 2000).

For other examples of studies that examine visual culture as it relates to empire and Orientalism, see Frederick Bohrer, *Orientalism and Visual Culture: Imagining Mesopotamia in Nineteenth-Century Europe* (Cambridge: Cambridge University Press, 2003); Jocelyn Hackforth-Jones and Mary Roberts, eds., *Edges of Empire: Orientalism and Visual Culture* (Malden: Wiley-Blackwell, 2005); and, Thomas Metcalf, *An Imperial Vision: Indian Architecture and Britain's Raj* (Oxford: Oxford University Press, 2002).

11. Warwick Anderson, *Colonial Pathologies: American Tropical Medicine, Race, and Hygiene in the Philippines* (Durham: Duke University Press, 2006); Bascara; Sharon Delmendo, *The Star-Entangled Banner: One Hundred Years of*

America in the Philippines (New Brunswick: Rutgers University Press, 2004); Kristin Hoganson, *Fighting for American Manhood: How Gender Politics Affected the Spanish-American and Philippine-American Wars* (New Haven: Yale University Press, 1998); Kramer; and Allan Punzalan Issac, *American Tropics: Articulating Filipino America* (Minneapolis: University of Minnesota Press, 2006).

For other books that assess US representations of Asia and the Middle East in popular culture, see Christina Klein, *Cold War Orientalism: Asia in the Middlebrow Imagination, 1945–1961* (Berkeley: University of California Press, 2003); Douglas Little, *American Orientalism: The United Sates and the Middle East Since 1945* (Chapel Hill: University of North Carolina Press, 2002); and, Melani McAlister, *Epic Encounters: Culture, Media, and U.S. Interests in the Middle East Since 1945* (Berkeley: University of California Press, 2005).

12. Kristin Hoganson, "Cosmopolitan Domesticity: Importing the American Dream, 1865–1920," *American Historical Review* 107, no. 1 (February 2002): 55–83. Hoganson further elaborates on this issue in her book *Consumer's Imperium: The Global Production of American Domesticity, 1865–1920* (Chapel Hill: University of North Carolina Press, 2007).

13. There are a number of books that examine America's obsession with Orientalism in visual culture and the arts, both fine and decorative. Although these scholars do not make interconnections between Orientalism and a larger imperial thrust, their work has been critical to the first two chapters of my book since they record how American material and visual culture turned toward Orientalist tropes at the turn of the century. See, for instance, Mary Blanchard, *Oscar Wilde's America: Counterculture in the Gilded Age* (New Haven: Yale University Press, 1998); Holly Edwards, *Noble Dreams, Wicked Pleasures: Orientalism in America, 1870–1930* (Princeton: Princeton University Press, 2000); Anthony Lee, *Picturing Chinatown: Art and Orientalism in San Francisco* (Berkeley: University of California Press, 2001); and Mari Yoshihara, *Embracing the East: White Women and American Orientalism* (Oxford: Oxford University Press, 2003).

14. Kaplan, 17.

15. See Gerald Linderman, *The Mirror of War: American Society and the Spanish-American War* (Ann Arbor: University of Michigan Press, 1974) for more on events that led to the war.

16. For more specifics on military history in relation to these events, see Brian McAllister Linn, *The U.S. Army and Counterinsurgency in the Philippine War, 1899–1902* (Chapel Hill: University of North Carolina Press, 1989).

17. These periodicals were enormously popular. The *World* and the *Evening Journal* had circulations that varied depending on the specific edition and the news cycle, but most estimates claim that Hearst and Pulitzer were selling millions of newspapers a week. For figures on Hearst, for instance, see

John Lawrence Tone, *War and Genocide in Cuba, 1895–1898* (Chapel Hill: University of North Carolina Press, 2006), 242.

18. Richard Ohman discusses this idea in his *Selling Culture: Magazines, Markets, and Class at the Turn of the Century* (London: Verso, 1996), 45.

19. For more on the Dewey phenomenon, see Wexler; and Michele Bogart, *Public Sculpture and the Civic Ideal in New York City, 1890–1930* (Chicago: University of Chicago Press, 1989). Also, see my "Celebrating Empire on the Home Front: New York City's Welcome-Home Party for Admiral Dewey," *Prospects* 25 (2000): 391–424.

20. For more on this event and other fairs, see Rydell. It should be noted that the Philippines was also represented at the 1901 Pan-American Exposition in Buffalo and the 1909 Alaska-Yukon-Pacific Exposition in Seattle. Jon A. Olivera, a PhD student in history at the University of Washington, told me about the 1909 fair. Part of Olivera's dissertation will focus on the Seattle fair.

21. For more on Burnham and his work in the Philippines, see Thomas Hines, *Burnham of Chicago: Architect and Planner* (Chicago: University of Chicago Press, 1979); and my "Building Empire: Architecture and American Imperialism in the Philippines," *Journal of Asian American Studies* 4, no. 2 (2001): 123–45.

22. Jill Beaulieu and Mary Roberts, eds., *Orientalism's Interlocutors: Painting, Architecture, Photography* (Durham: Duke University Press, 2002). Said, in his book *Culture and Imperialism* (New York: Alfred A. Knopf, 1993), also discusses the importance of this "response to Western dominance which culminated in the great movement of decolonization all across the Third World" (xii).

23. Clodualdo del Mundo Jr., *Native Resistance: Philippine Cinema and Colonialism, 1898–1941* (Manila: De La Salle University Press, 1998); and Rafael.

24. Frederick Jackson Turner, "The Significance of the Frontier in American History," in *America: One Land, One People*, ed. Robert C. Baron (Golden, CO: Fulcrum, 1987), 245.

25. A helpful discussion about manifest destiny, the mythic image of the West, and American colonialism in the Philippines can be found in Delmendo, 21–46.

CHAPTER ONE

1. He returned again in 1875 and 1891, but this chapter focuses on his first trip.

2. See the introduction of Christine Wallace Laidlaw, *Charles Appleton Longfellow: Twenty Months in Japan, 1871–1873* (Cambridge: Friends of the Longfellow House, 1998), 5–7; Christine Guth, "Charles Longfellow and Okakura Kakuzo: Cultural Cross-Dressing in Colonial Context," *Positions* 8, no. 3 (Winter 2000): 608; and, for a more in-depth analysis of Longfellow's

biography, see Christine Guth, *Longfellow's Tattoos: Tourism, Collecting, and Japan* (Seattle: University of Washington Press, 2004). Guth's book is indispensable for anyone interested in Charles Longfellow's life.

3. Charles Longfellow, telegram to H. W. Longfellow, June 1, 1871, in Laidlaw, 22.

4. Charles Longfellow, diary entry, September 19, 1871, in Laidlaw, 62.

5. A brief handwriting analysis shows that these were not written in Charley's hand. For more on the specifics of those photographers whom Charles Longfellow hired, see Laidlaw, 189. Additionally, Christine Guth writes about this photo album in her *Longfellow's Tattoos*, 66–72.

6. Richard Siddle, "Ainu History: An Overview," in *Ainu: Spirit of a Northern People*, ed. William W. Fitzhugh and Chisato O. Dubreuil (Washington D.C.: National Museum of Natural History, Smithsonian, 1999), 71–72.

7. David L. Howell, "Making 'Useful Citizens' of Ainu Subjects in Early Twentieth-Century Japan," *Journal of Asian Studies* 63, no. 1 (February 2004): 5–29.

8. I am using the term *ethnography* intentionally here, and relating it to anthropological theories about how cultural observation inevitably leads to power dynamics. For more on this, see James Clifford, *The Predicament of Culture: Twentieth-Century Ethnography, Literature, and Art* (Cambridge, Mass.: Harvard University Press, 1988).

9. For a brief and helpful reading of the hut, see Neil Levine, *The Architecture of Frank Lloyd Wright* (Princeton: Princeton University Press, 1996), 12.

10. Charles Longfellow, 1871 journal, in Laidlaw, 62.

11. Ibid., 74–75.

12. Susan Stewart, *On Longing* (1984; Durham: Duke University Press, 1998), 135.

13. The nineteenth-century American scientist and collector Edward Sylvester Morse also spent time with the Ainus. Morse's representation of the Ainus possessed the imprint of a popular press, while Longfellow's thoughts about the Ainus remained out of the public eye. Like Longfellow, however, Morse deployed stereotypes to portray the northern tribe. He noted that the Ainu "were all really intelligent-looking men, with their long, dignified beards, and it was impossible to realize that they were low, unlettered savages without moral courage, lazy, and strongly given to drunkenness, supporting themselves by hunting with bow and arrow and fishing." Morse also described the huts of the Ainus and provided his reader with drawings that visually detailed the Ainus' uncivilized nature. Morse brought his work to the public through what passed in the late nineteenth century as an accurate and careful ethnographic study. As personal as Longfellow's souvenirs were, Morse wanted his research to be seen and appreciated by a larger audience. See Edward S. Morse, *Japan Day by Day: 1877, 1878–79, 1882–83* (New York: Houghton Mifflin, 1917), 1.

14. Christine Guth, "Longfellow's Tattoos: Marks of a Cross-Cultural Encounter," *Orientations* 29, no. 11 (December 1998): 36.
15. Ibid., 36–42.
16. Guth, *Longfellow's Tattoos*, especially her fourth chapter.
17. Ibid., 42. Guth further discusses the tradition of Western tourists dressing in the garb of the Other throughout the Middle East, but also, of course, in Japan. For more on this, see her *Longfellow's Tattoos*, 127–30.
18. For more on this idea, see Anne McClintock, *Imperial Leather: Race, Gender, and Sexuality in the Colonial Contest* (New York: Routledge, 1995), especially chapters 3 and 4.
19. For more on stereotype and the idea of the cultural hybrid, see Homi Bhabha, *The Location of Culture* (London: Routledge, 1994).
20. For more on this image and its connotation of masculinity, see Guth, "Charles Longfellow and Okakura Kakuzo," 605–36.
21. Longfellow to Alice Mary Longfellow, August 3, 1871, in Laidlaw, 30.
22. Ibid.
23. Ibid.
24. According to records at the Longfellow National Historic Site, the individuals in this image, from left to right, are Edward Haven, Matahe, Metama, an unidentified woman, Charles, and Sokuhe. For more on Beato, see David Harris, *Of Battle and Beauty: Felice Beato's Photographs of China* (Santa Barbara: Santa Barbara Museum of Art, 1999).
25. Christine Laidlaw notes that a number of "Western men living in Japan in the Meiji era had Japanese mistresses. The photographs suggest that Charles, also, had one or more. Among the likely candidates are Ohanna, whose picture he kept in his bedroom on his return to Cambridge, and Sokuhe and Metama, who were photographed on his veranda." Laidlaw, 7. According to Guth, "Ohannasan may have been a geisha employed" at a teahouse Charles visited. See Guth, *Longfellow's Tattoos*, 80.
26. For the idea of the photograph as a form of currency, see McClintock, 123.
27. Marianna Torgovnick, *Gone Primitive: Modern Intellects, Savage Lives* (Chicago: University of Chicago Press, 1990), 229.
28. Malinowski quoted in Torgovnick, 227.
29. Torgovnick, 232.
30. Two images in the Longfellow archive have writing on their versos that reads, "Honiss Fotografo Manila," but the other nine images have been archived as "probably" representations of Filipinos. These other nine photographs do not have studio markings. The Philippine tradition of taking photographs in photo studios and circulating these images as gifts is discussed by Vicente Rafael in his book *White Love and Other Events in Filipino History* (Durham: Duke University Press, 2000), 76–102.
31. Here I am thinking of images such as Jan Steen's *The Dissolute Household*, ca. 1668, which sets figures in an interior and includes, on the floor of the scene, playing cards. The Steen image is overtly didactic in tone, but the

arrangement of figures in an interior with props is typical of the genre settings that the photography studio in Manila used as a model.

CHAPTER TWO

1. William Dean Howells, *A Hazard of New Fortunes* (1890; New York: Oxford University Press, 1990), 38–39.
2. Amy Kaplan, *The Anarchy of Empire in the Making of U.S. Culture* (Cambridge, Mass.: Harvard University Press, 2002).
3. Kristin Hoganson, "Cosmopolitan Domesticity: Importing the American Dream, 1865–1920," *American Historical Review* 107, no. 1 (February 2002): 65.
4. For more on Morse, see Robert Rosenstone, *Mirror in the Shrine: American Encounters with Meiji Japan* (Cambridge, Mass.: Harvard University Press, 1988).
5. Edward S. Morse, *First Book of Zoology* (1875; New York: D. Appleton, 1884), 49.
6. Ibid., 50.
7. Ibid., 50–51.
8. Ibid., 51.
9. Laura Rigal makes this connection in her *American Manufactory: Art, Labor, and the World of Things in the Early Republic* (Princeton: Princeton University Press, 1998), 110. The writing on this image is extensive. For another important reading of this painting, see Roger Stein, "Charles Willson Peale's Expressive Design: *The Artist in His Museum," Prospects: The Annual of American Cultural Studies* 6 (1981): 139–85.
10. Susan Stewart, *On Longing: Narratives of the Miniature, the Gigantic, the Souvenir, the Collection* (1984; Durham: Duke University Press, 1993), 151.
11. Ibid., 152.
12. Edward Morse, *Japanese Homes and Their Surroundings* (Boston: Ticknor, 1886), 159–60.
13. Ibid., 309.
14. James Clifford, *The Predicament of Culture: Twentieth Century Ethnography, Literature, and Art* (Cambridge, Mass.: Harvard University Press, 1988), 218.
15. Ibid., 23.
16. Morse also worked as an ethnographer and studied the people of Asia. See, for instance, his *Japan Day by Day: 1877, 1878–79, 1882–83* (New York: Houghton Mifflin, 1917).
17. "The Harmony of Colors," *Art Amateur* (June 1879): 10.
18. "A Superb Japanese Lacquer Screen," *Art Amateur* (September 1880): 81.
19. Thomas Kim, "Being Modern: The Circulation of Oriental Objects," *American Quarterly* 58, no. 2 (June 2006): 379–406. Kim also discusses Morse.
20. For a helpful source on the China trade, see Carl L. Crossman, *The Decorative Arts of the China Trade: Paintings, Furnishing, and Exotic Curiosities*

(Woodbridge, Suffolk: Antique Collectors' Club, 1991). And, for more on the popularization of Orientalism in American visual and material culture, see Holly Edwards, "A Million and One Nights: Orientalism in America, 1870–1930," in her edited volume *Noble Dreams, Wicked Pleasures: Orientalism in America, 1870–1930* (Princeton: University of Princeton Press, 2000), 11–57.

21. William Hosley, *The Japan Idea* (Hartford: Wadsworth Atheneum, 1990), see p. 36 for information on the '76 exposition and chapter 1 for more on Perry and the opening of Japan.

22. Cynthia A. Brandimarte, "Japanese Novelty Stores," *Winterthur Portfolio* 26, no. 1 (Spring 1991): 2.

23. For more on the explosion of Japanism in turn-of-the-century American material culture, see Brandimarte. Additionally, Jane Converse Brown describes the interest in Japanese taste at the turn of the century in her "'Fine Art and Fine People': The Japanese Taste in the American Home, 1876–1916," in *Making the American Home: Middle-Class Women and Domestic Material Culture, 1840–1940*, ed. Marilyn Ferris Motz and Pat Browne (Bowling Green, Ohio: Popular Press, 1988), 121–39. And for a discussion about the impact of Japanism on a very specific American decorative arts market, see Charles Venable's *Silver in America, 1840–1940* (New York: Abrams, 1995), 172–91.

24. Doreen Bolger Burke et. al., *In Pursuit of Beauty* (New York: The Metropolitan Museum of Art, 1986), 19.

25. Frank Luther Mott, *A History of American Magazines, 1885–1905* (Cambridge, Mass.: Harvard University Press, 1957), 146.

26. See J. M. Mancini, *Pre-Modernism: Art-World Change and American Culture from the Civil War to the Armory Show* (Princeton: Princeton University Press, 2005), esp. 91–97.

27. "An Oriental Lounging Room," *Art Amateur* (April 1886): 111.

28. Even locations in the Americas were marked with the term "Orient." On the case of Mexico, see, for instance, Gilbert Gonzalez, *Culture of Empire: American Writers, Mexico, and Mexican Immigrants, 1880–1930* (Austin: University of Texas Press, 2003), 75–80.

29. Anne McClintock explicates the connections between domesticity and race in her *Imperial Leather: Race, Gender, and Sexuality in the Colonial Contest* (New York: Routledge, 1995).

30. From June 1879 to December 1879, the journal was published in New York. From January 1880 to May 1880, the journal was published in New York and Boston. From June 1880 to October 1891, the journal was published only in New York. And finally, from November 1891 to September 1903, the journal was published in New York and London. Although London is mentioned as a publication site, *Art Amateur* continued to focus on an American audience.

31. "Rise of Art in the Household," *Art Amateur* (June 1879): 1.

32. Ibid., 2.
33. The details of this phenomenon, which historians usually place during the early to mid portion of the nineteenth century, have been well documented. For two helpful sources, see Paul Johnson's *A Shopkeeper's Millennium* (New York: Hill and Wang, 1978); and Sean Wilentz's *Chants Democratic* (New York: Oxford University Press, 1984).
34. "Rise of Art in the Household," *Art Amateur* (June 1879): 2.
35. The use of Eve can be located in other realms of Gilded Age, visual culture. I am thinking of, for example, Mary Cassatt's paintings of women picking apples (*Young Women Picking Fruit* [1891] and *Modern Women* [1893]).
36. For a discussion about the gendered discourse that surrounded nineteenth-century furnishings, see Mary Blanchard, *Oscar Wilde's America: Counterculture in the Gilded Age* (New Haven: Yale University Press, 1998). Also, for more on the idea of American women as consumers of Orientalism during this period, see Mari Yoshihara, *Embracing the East: White Women and American Orientalism* (Oxford: Oxford University Press, 2003).
37. *Art Amateur* (December 1881): p. 1 has the illustrations and the written description can be found on p. 2.
38. Mancini discusses these menu cards as an example of the international context that produced a form of "pre-modernism" in late nineteenth-century America. See Mancini, 6 and 12.
39. The term middle class is decidedly ambiguous, but in this context it connotes a group of magazine subscribers who would have had the leisure and finances to formulate a social position predicated on artistic taste. This definition of the middle class comes from Karen Halttunen's *Confidence Men and Painted Women: A Study of Middle-Class Culture in America, 1830–1870* (New Haven: Yale University Press, 1982), which argues that the domestic sphere became the stage setting for a self-conscious display of middle-class culture. For more on the notion of the middle class, see Stuart Blumin, *The Emergence of the Middle Class: Social Experience in the American City, 1760–1900* (Cambridge: Cambridge University Press, 1989).
40. The January 1881 edition of *Art Amateur* (24) discusses the cards under the heading "Holiday Premiums to Subscribers." It describes how customers will receive one of two sets of four cards with each subscription. The artist at Tiffany who designed the cards was Mr. Whitehouse, the head of Tiffany's stationery department.
41. John Kasson describes the menu card as a component of the carefully orchestrated, and well-mannered, nineteenth-century dinner party in his *Rudeness and Civility: Manners in Nineteenth-Century Urban America* (New York: Noonday Press, 1990), 204.
42. Eunyoung Cho, "The Selling of Japan: Race, Gender, and Cultural Politics in the American Art World, 1876–1915" (PhD diss., University of Delaware, 1998), 193.

43. Cori Schnittke Sherman, "Sex and Power: Gendered Messages in the Oral Imagery of Ukiyoe," in *Illusion and Reality: Edo Period Japanese Prints and Paintings* (Amarillo, Tex.: Amarillo Museum of Art, 1999), 28–36.

44. "An Oriental-Lounging Room," *Art Amateur* (April 1886): 111.

45. Ibid.

46. We could also think of J. D. Rockefeller's Moorish smoking room now at the Brooklyn Museum as an example of this phenomenon.

47. John Sweetman provides a helpful survey of the Islamic influence in Western art and design in his *The Oriental Obsession: Islamic Inspiration in British and American Art and Architecture, 1500–1920* (Cambridge: Cambridge University Press, 1988). Sweetman also describes the Western fascination with Muslim "excess" and militancy in his introduction; see p. 8.

48. Washington Irving, *The Alhambra* (1832; Boston: Twayne, 1983).

49. Again, see Stewart for more on the idea of the collection as a cultural construct.

50. See Karen Halttunen, "From Parlor to Living Room: Domestic Space, Interior Decoration, and the Culture of Personality," in *Consuming Visions: Accumulation and Display of Goods in America, 1880–1920*, ed. Simon Bronner (New York: W. W. Norton, 1989). For more on the parlor, see Halttunen's *Confidence Men and Painted Women*.

51. Halttunen, "From Parlor to Living Room"; and *Confidence Men and Painted Women*.

52. For more on furniture and its relationship to corporeal posture, see Kenneth Ames, *Death in the Dining Room and Other Tales of Victorian Culture* (Philadelphia: Temple University Press, 1992).

53. For the text that accompanies this image, see "Japanese Reception Room," *Art Amateur* (December 1897): 17.

54. Ibid.

55. Ibid.

56. McClintock, 35.

57. Laura Wexler, *Tender Violence: Domestic Visions in an Age of U.S. Imperialism* (Chapel Hill: University of North Carolina Press, 2000).

58. For more on this issue see Kaplan.

59. "Home Decoration and Furniture," *Art Amateur* (July 1888): 38.

60. Bradley C. Brooks, "Clarity, Contrast, and Simplicity: Changes in American Interiors, 1880–1930," in *The Arts and the American Home, 1890–1930*, ed. Jessica Foy and Karal Ann Marling (Knoxville: University of Tennessee Press, 1994), 14–43. For more on the Colonial Revival, see Alan Axelrod, ed., *The Colonial Revival in America* (New York: W. W. Norton, 1985); and Thomas Denenberg, *Wallace Nutting and the Invention of Old America* (New Haven: Yale University Press, 2003).

61. For this image see *Art Amateur* (March 1896): 95.

62. "Two Bedrooms and a Playroom," *Art Amateur* (February 1899): 68.

63. See Lisa Bloom, *Gender on Ice: American Ideologies of Polar Expeditions* (Minneapolis: University of Minnesota Press, 1993), 11. Bloom discusses the interconnections of these words in terms of science and polar exploration, but her analysis is particularly useful to my discussion of the Spanish-American War from the same period. After all, Bloom argues that polar travel is ultimately a form of colonization completed under the guise of science.

64. Thomas Denenberg, author of *Wallace Nutting and the Invention of Old America*, pointed this out to me.

65. "Two Bedrooms and a Playroom"; the image for the boy's room is on page 68 and the girl's room is on page 69.

66. Theodore Roosevelt, *The Strenuous Life* (1900; Bedford, MA: Applewood Books, 1991).

67. Angela Miller discusses the feminization of the landscape during the course of the nineteenth century in her book *The Empire of the Eye: Landscape Representation and American Cultural Politics, 1825–1875* (Ithaca: Cornell University Press, 1993), 243–88.

68. For the differences between the construction of male and female gender roles in nineteenth-century youth culture, see E. Anthony Rotundo, *American Manhood* (New York: Basic Books, 1993).

69. Again, see Bloom for more on turn-of-the-century masculinity. And for an excellent discussion of the Spanish-American War as a conflict "showcasing American masculinity," see Amy Kaplan, "Black and Blue on San Juan Hill," in *Cultures of US Imperialism*, Kaplan and Pease, eds. (Durham: Duke University Press, 1993), 219–36. For more on artistic representations of the Spanish-American War, see Alexander Nemerov, *Frederic Remington and Turn-of-the-Century America* (New Haven: Yale University Press, 1995).

70. For more about imagined notions of nationalism in relation to the media, see Benedict Anderson, *Imagined Communities* (London: Verso Books, 1991).

71. Mary Blanchard discusses this transformation in her "Boundaries of the Victorian Body: Aesthetic Fashion in Gilded Age America," *American Historical Review* 100, no. 21 (February 1995): 21–50.

72. G. D. Rice, "Art in the Philippines," *Art Amateur* (February 1902): 68.

73. Ibid.

74. The notion of teaching English to Filipinos became an important aspect of American educational reform in the colony. For a discussion of American colonial policy in relation to education, see Glenn Anthony May, *Social Engineering in the Philippines: The Aims, Execution, and Impact of American Colonial Policy*, (London: Greenwood Press, 1980).

75. Charles C. Niehaus, "The Making of the Dewey Triumphal Arch," *Art Amateur* (October 1899): 91–94.

76. *Art Amateur* (October 1899): 95.

77. Examples of Morse's later books include *Glimpses of China and Chinese Homes* (Boston: Little Brown, 1902); and *Japan Day by Day: 1877, 1878–79, 1882–83* (Boston: Houghton Mifflin, 1917).

CHAPTER THREE

1. George Reece, "Native Art in the Moro Country," in *Brush and Pencil* 10, no. 6 (September 1903): 345–46.
2. Ibid., 346–47.
3. Ibid., 348.
4. Vicente Rafael, *White Love and Other Events in Filipino History* (Durham: Duke University Press, 2000), 23.
5. Mark Twain, "To the Person Sitting in Darkness," in Mark Twain, *Following the Equator and Anti-Imperialist Essays*, ed. Shelley Fisher Fishkin (New York: Oxford University Press, 1996), 8.
6. For an overview of journalism and American empire at the turn of the century, see Gerald Linderman, *The Mirror of War: American Society and the Spanish-American War* (Ann Arbor: University of Michigan Press, 1974); and Charles Brown, *The Correspondents' War: Journalists in the Spanish-American War* (New York: Charles Scribner's Sons, 1967). Even though both the *World* and the *Evening Journal* used embellished language to sell newsprint throughout the period I discuss in this chapter, these popular newspapers each had their own editorial agenda. David Axeen explains that although the *World* was in favor of the Spanish-American War, the paper did contain some anti-imperialist sentiment. He claims that the reporting in Pulitzer's *World* was less raucous than that in Hearst's *Evening Journal*. See David Axeen, "'Heroes of the Engine Room': American 'Civilization' and the War with Spain," *American Quarterly* 36, no. 4 (Autumn 1984): 481–502. Additionally, for a helpful critique of more recent media representations of the "Orient," particularly the Middle East, see Melani McAlister, *Epic Encounters: Culture, Media, and U.S. Interests in the Middle East Since 1945* (Berkeley: University of California Press, 2005). In addition, Christina Klein examines the issue of the media and Orientalism in the larger cultural milieu in her *Cold War Orientalism: Asia in the Middlebrow Imagination, 1945–1961* (Berkeley: University of California Press, 2003).
7. *New York Evening Journal*, March 28, 1901.
8. Ibid.
9. John Kasson, *Rudeness and Civility: Manners in Nineteenth-Century Urban America* (New York: Noonday Press, 1990), 96.
10. For more on the idea of photography and its culturally constructed discourse of the "real," see Abigail Solomon-Godeau, *Photography at the Dock: Essays on Photographic History, Institutions, and Practices* (Minneapolis: University of Minnesota Press, 1991). Other scholars have engaged the American documentary tradition in a similar fashion. See, for example, Maren

Stange, *Symbols of Ideal Life: Social Documentary Photography in America, 1890–1950* (Cambridge: Cambridge University Press, 1989).

11. William Dinwiddie, "Aguinaldo as a Prisoner at $4 a Day," *World*, October 5, 1902.

12. *New York Evening Journal*, May 3, 1900.

13. Marion Wilcox, "Philippine Ethnology," *Harper's Weekly*, May 13, 1899, 487.

14. Lisa Bloom develops the idea of how an American audience gains knowledge of non-Western cultures through the photographic medium in *Gender on Ice: American Ideologies of Polar Expeditions* (Minneapolis: University of Minnesota, 1993), 60. Also, see Catherine Lutz, *Reading National Geographic* (Chicago: University of Chicago Press, 1993), for more on this issue.

15. *New York Evening Journal*, May 3, 1900.

16. Wilcox, 487.

17. *New York Evening Journal*, February 6, 1899.

18. John Dwyer, "To-Day's Real Life in the Philippines," *World*, May 1, 1898.

19. For more on popular representations of Native Americans, see John Coward, *The Newspaper Indian: Native American Identity in the Press, 1820–1890* (Champaign: University of Illinois Press, 1999).

    Amy Kaplan, in her book *The Anarchy of Empire in the Making of U.S. Culture* (Cambridge, Mass.: Harvard University Press, 2002), observes that American empire is not a discreet set of historical moments that transpired at the end of the nineteenth century, but rather goes beyond the boundaries of the Spanish-American and Philippine-American conflicts. The entire nineteenth century is, according to Kaplan, intricately linked to the history of empire and one of the more obvious examples of American empire was the decimation of the Native American population.

20. Sixto Lopez, *The "Wild Tribes" and Other Filipinos* (Boston: Anti-Imperialist League, 1911).

21. G. A., "Filipino Characteristics," *Harper's Weekly*, March 4, 1899, 226.

22. F. D. Millet, "The Filipino Republic," *Harper's Weekly*, November 12, 1898, 1110. While a correspondent for *Harper's Weekly*, Millet also published a book about the Philippines entitled *The Expedition to the Philippines* (New York: Harper & Brothers Publishers, 1899).

23. Edward Said employs Kipling as an important Orientalist in the context of the European literary canon in *Orientalism* (New York: Vintage Books, 1978), 226–28.

24. "The Revenge of the Filipino," *World*, January 22, 1899.

25. Ibid.

26. See Ann Laura Stoler, *Race and the Education of Desire: Foucault's History of Sexuality and the Colonial Order of Things* (Durham: Duke University Press, 1995), for more about empire and issues related to blood and miscegenation.

27. Warwick Anderson, *Colonial Pathologies: American Tropical Medicine, Race, and Hygiene in the Philippines* (Durham: Duke University Press, 2006), 60.

28. Again, see "The Revenge of the Filipino."

29. Dr. Henry C. Rowland, "Fighting Life in the Philippines," *McClure's Magazine*, July 1902. This narrative is, of course, very similar to discussions about Abu Ghraib prison during the recent Iraq War. For more on Rowland's essay, see Paul Kramer, *The Blood of Government: Race, Empire, the United States, and the Philippines* (Chapel Hill: University of North Carolina Press, 2006), 149–51.

30. Rowland, 242.

31. Ibid., 243.

32. Ibid., 244.

33. Ibid.

34. Ibid., 246.

35. Ibid., 247.

36. *New York Evening Journal*, April 15, 1902.

37. Ibid.

38. John Luther Long, "A 'Madame Butterfly' of the Philippines," *World*, June 7, 1903.

39. For more on the trope of Madame Butterfly in Western culture, see Maria Degabriele, "From Madame Butterfly to Miss Saigon: One Hundred Years of Popular Orientalism," *Critical Arts Journal* 10, no. 2 (1996): 105–19.

40. From the preface of Edward Stratemeyer, *The Campaign of the Jungle; or, Under Lawton through Luzon* (Boston: Lee and Shepard Publishers, 1903). For more on Stratemeyer, see Deidre Johnson, *Edward Stratemeyer and the Stratemeyer Syndicate* (New York: Twayne Publishers, 1993).

41. Stratemeyer, 17.

42. For more information on the Philippine Commission, see my sixth chapter and Glenn Anthony May's *Social Engineering in the Philippines: The Aims, Execution, and Impact of American Colonial Policy, 1900–1913* (Westport: Greenwood Press, 1980).

43. "The United States Engineer Corps in the Philippines," *Harper's Weekly*, June 21, 1902, 788.

44. Ibid.

45. Ibid., 789.

46. It is unclear whether the men are all American soldiers, or if Filipinos are also present.

47. William Dinwiddie, "Filipino Fireplaces," *Harper's Weekly*, December 29, 1900, 1272.

48. Ibid.

49. May, 5.

50. "Seeks Sole Power in the Philippines," *World*, December 17, 1901.

51. *World*, May 3, 1898.

52. *McClure's Magazine*, May–October 1898. As Amy Henderson pointed out to me, many Americans would have recognized this chair (not pictured). It is the Morris Chair, named after William Morris. Morris was a nineteenth-century British advocate for the Arts and Crafts movement.

53. For more on advertising and its ability to disseminate empire through visuality, see Anandi Ramamurthy, *Imperial Persuaders: Images of Africa and Asia in British Advertising* (Manchester: Manchester University Press, 2003).
54. John Barrett, "Manila and the Philippines," *Harper's Weekly*, August 6, 1898, 770. Barrett would later become the commissioner general for the display of Asian cultures at the 1904 St. Louis World's Fair. See Kramer, 239–40, for more on Barrett.
55. John Barrett, "The Philippines: Our Approach to Asia," *Harper's Weekly*, July 28, 1900, 702.
56. There is a lengthier discussion about this map in chapter 4, where I focus specifically on the issue of mapping the Philippine colony.
57. Barrett, 703.
58. William Jennings Bryan, "The Religious Argument," *Commoner*, December 30, 1904.
59. For the cartoon and these comments see Charles Nelan, *Cartoons of Our War with Spain* (New York: Frederick A. Stokes Company, 1898).
60. Grace Corneau, "American Women in the Philippines," *World*, October 23, 1898.
61. Vicente Rafael writes about American households and domesticity in the Philippines during the early colonial period. He also details the role of the Philippine servant in these domestic settings. See his *White Love and Other Events in Filipino History*, 52–75.
62. "Oriental Servants the Latest Fad of the 400," *New York Evening Journal*, February 1, 1899.
63. For more on this theme, see Laura Wexler, *Tender Violence: Domestic Visions in an Age of U.S. Imperialism* (Chapel Hill: University of North Carolina Press, 2000); Kaplan; and Anne McClintock, *Imperial Leather: Race, Gender, and Sexuality in the Colonial Contest* (New York: Routledge, 1995).
64. Wexler, 22.
65. Ibid., 53.
66. One of the most famous reactions to Aguinaldo's capture by Funston can be found in Mark Twain's satirical "A Defense of General Funtson," *North American Review* 174 (May 1902): 613–24.
67. Said, 166.

CHAPTER FOUR

1. McKinley, quoted in John Bancroft Devins, *An Observer in the Philippines; Or, Life in Our New Possessions* (Boston: American Tract Society, 1905), 71.
2. Ibid., 70.
3. J. B. Harley, *The New Nature of Maps: Essays in the History of Cartography* (Baltimore: Johns Hopkins University Press, 2001), 57. For further discussion about cartography, see Norman Joseph William Thrower, *Maps and Civilization: Cartography in Culture and Society* (Chicago: University of

Chicago Press, 1996); and Mark Monmonier, *How to Lie with Maps* (Chicago: University of Chicago Press, 1996).

4. Susan Schulten, *The Geographic Imagination in America, 1880–1950* (Chicago: University of Chicago Press, 2001), 7.

5. See the *World*, January 3, 1900.

6. The map of Africa would have signaled any number of colonial conflicts in Africa.

7. Schulten, 39.

8. The *New York Times* from November 6, 1899, has the Wanamaker's advertisement with the retail and discount prices. This ad also has a drawing of the "Century" bookcase, which was a special piece of furniture made to hold the multivolume set.

9. *The Century Dictionary and Cyclopedia : A Work of Universal Reference in All Departments of Knowledge, with a New Atlas of the World,* (New York: Century Company, 1899), 9:803.

10. *The Century Dictionary and Cyclopedia*, vol. 10, preface, no page.

11. Ibid., map no. 118.

12. Schulten, 26.

13. The publishers of the *Cyclopedia* also produced the *Century* during this same period. This quarterly magazine included articles about American empire in the Philippines written by supporters of imperialism. For instance, Dean C. Worcester, who served on the Philippine Commission and wrote several books about the archipelago, wrote "Knotty Problems of the Philippines" in the October 1898 issue of the magazine (56, no. 6, 873–80).

14. See *New York Evening Journal*, March 16 and November 18, 1899.

15. Ibid., November 21, 1898.

16. Ibid., November 26, 1898.

17. Ibid., December 5, 1898.

18. *World*, May 15, 1898.

19. The Scottish writer John Wilson coined the phrase "His Majesty's dominions, on which the sun never sets," which was later changed to the more popular phrase, "The sun never sets on the British Empire." He first published this infamous passage in a series of articles he wrote for *Blackwood's* magazine, using the pseudonym Christopher North. For more on Wilson, see Ralph Colby, "John Wilson: A Study of His Writings" (Ph.D. diss., University of Illinois, 1931).

20. Early images of America, in books by Vespucci and Columbus, reveal a similar project. See Stephen Greenblatt, *Marvelous Possessions: The Wonder of the New World* (Chicago: University of Chicago Press, 1991).

21. "The United States Engineer Corps in the Philippines," *Harper's Weekly*, June 21, 1902, 788.

22. Warren Du Pré Smith, "Geographical Work in the Philippines," *Geographical Journal* 34, no. 5 (November 1909): 540–41.

23. The largest group of these military maps can be found in record group 395 at the National Archives II in College Park, Maryland, in the Cartographic and Architectural Records Division.

24. "Road Sketch from Tacloban to Carigara," 1904, Cartographic and Architectural Records, Record Group 395, National Archives II, College Park, Maryland.

25. Joseph Kay, "BayBay, Leyte, P.I.," December 3, 1902, Cartographic and Architectural Records, Record Group 395, National Archives II, College Park, Maryland.

26. The ethnology of the Filipinos on the island of Leyte had been the topic of academic discussion. See, for instance, Frederic H. Sawyer, *The Inhabitants of the Philippines* (London: Sampson Low, Martson and Company, 1900), 300–306.

27. "Route of Expedition from Abuyog Leaving Nov. 7th 1906," Cartographic and Architectural Records, Record Group 395, National Archives II, College Park, Maryland.

28. There are several period reports on this tribe, but a later *New York Times* article titled "Tribes in the Philippines Often Cause Trouble" (from January 18, 1931), offers the clearest explanation of the Pulajanes. William Howard Taft also commented on this group, which he referred to as Pulahanes. In a report written while secretary of war to President Roosevelt, Taft explains, "Whenever Filipino municipal officials come into contact either with non-Christian tribes or with inferior people of their own race like those who live in the mountains of Samar and Leyte, known as 'Pulihanes,' they are likely to exercise official authority for their own profit and to the detriment of the inferior people." See William Howard Taft, *Special Report of William H. Taft Secretary of War to the President on the Philippines* (Washington: Government Printing Office, 1908), 12.

29. Robert Bennett Bean, *The Racial Anatomy of the Philippine Islanders* (Philadelphia: J. B. Lippincott Company, 1910), 228–29.

30. Ibid., 7.

31. R. J. Terry, "Robert Bennett Bean, 1874–1944," *American Anthropologist* 48, no. 1 (January–March 1946): 70–74. Bean's interest in race went beyond the Philippines. Victoria Hattam, for instance, in her book *In The Shadow of Race: Jews, Latinos, and Immigrant Politics in the United States* (Chicago: University of Chicago Press, 2007), 39, discusses Bean's use of Lamarckianism to study "the racial characteristics of the Jews, in which he insisted on the heritability of acquired characteristics."

32. Bean, 15.

33. Ibid., 40–45.

34. Ibid., 75.

35. Ibid., 90.

36. Ibid., 221.

37. Ibid., 224.

38. William Churchill, "Reviewed Work(s): *The Racial Anatomy of the Philippine Islanders* by Robert Bennett Bean," *Bulletin of the American Geographical Society* 43, no. 10 (1911): 783.

39. Bean, 234, and see 231–32 for the chart.

40. Ibid., 229.

41. John Tagg, *The Burden of Representation: Essays on Photographies and Histories* (Amherst: University of Massachusetts Press, 1988), 85. Allan Sekula has also written about the relationship between photography and the mug shot, see his "The Traffic in Photographs," *Art Journal* 41, no. 1 (Spring 1981): 15–25. Laura Auricchio pointed the mug-shot-like quality of these photographs out to me.

42. There are other examples of photography's role in creating putative evidence of links to earlier forms of man found in a variety of colonized regions. Anne Maxwell discusses this phenomenon in her book *Colonial Photography and Exhibitions: Representations of the "Native" and the Making of European Identities* (Leicester: Leicester University Press, 1999), 55–59.

43. Bean, 234.

44. Ibid., 228.

45. John Gray, "The Differences and Affinities of Paleolithic Man and the Anthropoid Ape," *Man* 11 (1911): 120.

46. Gustaf Retzius, "The So-Called North European Race of Mankind: A Review of, and Views on, the Development of Some Anthropological Questions," *Journal of the Royal Anthropological Institute of Great Britain and Ireland* 39 (July–December 1909): 297.

47. Erik Trinkaus and Pat Shipman, *The Neanderthals: Changing the Image of Mankind* (New York: Knopf, 1993).

48. Ibid., 105.

49. The debate about cannibalism and Neanderthals continues today, but now the connection between Neanderthals and *Homo sapiens* has been revised. See, for instance, B. Chiarelli, "Spongiform encephalopathy, cannibalism and Neanderthals extinction," *Human Evolution* 19, no. 2 (April 2004): 81–91.

50. George F. Becker, "Conditions Requisite to Our Success in the Philippine Islands," *American Geographical Society* 33, no. 2 (1901): 114.

51. Rob Shields describes a place-image as "images and stereotypes, an imaginary geography of places and spaces, [that] are shown to have social impacts which are empirically specifiable and located not only at the level of individual proxemics . . . but also at the level of social discourses." For this definition, see his *Places on the Margin: Alternative Geographies of Modernity* (London: Routledge, 1992), 6. For a discussion and use of Shields's theory, see Krista Thompson, *An Eye for the Tropics: Tourism, Photography, and the Framing of the Caribbean Picturesque* (Durham: Duke University Press, 2006).

CHAPTER FIVE

1. *Harper's Weekly*, September 30, 1899.
2. Rudyard Kipling, "The White Man's Burden." *McClure's Magazine*, February 1899.
3. See Laura Wexler, *Tender Violence: Domestic Visions in an Age of U.S. Imperialism* (Chapel Hill: University of North Carolina Press, 2000). Wexler mentions and shows the Pears' image on pages 44–45, and the entire first chapter of her book focuses on Dewey in relation to her argument about "tender violence." Specifically, Wexler interrogates a series of photographs that Frances Johnston took of Dewey and his crew on the Olympia. She contends that these images domesticated Dewey and his men, while concomitantly connoting the violence of imperialism. Anne McClintock also discusses the Pears' advertisement from the perspective of domesticity in her *Imperial Leather: Race, Gender, and Sexuality in the Colonial Contest* (New York: Routledge, 1995), 32. Finally, Richard Ohmann examines this ad in his *Selling Culture: Magazines, Markets, and Class at the Turn of the Century* (London: Verso, 1996), 203–4.
4. For an excellent survey of Pears' advertisements in relation to the history of empire, see Anandi Ramamurthy, *Imperial Persuaders: Images of Africa and Asia in British Advertising* (Manchester: Manchester University Press, 2003), especially pages 24–62.
5. " 'I Am Not a Politician, But a Sailor'—Dewey, When Asked about the Presidency," *World*, September 27, 1899.
6. Kirk Savage, *Standing Soldiers, Kneeling Slaves: Race, War, and Monument in Nineteenth-Century America* (Princeton: Princeton University Press, 1997), 7.
7. "Opposed Dewey Appropriation," *World*, June 7, 1899, in *Charles R. Lamb Scrapbook on the Dewey Arch*, Archives of American Art.
8. *Proceedings of the Board of Aldermen of the Municipal Assembly of the City of New York*, vol. 3, July 11, 1899, 20, The New-York Historical Society, New York, New York (NYHS).
9. "Dewey Wants No Fetes at Home," *World*, August 9, 1899.
10. "Dewey the Boy," *World*, September 24, 1899.
11. Ibid.
12. Ibid.
13. Mabel Borton Beebe, *The Story of George Dewey for Young Readers* (Chicago: Werner School Books, 1899), 21.
14. This concern over masculine culture was especially critical in relation to boyhood culture. For more on this, see E. Anthony Rotundo, *American Manhood: Transformations in Masculinity from the Revolution to the Modern Era* (New York: Basic Books, 1993). Also, for more on the relationship between American wars for empire and masculinity, see Kristin Hoganson, *Fighting*

for American Manhood: How Gender Politics Provoked the Spanish-American and Philippine-American Wars (New Haven: Yale University Press, 1998).

15. "George Dewey, the Man, at Close Range; Minutely Described by World Reporters," *World*, September 28, 1899.

16. William Hearst, "Dewey as Modest as He Is Brave," *New York Evening Journal*, September 27, 1899.

17. Ibid.

18. An anonymous reader pointed out this possible anti-imperialist reading of this image.

19. For this image, see the *World*, September 18, 1899. This issue of "separate spheres," or the historical notion of the nineteenth-century domestic realm versus the world outside the home, has an enormous historiography. For a helpful and critical review of this material, see Linda Kerber, "Separate Spheres, Female Worlds, Women's Place: The Rhetoric of Women's History," *Journal of American History* 75, no. 1 (June 1988): 9–39.

20. "Dewey Playing with His Pet Dog Bob," *World*, August 21, 1899.

21. For this image, see the *New York Evening Journal*, September 11, 1899. A similar map can be found in the *New York Evening Journal* with the headline "Dewey at Villefrance" in the August 22, 1899, edition.

22. *Proceedings of the Board of Aldermen of the Municipal Assembly of the City of New York*, vol. 3, September 5, 1899, 415, NYHS.

23. See "Dewey Celebration," *New York Mail and Express*, July 29, 1899, National Sculpture Society Records, Archives of American Art.

24. *Proceedings of the Board of Aldermen of the Municipal Assembly of the City of New York*, vol. 3, September 5, 1899, 413, NYHS.

25. Susan Stewart examines the dichotomy of the carnivalesque (hiatus in the law) and the parade in her *On Longing: Narratives of the Miniature, the Gigantic, the Souvenir, the Collection* (1984; Durham: Duke University Press, 1994), 84–85. Stewart's work with this trope comes from Mikhail Bakhtin, who explores the realm of carnival in his *Problems with Dostoevsky's Poetics* (Minneapolis: University of Minnesota Press, 1984).

26. "You Can Go and See Dewey," *New York Evening Journal*, September 26, 1899.

27. *Official Programme of the Reception to Admiral George Dewey by the City of New York*, 1899, Daniel Chester French Papers, Library of Congress, Washington, D.C., Library of Congress.

28. "Official Route of the Dewey Land Parade," *World*, September 7, 1899.

29. Again, see Stewart, 84–85.

30. Moses King, *The Dewey Reception: New York* (New York: Chasmar-Winchell, 1899).

31. "Women's Plans to Welcome Dewey," *New York Evening Journal*, August 30, 1899.

32. Carroll Smith-Rosenberg, *Disorderly Conduct: Visions of Gender in Victorian America* (Oxford: Oxford University Press, 1985), 246.

33. See Graham Dawson, *Soldier Heroes: British Adventure, Empire and the Imagining of Masculinities* (London: Routledge, 1994). Dawson explains how imperialism demands a home-front celebration of a culturally constructed, masculine "soldier hero."

34. "Women's Plans to Welcome Dewey."

35. For this front page, see the *World*, September 30, 1899.

36. "City Ablaze with Flags to Welcome Admiral Dewey," *New York Evening Journal*, September 25, 1899. Although the Arabic term *fakir* means an ascetic who follows Allah, here it is used to mean street vendor.

37. Ibid.

38. This advertisement for "The Wanamaker Store" can be found in the *World*, September 28, 1899.

39. The Siegel Cooper Co. advertisement can be found in the *New York Evening Journal*, September 20, 1899; The Hunter advertisement can be found in the *World*, September 29, 1899; and, the Childs Cigar advertisement can be found in the *New York Evening Journal*, September 28, 1899.

40. This hyperbolic use of Dewey to sell goods did lead to some controversy. Laura Baker discusses the problematic outdoor advertising associated with the Dewey festivities in her "Public Sites versus Public Sights: The Progressive Reponse to Outdoor Advertising and the Commercialization of Public Space," *American Quarterly* 59, no. 4 (December 2007): 1187–1213.

41. Again, see the Wanamaker ad.

42. *Art Amateur* (October 1899): 95.

43. "The Sculptors' Patriotism," *Harper's Weekly*, August 9, 1899, in *Charles R. Lamb Scrapbook on the Dewey Arch*, Archives of American Art.

44. Michele Bogart defines the arch in relation to an imperialist imagination in her *Public Sculpture and the Civic Ideal in New York City, 1890–1930* (Chicago: University of Chicago Press, 1989), 97–110. Bogart's work on the arch has been critical for my project.

45. Bogart, 5. Also, see Robert Wiebe, *The Search for Order, 1877–1920* (New York: Hill and Wang, 1967), for more on the professionalization of American culture.

46. Charles Lamb, *Charles R. Lamb Scrapbook on the Dewey Arch*, Archives of American Art.

47. "Dewey Day to Be a Record Breaker," *World*, July 21, 1899, in the *Charles R. Lamb Scrapbook on the Dewey Arch*, Archives of American Art.

48. "Work on Dewey Arch Begun," *New York Telegraph*, July 29, 1899, National Sculpture Society Records, Archives of American Art.

49. "Aldermen Hold Up Dewey Ceremonies," *New York Journal*, August 5, 1899, National Sculpture Society Records, Archives of American Art.

50. *Proceedings of the Board of Aldermen of the Municipal Assembly of the City of New York*, vol. 3, August 9, 1899, 241, NYHS.

51. "Work on the Dewey Arch Is Progressing Slowly," *Brooklyn, NY Eagle*, August 27, 1899, National Sculpture Society Records, Archives of American Art.

52. "Progress of the Dewey Arch," *New York Evening Journal*, September 22, 1899.

53. "How the Dewey Arch Looks To-Day," *New York Evening Journal*, September 26, 1899.

54. "New York's Stolen Arch," undated and without source, National Sculpture Society Records, Archives of American Art.

55. See, for example, Henri Pene Du Bois, "Arch of Dewey Like That of Titus," *New York Journal*, September 1899, National Sculpture Society Records, Archives of American Art.

56. "Dewey Arch Completed," *Boston Globe*, September 30, 1899, National Sculpture Society Records, Archives of American Art.

57. See Alan Trachtenberg, *The Incorporation of America: Culture and Society in the Gilded Age* (New York: Hill and Wang, 1982). His final chapter focuses on the 1893 fair.

58. Bogart, 103.

59. Ibid., 104.

60. Charles H. Caffin, *The Dewey Triumphal Arch* (New York: Noonday, 1899).

61. For this image, see King, *The Dewey Reception: New York*. For a short film that shows tourists and New Yorkers traveling around and through the arch the day after the Dewey parade, see *The Dewey Arch*, 52 sec., American Mutoscope and Biograph Company, 1899, from the Library of Congress, American Memory, http://memory.loc.gov/ammem/index.html (search for "Dewey Arch").

62. Bogart, 106. See the front cover of *Harper's Weekly*, October 7, 1899, for an image of Dewey reviewing the parade from the arch.

63. Bogart, 108. G. Kurt Piehler makes a similar argument in his *Remembering War the American Way* (Washington, D.C.: Smithsonian Institution Press, 1995), 89. The Board of Aldermen did, however, try to save the arch. See *Proceedings of the Board of Aldermen of the Municipal Assembly of the City of New York:* vol. 4, December 29, 1899, 1062, NYHS.

64. "Vandals with Knives Hack Dewey Arch," *World*, October 2, 1899, National Sculpture Society Records, Archives of American Art. See also Bogart, 108.

65. "Dewey Arch Is Disappearing," *New York Telegraph*, October 5, 1899, National Sculpture Society Records, Archives of American Art.

66. For more on the cultural significance of the photograph as a material object during the nineteenth century, see Shirley Teresa Wajda's American studies dissertation (PhD) " 'Social Currency': A Domestic History of the Portrait Photograph in the United States, 1839–1889" (University of Pennsylvania, 1992).

67. Stewart, 135.

68. W. J. T. Mitchell, *Picture Theory* (Chicago: University of Chicago Press, 1994), 378.

69. City of New York, *Triumphal Arch Erected in Honor of Admiral Dewey* (New York, 1899).

70. Again, for more on masculinity and American militarism during this period, see Hoganson.

CHAPTER SIX

1. "The Revenge of the Filipino," *World*, January 22, 1899.
2. Henry Watterson, *History of the Spanish-American War* (New York: Western W. Wilson, 1898), 39.
3. Amy Kaplan, *The Anarchy of Empire in the Making of U.S. Culture* (Cambridge, Mass.: Harvard University Press, 2002).
4. Robert Rydell, *All the World's a Fair: Visions of Empire at American International Expositions, 1876–1916* (Chicago: University of Chicago Press, 1984), 154–83.
5. John Wesley Hanson, *The Official History of the Fair: St. Louis, 1904* (St. Louis: St. Louis Fair Officials, 1904), 296.
6. Ibid., 297.
7. *Philippine Exposition*, 1904, Warshaw Collection, Archives Center, National Museum of American History, Smithsonian Institution, Washington, D.C.
8. Ibid.
9. C. S. Jackson and Charles Walter Brown, *Jackson's Famous Photographs of the Louisiana Purchase Exposition*, 1904, Warshaw Collection, Archives Center, National Museum of American History, Smithsonian Institution, Washington D.C.
10. Ibid.
11. For more on the issue of photography at the 1904 fair, see Sharon Delmendo, *The Star-Entangled Banner: One Hundred Years of America in the Philippines* (Rutgers: Rutgers University Press, 2004), 47–85. Other photographers, such as Frances Benjamin Johnston, also photographed the ethnographic spectacle at this and other fairs. For more on Johnston's photographs at world's fairs, see Bettina Berch, *The Woman Behind the Lens: The Life and Work of Frances Benjamin Johnston* (Charlottesville: University of Virginia Press, 2000). And, for more about her imagery and that of other photographers at the 1904 fair, see Eric Breitbart, *A World on Display 1904: Photographs from the St. Louis World's Fair* (Albuquerque: University of New Mexico Press, 1997). For a survey of the use of photography at various nineteenth-century fairs, see Julie K. Brown, *Making Culture Visible: The Public Display of Photography at Fairs, Expositions and Exhibitions in the United States, 1847–1900* (Amsterdam: Harwood Academic Publishers, 2001). Additionally, Benito Vergara discusses the role of photography in the American colonial enterprise in his *Displaying Filipinos: Photography and Colonialism in Early Twentieth Century Philippines* (Quezon City: University of Philippines Press, 1996).
12. For this souvenir book, see *The Philippine Exposition*, Warshaw Collection, Archives Center, National Museum of American History, Smithsonian

Institution, Washington D.C. Note that this book does not include an author's name or publication information, but has a cover with a drawing of visitors to the fair going into a hut on the Philippine Reservation. Seven photographs (three at the top, of Wilson, Taft, and Niederlein, and four at the bottom, of Zamora, Paterno, Guerrera, and Escamilla) surround the central hut scene.

13. Anne Maxwell, *Colonial Photography and Exhibitions: Representations of the 'Native' and the Making of European Identities* (Leicester: Leicester University Press, 1999), 7. Maxwell also discusses the specific role of photography at the 1904 fair; see pages 84–86 of her book.

14. For more on benevolent assimilation, see chapter 3 and Vicente Rafael, *White Love and Other Events in Filipino History* (Durham: Duke University Press, 2000).

15. Robert Reid, *The Universal Exposition Beautifully Illustrated* (St. Louis: Louisiana Purchase Exposition, 1904).

16. Hanson, 296.

17. Ibid., 304 and 313.

18. Ibid., 313.

19. Paul Kramer, "Making Concessions: Race and Empire Revisited at the Philippine Exposition, St. Louis, 1901–1905," *Radical History Review* 73 (1999): 74–114. Kramer also discusses the fair's failures in his book *The Blood of Government: Race, Empire, the United States, and the Philippines* (Chapel Hill: University of North Carolina Press, 2006), 229–84.

20. Burnham to Forbes, April 4, 1904, Burnham Papers, Chicago Art Institute, Chicago, IL (hereafter Burnham Papers, CAI).

21. Burnham to Forbes, April 15, 1904, Burnham Papers, CAI.

22. P. G. McDonnell, "Committee Report of the City of Manila Office of the Municipal Board," October 19, 1903, Burnham Papers, The National Library of the Philippines, Manila, Philippines (hereafter Burnham Papers, The National Library of the Philippines).

23. Melvin Kalfus, *Frederick Law Olmsted: The Passion of a Public Artist* (New York: New York University Press, 1990), 81–86. By this time, Olmsted Jr. had already worked with Daniel Burnham and Charles McKim on the replanning of Washington, D.C. (The McMillan Commission, c. 1902).

24. Olmsted to Taft, March 24, 1904, Burnham Papers, The National Library of the Philippines.

25. Forbes to Taft, March 25, 1904, Burnham Papers, The National Library of the Philippines.

26. See Thomas Hines, *Burnham of Chicago: Architect and Planner* (Chicago: University of Chicago Press, 1979), 199. Hines mentions that Charles McKim also wanted the Philippine architectural post, but Forbes had already decided on retaining Burnham.

27. Burnham to Margaret Burnham, December 7, 1904, Burnham Papers, CAI.

28. Burnham Diary, December 30, 1904, in Charles Moore, *Daniel Hudson Burn-ham: Architect Planner of Cities* (New York: De Capo Press, 1968), 240.

29. Forbes Journal, December 26, 1904, Forbes Papers, Houghton Library, Har-vard University, Cambridge, MA (hereafter Forbes Papers).

30. Ibid.

31. Burnham to Charles Moore, March 13, 1905, in Moore, 245.

32. Daniel H. Burnham, "The Development of Manila," *Western Architect* 9 (January 1906): 7.

33. David Lowenthal, *The Past Is a Foreign Country* (Cambridge: Cambridge University Press, 1985), 325.

34. Daniel H. Burnham and Peirce Anderson, "Report on Proposed Improve-ments at Manila," in Moore, 179. Although both names are on this report and the Baguio report, I refer to Burnham as the author in my text.

35. Ibid., 180.

36. For more on the City Beautiful in relation to the 1893 fair, see Mario Manieri-Elia, "Toward an 'Imperial City': Daniel H. Burnham and the City Beautiful Movement," *The American City: From the Civil War to the New Deal,* Giorgio Ciucci, et. al. eds. (Cambridge: MIT Press, 1983), 1–142; Helen Lefkowitz Horowitz, *Culture and the City: Cultural Philanthropy in Chicago from the 1880s to 1917* (Lexington: University of Kentucky Press, 1976); William H. Wilson, *The City Beautiful Movement* (Baltimore: Johns Hopkins University Press, 1989).

37. Burnham and Anderson, "Report on Proposed Improvements at Manila," 184.

38. Ibid., 186.

39. Ibid., 193.

40. Ibid., 193.

41. Burnham, "Report on Proposed Passenger Station and Track Connections at Manila, P.I., DH Burnham & Co., Architects. Chicago, Illinois," 1906, Burnham Papers, CAI.

42. Daniel Burnham and Peirce Anderson, "Report on the Proposed Plan of the City of Baguio Province of Benguet, P.I.," in Moore, 196.

43. Ibid. For a discussion about how the implementation of imperialism is of-ten predicated on the cultural construction of a colony as an anachronistic space, see Anne McClintock, *Imperial Leather: Race, Gender, and Sexuality in the Colonial Contest* (New York: Routledge, 1995).

44. Burnham and Anderson, "Report on the Proposed Plan of the City of Ba-guio Province of Benguet, P.I.," 199.

45. For more on the City Beautiful in Washington, see Richard Longstreth, ed., *The Mall in Washington, 1791–1991* (Hanover: University Press of New England, 1991).

46. Burnham and Anderson, "Report on the Proposed Plan of the City of Ba-guio Province of Benguet, P.I.," in Moore, 199.

47. Paul Rabinow discusses this issue in his *French Modern: Norms and Forms of the Social Environment* (Chicago: University of Chicago Press, 1989).

48. For more on urban-housing reform in America, see Richard Plunz, *A History of Housing in New York City: Dwelling Type and Social Change in the American Metropolis* (New York: Columbia University Press, 1990); Roy Lubove, *The Progressives and the Slums: Tenement House Reform in New York City, 1890–1917* (Pittsburgh: University of Pittsburgh Press, 1962).

49. William Howard Taft, *Special Report of WM. H. Taft Secretary of War to the President on the Philippines* (Washington: Government Printing Office, 1908), 56.

50. Warwick Anderson, *Colonial Pathologies: American Tropical Medicine, Race, and Hygiene in the Philippines* (Durham: Duke University Press, 2006), 142.

51. Robert Reed provides a variety of details about Baguio's history in his *City of Pines: The Origins of Baguio as a Colonial Hill Station and Regional Capital* (Baguio City: A-Seven Publishing, 1999).

52. Taft, 57.

53. "Fence Thrown Round Baguio," *Manila Times*, December 29, 1904.

54. Forbes to Burnham, May 28, 1905, Forbes Papers.

55. The idea of Filipino elites owning land in Baguio was integral to the American imperial policy that favored the most privileged segment of Philippine society. For more on Filipino elites during the early colonial period, see Julian Go, *American Empire and the Politics of Meaning: Elite Political Cultures in the Philippines and Puerto Rico during U.S. Colonialism* (Durham: Duke University Press, 2008).

56. See Thomas Hines, *Burnham of Chicago: Architect and Planner* (New York: Oxford University Press, 1974), 211. For a more detailed look at Parsons's life, see Thomas Hines, "American Modernism in the Philippines: The Forgotten Architecture of William E. Parsons," *Journal of the Society of Architectural Historians* 32 (December 1973): 316–26.

57. Forbes to Parsons, October 27, 1905, Forbes Papers.

58. Act no. 1495 of the Philippine Commission, enacted May 26, 1906. A copy of this law can be found at the National Archives II, Record Group 350, College Park, Maryland.

59. Forbes Journal, March 12, 1906, Forbes Papers.

60. Forbes to Burnham, April 22, 1906, Forbes Papers.

61. Burnham to Parsons, April 28, 1906, Burnham Papers, CAI.

62. Burnham to Parsons, October 6, 1906, Burnham Papers, CAI.

63. William Parsons, "Annual Report of the Consulting Architect for the Period Extending November 17, 1905–June 30, 1906, To the Honorable, The Secretary of Commerce and Police, Manila, P.I.," Burnham Papers, CAI.

64. Ibid.

65. For more on concrete, see Reyner Banham, *A Concrete Atlantis: U.S. Industrial Building and European Modern Architecture* (Cambridge: MIT Press, 1989). For more information on the historical development of concrete as a

building material, see Peter Collins, *Concrete: The Vision of a New Architecture* (Glasgow, Scotland: University of Glasgow, 1959).

66. A. N. Rebori, "The Work of William Parsons in the Philippine Islands: Part II," *Architectural Record* 41 (May 1917): 433.

67. Again, Kaplan assesses the anarchic discord inherent to the American colonial process.

68. Taft, 55.

69. "Secretary Dickinson to Lay Corner Stone of New Hotel Which Will Be Most Complete Building in Orient," *Manila Times*, August 29, 1910, Burnham Papers, CAI.

70. "New Luneta, Hotel and Clubs will Give Manila's Sea Front Striking Appearance to the Incoming Traveler and Tourist," *The Manila Times*, August 30, 1910, Burnham Papers, CAI.

71. These floor plans can be found in Parsons's article "Manila Old and New," *Western Architect* 17 (January 1911): 9–11.

72. Beth Day, *The Manila Hotel: The Heart and Memory of a City* (Manila: Beth Day, 1979), 11. This self-published book, which contains period photographs and quotations attributed to Parsons, can be found at the National Library in Manila.

73. See A. N. Rebori, "The Work of William E. Parsons in the Philippine Islands, part I," *Architectural Record* 41 (April 1917): 315. Parsons constructed several other buildings in Manila, even though his work never moved far beyond the area of the New Luneta. He built schools, social clubs, a hospital, and structures for the University of the Philippines. Most of these projects, such as the Normal School (1912) and the colonial hospital (1912), have a configuration similar to that of the Manila Hotel. These edifices have unembellished facades (the result of using reinforced concrete) with large windows, and their rigid, boxlike geometry signifies a modern sensibility.

74. Thomas Hines connects Parsons work to "'modern' architecture." Hines contends that Parsons "worked with plain unornamented reinforced concrete, creating effects that suggested the better-known contemporary work of Gill [Irving Gill] in California and Adolf Loos in Austria." See Hines, "American Modernism in the Philippines," 316 and 323.

75. Ralph Harrington Doane, "The Story of American Architecture in the Philippines: Part II," in *Architectural Review* 8 (February–May 1919): 116.

76. Ibid., 115.

77. Ibid., 120.

78. McClintock, 40.

79. Parsons to Forbes, February 21, 1913, Forbes Papers.

80. Forbes to Edward Ayer, March 8, 1913, Forbes Papers. Ayer was an anthropologist who was very enthusiastic about imperialism and became obsessed with collecting artifacts from the Philippines. For more on Ayer, see Horowitz, 65–69.

81. The ways in which Filipinos remember their historic connections to empire are, of course, multifarious. This is one example and should not be taken as indicative of the typical postcolonial reaction in the Philippines.

CONCLUSION

1. William Howard Taft, "The Philippines," *National Geographic* 16, no. 8 (August 1905): 366.
2. For more on Taft and his role in the Philippines, see Ralph Eldin Minger, *William Howard Taft and United States Foreign Policy: The Apprenticeship Years, 1900–1908* (Urbana: University of Illinois Press, 1975); and Paul Hutchcroft, "Colonial Masters, National Politicos, and Provincial Lords: Central Authority and Local Autonomy in the American Philippines, 1900–1913," *Journal of Asian Studies* 59, no. 2 (May 2000): 277–306.
3. William Howard Taft, *Special Report of William Howard Taft Secretary of War to the President on the Philippines* (Washington: Government Printing Office, 1908), 75.
4. Ibid., 75.
5. Ibid., 49.
6. Ibdi., 53.
7. Ibid., 66. Taft also discussed the specifics of American infrastructure in the Philippines in his article "The Philippines."
8. Ibid., 61. Taft also discusses his opinions about reducing tariffs on Philippine goods in his *Letter of the Secretary of War to the Committee on Ways and Means in RE Reduction of the United States Tariff on Importations of Philippine Products* (Washington: Government Printing Office, 1905).
9. William Howard Taft, "The Philippine Islands: An Address Delivered before the Chamber of Commerce of the State of New-York" (New York, 1904), 10.
10. Ibid., 20.
11. For a discussion of Taft's phrase "little brown brothers," and its paternalistic connotations, see Stuart Creighton Miller, *Benevolent Assimilation: The American Conquest of the Philippines, 1899–1903* (New Haven: Yale University Press, 1982), 134.
12. I first heard about the Taft decorating project during a conversation with Dennis Hranitzky. Following his tip, I looked at William Seale's *The President's House: A History*, vol. 2 (New York: Harry N. Abrams, 1986), and p. 746 is where Seale mentions the Filipino furnishings in the Yellow Oval Room. Additionally, Helen Herron Taft, the First Lady, mentions White House furniture from the "Far East" and "Orient" in her memoir, *Recollections of Full Years* (New York: Dodd, Mead & Company), 338. She does not discuss the specific items included here, but she does claim to have "put in" many Asian pieces.

13. This information came from a telephone interview with Donna A. Hayashi, assistant to the curator of the White House, July 27, 1996.

14. "The New Executive Offices for the President," *New York Times*, November 7, 1909.

15. "White House Reforms," *New York Times*, September 5, 1909. My use of the word "tender," is, of course, a reference to Laura Wexler's book *Tender Violence: Domestic Visions in an Age of U.S. Imperialism* (Chapel Hill: University of North Carolina Press, 2000), which I discuss in earlier chapters.

16. William Howard Taft, *Census of the Philippine Islands* (Washington: Government Printing Office, 1905), 1:530, quoted in Vicente Rafael, *White Love and Other Events in Filipino History* (Durham: Duke University Press, 2000), 34.

17. Renato Rosaldo, *Culture and Truth: The Remaking of Social Analysis* (1989; Boston: Beacon Press, 1993), 69.

18. Ibid., 70.

Index

Page numbers followed by f refer to figures.